TEACHI...

E...

General Ea... . Peter King

POETRY EXPERIENCE

POETRY EXPERIENCE

Teaching and writing poetry
in secondary schools

STEPHEN TUNNICLIFFE

London · METHUEN · *New York*

First published in 1984 by
Methuen & Co. Ltd
11 New Fetter Lane, London EC4P 4EE

Published in the USA by
Methuen & Co.
in association with Methuen, Inc.
733 Third Avenue, New York, NY 10017

© 1984, Stephen Tunnicliffe

Phototypeset by Tradespools Ltd,
Frome, Somerset
Printed in Great Britain by
Richard Clay (The Chaucer Press)
Bungay, Suffolk

British Library Cataloguing in
Publication Data

Tunnicliffe, Stephen
Poetry experience.—(Teaching secondary
English)
1. Poetics—Study and teaching—Great
Britain 2. English literature—Study and
teaching—Great Britain
I. Title II. Series
808.1 PN1101

ISBN 0-416-34600-6
ISBN 0-416-34610-3 Pbk

CONTENTS

GENERAL EDITOR'S PREFACE

English remains a core subject in the secondary school curriculum as the confident words of a recent HMI document reveal:—

> English is of vital importance in the development of pupils as individuals and as members of society: our language is our principal means of making sense of our experience and communication with others. The teaching of English is concerned with the essential skills of speech, reading and writing, and with literature. Schools will doubtless continue to give them high priority.
>
> (*The School Curriculum*, DES, 1981)

Such confidence belies the fact that there has been, and continues to be, much debate among practitioners as to exactly what constitutes English. If the desired consensus remains rather far off at least the interested teacher now has a large and useful literature on which he or she can profitably reflect in the attempt to answer the question 'What is English?' There have been notable books designed to reorientate teachers' thinking about the subject ranging from those absorbed by the necessary theoretical analysis, like John Dixon's *Growth Through English* (Oxford, rev. edn 1975), to those working outwards from new research into classroom language, like *From Communication to Curriculum*, by Douglas Barnes (Penguin, 1976); but there are not so many books intended to help teachers get a purchase on their day-to-day activities (a fine exception is *The English Department Handbook* recently published by the ILEA English Centre). To gain such a purchase requires confidence built not from making 'everything new' so much as learning to combine the best from the older traditions with some of those newer ideas. And preferably these ideas have to be seen to have emerged from effective classroom teaching. The English teacher's aims have to be continually reworked in the light of new experience, and the assurance necessary to manage this is bred out of the convictions of other experienced practitioners. This is of particular importance to the new and inexperienced teacher. It is to such teachers and student teachers that this series is primarily directed.

The books in this series are intended to give practical guidance in the various areas of the English curriculum. Each area is treated in a separate volume in order to gain the necessary space in which to discuss it at some length. The aim of the series is twofold: to describe good practice by exploring the approaches and activities reflected in the daily work of an English teacher in the comprehensive school; and to give a practical lead to teachers who wish to try out for themselves a wider repertoire of teaching skills and ways of organizing syllabuses and lessons. Taken as a whole, the series does not press upon the reader a ready-made philosophy, but attempts to provide a map of the English teaching landscape in which the separate volumes highlight an individual feature of that terrain, representing its particular characteristics while reminding us of the continuity between these differing elements in the overall topography.

The series addresses itself to the 11–16 age range with an additional volume on sixth-form work, and assumes a mixed ability grouping, at least in the first two years of schooling. Each volume begins with a discussion of the problems and rationale of its chosen aspect of English and goes on to describe practical ways in which the teachers can organize their syllabus and lessons to achieve their intended goals, and ends with a brief guide to books, resources, etc. The individual volumes are written by experienced teachers with a particular interest in their chosen area and the ideas they express have been proved by them or their colleagues in their own classrooms.

It is at the level of the practical that any synthesis of the various approaches to English can be gained, and to accomplish this every teacher must be in possession of a rationale and an awareness of good methods wherever and however they have been achieved. By reading the books in this series it is to be hoped that teachers will be encouraged to try out for themselves ideas found effective by their colleagues so gaining the confidence to make their own informed choice and planning in their own classrooms.

Peter King
July 1983

ACKNOWLEDGEMENTS

The author and publishers would like to express their thanks to the following for permission to reproduce the poems and extracts in this book, and to offer their apologies to those who, despite every effort, could not be traced:

Peter Abbs for extracts from an article in *The Use of English* 26,4; Agenda Magazine Editions for extracts from *Agenda*; Committee of BATE for 'The Pebble', Francis Le Fevre, from *Poems from Bristol Schools*; Pamela Beattie 'Alone', source unknown; James Berry 'Seeing Granny' (*Poetry Review* June 1983); Ruth Bidgood 'Swallows' (from R. Bidgood *Not Without Homage*, Dyfed, Christopher Davies (Publishers) Ltd); Alan Brownjohn 'Representational' (from A. Brownjohn *A Night in the Gazebo*, London Secker & Warburg); Sandy Brownjohn for extracts from *Does It Have To Rhyme?* and *What Rhymes With 'Secret'?*, London, Hodder & Stoughton; Cambridge University Press for passages from Stephen Tunnicliffe *Stone, Wood, Metal, Plastic*; Stanley Cook 'Fallen Leaves' (from S. Cook *Word Houses*, Huddersfield, The Polytechnic

Department of English); C. J. Driver for extracts from an article in *The Use of English* 28,3; Douglas Dunn for extracts from 'A Removal from Terry Street'(reprinted by permission of Faber and Faber Ltd from *Terry Street* by Douglas Dunn); Alistair Elliot 'Touch of Death' (from A. Elliot *Talking Back*, London, Secker & Warburg); Geoffrey Fenwick for passages from unpublished material; Catriona Ferguson 'Candlelight' (from S. Brownjohn *Does It Have To Rhyme?*, London, Hodder & Stoughton); Bernadette Fitzgerald for extracts from *Approaches to Poetry*, Bristol, Avon Resources for Learning Development Unit; Raymond Garlick 'Baling Out' (from R. Garlick *A Sense of Europe*, Llandysul, Gwasg Gomer); Andrew Hall for Haiku (from S. Brownjohn *Does It Have To Rhyme?*, London, Hodder & Stoughton); Desmond Heath 'Flame' (from D. Heath *Rise Down Water*, unpublished); Ted Hughes, Faber and Faber Ltd and Harper & Row, Publishers, Inc. for lines from 'The Mirror' from *Crossing the Water* by Sylvia Plath; Elizabeth Jennings 'Rhyme for Children' (from E. Jennings *The Secret Brother*, London and Basingstoke, Macmillan); Linton Kwesi Johnson for lines from 'Wat About di Workin Claas' (*Race Today Review*, 1983); Karen Elizabeth Kirk 'My Love' (from Bartlett (ed.) *Mirror Poems*, Aylesbury, Ginn & Co.); Philip Larkin 'Toads' (quotations from 'Toads' are reprinted from *The Less Deceived* by Philip Larkin by permission of the Marvell Press); the executors of the estate of C. Day Lewis for lines from 'The Whispering Roots' (from C. Day Lewis *The Whispering Roots*, London, Jonathan Cape Ltd); Robert Lowell's executors for lines from 'Sailing Home from Rapallo' and for 'Terminal Days at Beverley Farms' (reprinted by permission of Faber and Faber Ltd from *Life Studies* by Robert Lowell. Copyright © 1956, 1959 by Robert Lowell. Reprinted by permission of Farrar, Straus and Giroux, Inc.); Meta Mayne-Reid 'No Ivory Tower' (from M. Mayne-Reid *No Ivory Tower*, Walton-on-Thames, Outposts Press); Adrian Mitchell 'A Good Idea' (from A. Mitchell *For Beauty*

Douglas: Collected Poems 1953–1978, London, Allison &
Busby); Edwin Morgan 'Glasgow Sonnets i' (from E. Morgan
From Glasgow to Saturn, Manchester, Carcanet); Richard
Murphy 'The Reading Lesson' (reprinted by permission of
Faber and Faber Ltd from *High Island* by Richard Murphy);
Marcus Natten for lines from 'They Sent Us Off to Ireland'
(from E. Lowbury (ed.) *Night Ride and Sunrise*, Aberystwyth,
Celtion Press); Ben Owen 'Last Thoughts' (from S. Brownjohn
What Rhymes With Secret?, London, Hodder & Stoughton);
Michael V. Sharpe 'Flood Tide in My Affairs' (from E.
Lowbury (ed.) *Night Ride and Sunrise*, Aberystwyth, Celtion
Press); R. S. Thomas 'Ffynnon Fair' (St Mary's Well) (from
R. S. Thomas *Laboratories of the Spirit*, London and Bas-
ingstoke, Macmillan) and 'The Empty Church' (from R. S.
Thomas *Frequencies*, London and Basingstoke, Macmillan);
Anthony Thwaite for stanzas from 'A Haiku Yearbook':
Anthony Thwaite, *Poems 1953–1983* (Secker & Warburg,
1984); Charles Tomlinson 'Winter-Piece' (© Oxford Univer-
sity Press 1963. Reprinted from *A Peopled Landscape* by
Charles Tomlinson (1963) by permission of Oxford University
Press); Chris Torrance 'South London Prose Poem' (from
Children of Albion, Harmondsworth, Penguin); Barrie Wade,
David Young and Robert Protherough (eds) for extracts from
English in Education, 9,2 and 9,3; Anthony Wakefield 'News
Flash' (from S. Brownjohn *Does It Have To Rhyme?*, London,
Hodder & Stoughton); J. P. Ward 'The M1 Dream' (from J. P.
Ward *To Get Clear*, Bridgend, Poetry Wales Press); W. B.
Yeats's executors for lines from 'In Memory of Major Robert
Gregory' (from *Collected Poems of W. B. Yeats*, London and
Basingstoke, Macmillan) by permission of Michael B. Yeats
and Macmillan London Ltd and Macmillan, Inc.

Baling Out

Be my escape, my parachute,
fabric of words; unshut for me
your cupola to catch my shout

and calm it to a silver curve.
Harness of great verbs, carry me;
your ropes must float me down the cave

of silence to the vowelled earth.
Along the screaming fuselage
I grope towards the sun's square hearth.

Now at the hatchway, at the lip
of language, I look down and see
the green nouns of reality, and leap.

Raymond Garlick

PART ONE
POETRY MATTERS

1

INTRODUCTION

Poetry matters. At the deepest level, poetic modes of apprehension form an essential part of our grasp of reality, and any systematic denial or attempted suppression of the poetic side of our nature can have dire consequences. We dream of 'technological Man', computerized, genetically selected and culturally enlightened. But dreams – even such dreams as those – are the realm of poets, and however sophisticated the machines become, however big the distance we manage to put between ourselves and the earth we spring from, we cannot escape the sensuous, emotion-filled, numinous, earthy world that poets inhabit and apprehend for us.

This book is a response to that conviction. It is concerned with the job of restoring the poetry experience to its rightful place in the teaching of English. I believe that any so-called English teacher who refuses to accept this central role of the poetic in language is failing in his or her chosen task. Yet I am aware that it is commonplace for English teachers to feel uneasy, bewildered or even embarrassed at the idea of teaching poetry to kids. Somehow it has come about that a potential teacher of English can spend three, four or five years in institutes of higher education and can emerge at the end with letters after his or her name, a 'qualified' English teacher and still be unaware of the proper place and function of poetry. Moreover, even those more enlightened, and more fortunate ones who enter the schools ready to teach poetry are often discouraged from doing so, first by their more experienced colleagues – some of whom have comfortably settled themselves into the exam 'rut-race', where poetry has no significant place (see Chapter 14), and secondly by the lack of practical guidance on how to set about the task.

I hope this book may go some way towards filling the gap. In it I have tried to present in systematic form some of the fruits of a quarter of a century of secondary English teaching. During that time I have been very conscious of the proliferation of books *about* English teaching, as well as of English text-books whose methods and format frequently contradict the former. I know how easy it is for hard-pressed English teachers to ignore the 'books about' – especially when they are more concerned with theory than practice – and to take refuge in text-books, however unimaginative and Procrustean their offerings. The present work is, I suppose, a book *about* poetry teaching, and may suffer the same fate. I have, however, tried to place the emphasis on practice rather than theory, and the central part of the book (Chapters 4 to 14) is very much concerned with what goes on in the classroom and how poetry can take its place in that familiar environment.

In Part Three are assembled references, book-lists and other strictly practical bits of information to back up the suggestions in Part Two, together with a small collection of the poems referred to that are not easily accessible elsewhere. Some of the information in this part derives from facts gathered directly from secondary-school English departments, so will, I hope, have enough of the smell of the classroom about them to encourage teachers to look further into the book.

Poetry is often discussed as if it were no more than a branch of literature, i.e. something one finds in books. It may be partly the narrowing effect of this, in an age of oral and visual communication, for most people unmediated by print, that gives it its rather questionable status in English teaching. What has that esoteric, solitary, bookish stuff to do with the throbbing world of the living language, of instant satellite communication, TV newscasters and 'information technology'? I hope the emphasis in the following pages on poetry spoken, performed and composed by children, as well as that on the written or printed page, may help to counteract that tendency. Another way of combating dismissive attitudes to poetry is to bring practising poets into our classrooms, and there are nowadays many opportunities for doing so (see Part Three). Poetry 'performances' are also gaining ground in the world of entertainment. I refer later to the magnetic effect of such performers of their own work as the West Indian poet Linton Kwesi Johnson (see Chapter 12). Pub poetry, and even travelling troupes of poets, like the enterprising 'Versewaggon', are extending the folk element of popular poetry outside the literary context altogether, and reminding us of the vitality and fun to be derived from playing with words sometimes, rather than reducing them always to the drudge status of a means to an end – usually in our world the acquisition of possessions or cash.

In an age of consumer goods and 'value for money', poetry is a refreshing reminder of the existence of different, more truly human values. It also shows us, in an age of conformity, consensus attitudes and mass media, that our full humanity derives not from mass responses or the submersion of individuality, but from our uniqueness. A poet is a supreme individualist. This does not, or at least should not, make him or her an egotist. Many of the poets I know are amongst the humblest and least assertive people of my acquaintance. There are bumptious, self-confident poets as well, of course, just as there are bumptious bank clerks and self-confident engineers. But poets have more safeguards than most against egocentricity, because their very occupation discourages so myopic a view of life. Our teaching of poetry should be directed towards lifting it out of its academic niche or literary featherbed into the world of our pupils' and our own experience. Thus the teaching of poetry becomes poetry experience.

2

POETRY AND POETS
IN OUR SOCIETY

One of our first tasks as teachers involved with word skill – and hence inescapably also with poetry – is to discredit the Romantic myth of the poet as a more or less willing aesthetic outcast from society. This myth is more deep-rooted than we may be aware of; it persists even – and perhaps especially – where poetry is commonly believed to have more status, as for instance in Wales today, with its increasingly ingrown cultivation of competitive verse in the *eisteddfodau*. Yet it is one of the most original English-language Welsh poets of our century, David Jones, who more than any other recognized the down-to-earth, practical nature of poetry making. It may be that in a period like ours, of industrial decline, when the rigid puritanism of the Victorian work ethos is being exposed for the sham it always was, we are in a better position to restore poetry to its rightful place as both art and craft, and hence encourage our pupils to accept the occupation of 'poet' as readily as that of plumber, electrician, bricklayer or woodworker. The many opportunities now available for inviting poets into schools make it easy for English teachers to ensure that all their pupils have seen, heard and spoken with practising poets before they leave school.

Poetry, like all other art, is concerned with the actual stuff and substance of the world around us – its 'thereness'.

> These facts that we knock against, when we wake up in the morning, whatever we feel like, and whatever we hope for and whatever we're dreaming, of whatever fancy ideas we have about the curvature of time, these facts, the solid floor beneath our feet and these things on the table – that's the stuff of painters [and poets]. This recalcitrant, inescapable 'thereness' of what I call everyday objects, which to people with an imagination seem about the most amazing thing.

This is the painter Frank Auerbach, but his emphasis on the actual is equally true of poets and their work. And the urgency which drives Auerbach on as a painter might also be seen as typical of all genuine poets. I tried to embody this primacy of things we can see, touch, feel and smell in the first theme kit collection I prepared for Cambridge University Press with the title *Stone, Wood, Metal, Plastic* (see Chapter 6).

One way of distinguishing genuine poetry, or perhaps I should say the genuine poet, is to be aware of the way that words and patterns of words become 'things', become valued for their 'thereness'. William Carlos Williams, a normal sports-mad teenager, found himself forced by illness to stay in bed and read. Once, in his reading, a phrase of R.L. Stevenson's – unlikely enough, it might seem, as a talisman – stuck in his mind. 'There was a young man and an upset canoe and a line that said, "I never let go of that paddle". I was crazy about that line. I'd say it over and over to myself. I wrote a theme about it and Uncle Billy Abbott gave me an A minus, the best mark I'd ever had. I was thrilled.' When he was fifteen, W.H. Auden's favourite books were about geology.

> I began writing poetry myself because one Sunday afternoon in March 1922, a friend suggested that I should: the thought

had never occurred to me. . . . Looking back, however, I now realize that I had read the technological prose of my favourite books in a peculiar way. A word like *pyrites*, for example, was for me, not simply an indicative sign; it was the Proper Name of a Sacred Being, so that, when I heard an aunt pronounce it *pirrits*, I was shocked. Her pronunciation was more than wrong, it was ugly. Ignorance was impiety.

Both these poets were able almost to pinpoint the moment when words began to be valued as the 'bricks' of which poetry is made. Interestingly, for both it was in early adolescence. The unpredictability of such moments should help us to realize both the importance of our work as English teachers and the impossibility of prescribing too closely the stages of our teaching, or its 'progressiveness' as the text-book makers like to call it. Once such awareness is aroused, creativity and criticism – Auden's revulsion to the 'ugliness' of '*pirrits*' – become part of the same process.

Much of this book will be concerned with the way words are *mani*pulated and the *manu*facture of poetry and verse. (I use these words to remind us of the degradation of the latter in current usage to describe machine 'facture'.) For convenience it will be helpful to isolate the techniques associated with this process. However, we find that amongst poets – 'carpenters of song' as the old Welsh bards called themselves – such skills are acquired as the need arises and are related strictly to the demands the work in hand makes. Auden, once again, has some timely remarks to make here:

> Rhymes, metres, stanza forms, etc., are like servants. If the master is fair enough to win their affection and firm enough to command their respect, the result is an orderly happy household. If he is too tyrannical, they give notice; if he lacks authority, they become slovenly, impertinent, drunk and dishonest.

He goes on to comment on 'free verse':

The poet who writes 'free verse' is like Robinson Crusoe on his desert island: he must do all his cooking, laundry and darning for himself. In a few exceptional cases, this manly independence produces something original and impressive, but more often the result is squalor – dirty sheets on the unmade bed and empty bottles on the unswept floor.

The 'manly independence' of Crusoe forms a useful image leading to the next point about poets in our time, their relationship with tradition, with writers of the past. One particularly pernicious effect of the exponential rate of technological change and the domestic 'spin-offs' of ever more marginal improvements in our material standard of living, is the growing tendency either to devalue tradition, or to discredit it by presenting it to children as something separate from today's world, a museum of curiosities. Shakespeare, Keats, Browning, even G.M. Hopkins, are seen as suitable texts for study, not as predecessors in a process that still goes on. It may be that Leavisite critical analysis, for all its sensitivity and intellectual rigour, has contributed to this by encouraging English teachers to see poetry as dissection material. I shall consider this further in Chapter 13.

For reasons that will become clear as the book progresses, our poetry teaching with children up to the age of fifteen or sixteen will tend to involve contemporary poetry more than poetry of the past. It is particularly important, therefore, for us to be aware of the continuity of imaginative literature and the active involvement of significant poets of our time with their predecessors. In the nineteenth and early twentieth centuries, when most published poetry developed within a self-consciously bookish environment, this often took the form of imitation and many poets of this time testify to their efforts to break free from the shackles such 'sedulous apeing' imposed on their work. William Carlos Williams records amusingly an early interview with an English professor who had expressed interest in his writing:

This was my Keats period. Everything I wrote was bad Keats. I arrived at Mr Bates's house with my *Endymion* imitation, a big bulky manuscript I'd been slaving over; I don't even remember the name of it. A butler let me in Mr Bates's bachelor apartment. He was sitting at a desk, the picture of a distinguished man. There was a step down and I tripped and dropped the manuscript. It rolled all over the floor. Mr Bates was kind. He perused the sonnets and said, 'I see you have been reading Keats.' 'I don't read anything else but him,' I said. He said, 'Well, you certainly have paid attention to how the sonnet is constructed. I'll tell you a little story. I myself write poems. When I've finished them to my satisfaction I place them in this drawer and there they remain. You may, I can't tell, develop into a writer but you have a lot to learn. Maybe in time you'll write some good verse. Go on writing but don't give up medicine. Writing alone is not an easy occupation for a man to follow.' This was a turning point in my life.

Significantly, Williams's account of this rather awkward meeting is followed by his first encounter with Ezra Pound. 'Before meeting Ezra Pound is like BC and AD' – emphasizing the dynamic way in which he interpreted the influences which shaped his work – Keats the poet, Pound the poet. He records that Pound was not at all impressed by his (Williams's) eighteen volumes of manuscript poetry. 'He was impressed with his own poetry; but then I was impressed with my own poetry, too, so we got along all right.'

Once again the painter Frank Auerbach provides further evidence of the centrality of tradition to a serious artist:

All sorts of things affect me. I draw from Constables and from Philips Koninck and from hundreds of paintings. I think it's an essential part of the diet. It would be ludicrous to imagine that paintings come out of thin air and the people who attempt to keep themselves innocent, I think you will find, do paintings that look tremendously like pictures that already exist. I think one's only hope of doing things that have a new presence, or at least a new accent, is to know what exists and to work one's way through it and to know that it is not necessary to do that thing.

Nowadays our increasing recognition of the importance of oral poetry (see Chapter 8), and the range of non-literary forms of poetry, together with the ascendancy and pervasive influence of oral rather than printed mass media, have tended to shift the emphasis away from literacy as the seed-bed of poetry, and this may tempt English teachers to assume that tradition as embodied in the poetry of the past has become less important. If anything, the reverse is true. For one thing, all poetry needs language, that living, growing, ever-changing organism, with its roots deep in our culture. For another, oral poetry, as I shall show, demands memory. There is little doubt that poetry was a more potent – perhaps the most potent – form of language in pre-literate times. Prose is a by-product of the printing press and its status as the language of 'real' life is far from unchallengeable. It will be part of my task in this book to redress the balance in favour of poetic forms of language.

We have reached a point at which it may be helpful to pause, and try to pin down a little more precisely what we mean by poetry. I don't wish to attempt a definition; there have been so many, and each has tended to reveal both its validity within its own context and its limitations as a comprehensive statement about what poetry really is, and what kinds of writing constitute poetry. This is partly because the mere act of definition is at the opposite pole of language from poetry making, striving as it does towards universality where poetry strives towards uniqueness. However, if the word 'poetry' is to hold any meaning in this book it must be susceptible to some kind of summing up. I think we can reasonably start with the idea of 'charged' or significant language. Auden can help us here.

We are told in the first chapter of Genesis that the Lord

brought to unfallen Adam all the creatures that he might name them and whatsoever Adam called every living creature, that was the name thereof, which is to say, its Proper Name. Here Adam plays the role of Proto-poet, not the Proto-prose writer. The Proper Name must not only refer, it must refer aptly and this aptness must be publicly recognizable. It is curious to observe, for instance, that when a person has been christened inaptly, he and his friends instinctively call him by some other name. Like a line of poetry, a Proper Name is untranslateable. Language is prosaic to the degree that 'it does not matter what particular word is associated with an idea provided the association, once made, is permanent'. Language is poetic to the degree that it does matter.

This responsibility towards language, leading at its most potent to the magic of the Proper Name, is something I believe to be central to poetry.

In an article about the idiosyncratic and provocative poet Ian Hamilton Finlay, Geoffrey Summerfield describes Finlay's one-word and emblematic 'poems' as *signs*.

It is precisely because our culture is disintegrated, because it cannot depend on a shared consensus, that Finlay seems to have been forced to start with very simple, primal emblems, carrying an absolutely minimal, pared down, cultural load. It is as if he began by saying, 'Surely you'll recognize this resonance, this analogy?', yet, so atrophied is the life of metaphor in England, as opposed to, say, Ireland, where metaphor, like the story, is a way of thought – so attenuated the capacity for the emblematic outside contexts where they are dinned in (as is the iconography of football clubs) that far from being too obvious, Finlay's simplest poems cause puzzlement and even angered bewilderment.

I am not as despairing of our culture as Summerfield, though I recognize what led him to his somewhat pessimistic conclusions here. Finlay can provide us with a good starting-point for our consideration of the nature of poetry. Geoffrey Summerfield refers, in the same article, to a feature series in *POTH* (*Poor Old Tired Horse*), the poetry magazine Finlay edited for a while, where contributors were asked to submit one-word poems. Those poets who attempted it successfully did so by making the titles carry a significant pointer. One of Finlay's own contributions illustrates the point:

> *One (Orange) Arm of the World's Oldest Windmill*
>
> autumn

Summerfield comments thus: 'The appropriation of the mill requires a metaphorical leap; the metamorphosis is supported by happy, chance coincidence – the four arms of the mill turn in time and correspond in their quarterings to the four cardinal points of the compass and to the four seasons.' However 'pared down' the one-word poem 'autumn' may have become, it still demonstrates what we have been discussing earlier – its dependence on the past for meaning. We cannot say or hear the word without a resonance that includes falling leaves, golden colours, harvest and all that implies in terms of reaping, gathering, storing, as well as remembrances of Keats and other writers. It is this trail of associations that makes possible the 'metaphorical leap' and in fact enriches the association between windmill and autumn.

In an age when instant 'communication' is regarded as desirable, and teams of clever people are engaged on the design of translation machines, poetry celebrates the richness of language and the uniqueness of each of its constituent parts. This is why Robert Frost defines it as the untranslatable element in language. Auden challenges the definition on the grounds that the uniqueness of language is the reflection of the uniqueness of man. 'Because one characteristic that all men, whatever their culture, have in common is uniqueness – every man is a member of a class of one – the unique perspective on the world which every genuine poet has survives translation.' But it is this uniqueness that is under attack in our age. The machine's ability to make thousands or millions of identical products has beguiled us into behaving as though man also comes off an assembly line in his millions. Our hostile, uncomprehending national rivalries notwithstanding, we persist in trying to annihilate distance, whether in space or between human cultures and societies and to pretend that instant accessibility means instant understanding. Poetry, well taught, which means poetry shared with our pupils, can help to restore the differences and make us newly aware of the rich diversity of the world we inhabit.

We have moved some way away from the more modest purpose of this book. I plead in my defence E.M. Forster's 'only connect!' I believe that poetry can become the holistic element in English teaching, drawing together the various aspects of language and showing how, by learning to control, understand and build with words children can both express – and therefore enjoy – themselves and grow as individuals within their society.

3

THE TEACHER'S
AND THE PUPIL'S ROLE

Poetry in school shares features that are common to all aspects
of the educational process involving language as a key element.
Like all other human processes it is untidy, and does not lend
itself too readily to rational analysis, or to formalization into
the step-by-step 'progressive course' treatment beloved of
traditionalists. This does not mean – as some teachers seem to
believe – that anarchy rules in poetry lessons, or that the
teaching of poetry is by definition a hopeless task. It does mean,
however, that in teaching poetry one needs to be adaptable,
opportunistic, flexible, open to suggestion, alert to possibilities
for change. In no branch of English teaching is one more aware
of the potential diversity of a classroom full of children; and in
no branch can that very diversity contribute more to the
learning process if the teacher will allow it to.

By way of comparison and contrast let us look at another
teaching process that involves language: learning a foreign
language. This probably begins these days before any formal
lessons, by picking up chance words, overhearing native
speakers, coming to recognize the characteristic intonations of

the language. Most modern language teachers will capitalize on this by starting with oral practice – question and answer, naming things and actions, gradually building up knowledge and confidence, but in quite a piecemeal fashion. The pupil first *listens* with understanding, then begins (fumblingly) to *talk*, then to *read and write*. At every point the pupil is encouraged to relate the new language to his own, to translate the unfamiliar into the familiar. As knowledge grows each of the three activities – listening, talking, writing – is refined and expanded, and increasingly each informs the others, so that the pupil comes to see the language as an organic whole. The teacher, from his acquired store of language experience, controls and directs the learning of his pupils at every new stage. If we transfer this description to secondary-school poetry teaching and learning we can see both similarities and differences. The most important of the latter is that the initial stages will all have taken place long before our pupils reach us, so that they will already have considerable experience of poetry, even though they themselves may not realize it. Sadly, they may sometimes have been taught that 'poetry' is some-thing apart and different from experiences that we shall need to show them are in fact poetic. For instance, the constant groping and verbal exploration involved in shaping replies to questions of the 'what's it like?' variety often involve an essentially poetic process. Repeated words and phrases and chants, advertising jingles on TV, nursery rhymes, playground games – all these can involve crude applications of techniques our pupils will come to recognize as facets of the poetry experience. The ability to recognize and respond to tone, to appreciate word-shapes and the sound-patterns they create – all these will come to be seen as ingredients in poetry. Nevertheless, as with learning a language, the teacher's first task is to help his pupils recognize what they already know, to identify and share such use and enjoyment as they have already experienced from poetic modes of language. Listening, speaking and writing are again the means to acquiring confidence and experience, but after eight or nine years' practice in the language that is to be seen by them as the medium of poetry, both their own and that of other poem-makers, pupils approach these activities at quite a sophisticated level.

It has been said that all poetry involves translation. When we *make* poetry we are translating experience into words, translating our recognition of order and pattern in our world into an ordering and patterning of language. (We may also be creating an order and a pattern out of the less satisfying flux of our daily experience.) When we read or hear poetry we translate what we hear in terms of what we know and what we are. Imagery in particular works through a form of translation. 'What's it like?' 'Yes, it *is* like that.' Here, however, we come to the second big difference between teaching poetry and teaching a foreign language. It is a difference of degree rather than of kind, but is none the less significant. I refer to the standpoint of the teacher. Because poetry works within and develops from a familiar language environment, the teacher cannot rely on or take refuge in superior knowledge in the way a modern language teacher can. This doesn't mean that a poetry teacher need not be more knowledgeable about poetry than his pupils; it *does* mean that he has always to recognize the vital – and individual – contribution each of his pupils will make to the poetry learning process by virtue of his or her unique background of language and feeling. This is true, of course, in other aspects of English teaching as well; in poetry teaching, which involves pupils and teacher alike in creative responses to experience both in the making and the appreciation of poetry, it becomes paramount. Not until one is involved in the close study of literary texts with 15- to 18-year-old students (e.g. for external examinations) does the teacher's accumulated literary knowledge need to be consciously deployed in the teaching of poetry.

Let us leave generalizations about poetry teaching. The Yorkshire poet Stanley Cook has a clearer grasp than most of how a child apprehends reality, partly because he is also a teacher, but mainly, I think, because of a rare honesty and directness of language. For this reason his work provides a good jumping-off point. This poem is from *Word Houses*, a short collection of 'Poems for Juniors':

> *Fallen Leaves*
> The leaves that made a picture on the trees
> One by one have fallen down
> And lie like pieces of jigsaw
> Scattered on the ground.
>
> Winds blow them here and there
> To put the picture together again
> Before they are pasted in place
> By the first sharp frost or shower of rain.

A modest and unpretentious statement. There is a sense in which this little poem is so complete that all we can do is read it – for example in the course of a discussion or work on 'seasons' or on the countryside, or as an example of the value and precision of comparisons, or of sound-patterns in words. I quote it here as a very clear example of how one can use the 'common land' of shared language in poetry teaching. Children and grown-ups both enjoy jigsaws. 'Making pictures' is an activity as valid in a 7-year-old as in David Hockney. And the poem *demonstrates* making pictures as well as using the idea as an image. The wrong way to present it to a class would be to assume that you had to 'teach' it. One can imagine what would happen: 'Now children, here is a poem about fallen leaves. Mr Cook thinks that a tree full of leaves can make a pretty picture. You've got a picture like that in your books, haven't you? Yes, Johnny, that's the picture. Well, who can show me in the poem where Mr Cook is thinking about a picture like that? That's right, Penny, "made a picture on the trees" ...' and so on remorselessly. This is a caricature, but one that many of those involved in teaching, or remembering their own schooldays, may recognize. What such a method ignores – fatally from the point of view of effective poetry teaching – is the variety of response even so slight a poem as this would elicit from a receptive class of 10- or 11-year-olds (or younger). For one, a tree might be the first thing she set eyes on every morning as she woke; another might have been doing a jigsaw an hour before hearing the poem; a third may have cycled to school that morning and felt the random force of a gust of wind. Each of these will respond differently to the poem. The essential task of the teacher will be to create and maintain a classroom environment in which such correspondences can be discovered and shared by individuals in the class. It might start in a silence following a reading aloud. It might arise from – or the silence might lead into – group discussions. A full appreciation of the poem may only be arrived at after children have been writing something of their own. 'Wasn't there a poem we read the other day about that? How did *he* use the idea of autumn leaves?' In Part Two we shall be looking more closely at the various strategies a poetry teacher might be able to employ in relation to such poems.

A further point here concerns word-patterning; but before considering this we need to tackle what I call the 'so what?' syndrome. An important part of the poetry teacher's job will be to convince pupils that there is a point in using language poetically, that there are, in fact, many practical justifications for developing the skills and insights associated with poetry. The 'so what?' syndrome applied to this poem might go like this: 'like pieces of jigsaw/pasted in place by … frost or … rain.' 'Yes, I see he's comparing the fallen leaves on the ground to pieces of jigsaw. So what? I agree that frost fastens dead leaves to the ground like bits of paper pasted into a scrap-book or on to a collage – so what?'

This may be merely a smart-alec way of evading the hard work of poetry. But it does represent a widely held view of poetry as being by its very nature useless or frivolous, compared with the 'real' world of jobs (or dole), money, technology and consumer goods. One of the best antidotes will always be the teacher's own commitment to poetry as an important mode of perception and illumination; its potency will be directly related to the teacher's credibility with his pupils, how far he or she is taken seriously as a person. Another resource open to him is his ability to draw children's attention to the importance they have in fact placed on such things as image-making, precision with words, and the poetic power of words in their own familiar uses of language and in their pursuit of human relationships. If they need this image-making ability in order to explain a new toy, or sport, or occupation, or to express how they feel about something, or to persuade a parent or friend, is it not worthwhile looking at the way others can make language work for them?

A poem is also a thing, a *made* pattern of words on a page, that can (and almost always should) be also a pattern of sounds in time. Poems achieve greater effectiveness, are more success- ful, as the pattern is perceived to be more consonant with the subject-matter – or to put it another way, as what the poem *is* more closely corresponds to what it is *about*. Perception is the key: a poem has no existence as a thing in itself. (Ian Hamilton Finlay may challenge this, with his emblematic poems often literally solid to the touch. But with his poems, as with others, their essential 'poem-ness', their 'inscape' must be realized (*real*-ized) by the reader/listener/observer.) Let us look at Stanley Cook's pattern. The rhythm follows the meaning closely. The steady iambs of the first line suggest the orderliness of a two-dimensional picture, and the switch to trochaic measure in the second line gives an ironic inevitability to the falling leaves. 'Pieces of jigsaw/Scattered' echoes its meaning exactly, and the heavy emphasis on 'Winds blow . . .' is equally pictorially just, the open sounds contrasting with the more urgent hammering of 'first sharp frost'. Yes, there is no doubt that this poet knows what he is doing. The point of this is not to suggest that we need such an analysis at every level of poetry teaching. This poem will probably elicit its best responses from 10- to 12-year-olds, for most of whom stopping to dissect the poem in this way would seem finicking and artificial. Yet the 13-year-old boy who started his poem 'Machines that die' like this would appreciate what Stanley Cook was doing through his rhythmic sound-patterns:

> All is quiet now the place is still.
> The drilling machine a minute ago
> Spinning and screaming through bright metal
> Is still as if touched by a witch's wand.

Similarly, it should be possible to guide the boy who wrote this about his cat to an appreciation of Stanley Cook's imagery:

> It pater across the floor softer and softer
> like throwing stone cross the water scimming

I have tried in this chapter to indicate the kind of give-and-take that is necessary in a productive poetry class. The practical examples in Part Two will translate these principles into classroom practice. Let us sum up the main points:

1 Because the medium of poetry is language – and for the majority of our pupils the mother-tongue at that – a poetry teacher has to be prepared to respond in as many different ways to a class of children as there are different language experiences amongst them.
2 Pupils of 11 and over already have wide language experience, and have (unconsciously) often used language poetically. Their formal poetry lessons so far may not have made them aware of this.
3 Listening, talking, reading and writing will all take their place in poetry teaching.
4 Making our own poems and responding to the poems of others involve a similar sensitivity to words, rhythm and imagery. They should therefore be complementary activities in a poetry classroom.
5 Because 'the medium is the message' to so great an extent in poetry teaching the teacher cannot take refuge in a superior

body of knowledge, as he might with other subjects.

6   The above point carries with it a warning against assuming too readily that our pupils are less responsive to any particular poem than we are. The reverse may well be the case.

7   We need to be prepared for, and to know how to counter, the 'so what?' syndrome.

8   A poem exists in its own right as an artefact, as well as having a subject-matter. Both are made manifest in the response of an appreciative reader or listener. The poem's success can be measured by the degree of correspondence between the two.

PART TWO
PUTTING IT
INTO PRACTICE

4

INTRODUCTION

In the chapters that follow we shall be interpreting in practical classroom terms concepts of poetry and poetry teaching and learning which have been outlined in Part One; Chapters 6 to 11 in particular include detailed suggestions for 'poetry lessons'. The inverted commas round that expression indicate certain reservations about its slightly old-fashioned ring, and also about the implication that one can somehow relegate 'poetry' to a sort of unwanted corner of the English room, to be taken out and dusted now and again in a 'poetry lesson'. The poetic, as many modern English scholars have reminded us, is a central mode of using language, and hence of our perception of world and society. Poetic uses of language will continue to take place whether or not English teachers bring them within the context of their day-to-day teaching experience. Good English teaching therefore *must* take note of the phenomenon. The relationship between poetry and experience must be faced up to, even though – indeed, especially because – in some respects it undermines the authoritarian role of the teacher, putting teacher and taught on an equal footing, as Barrie Wade acknowledges when he calls one poetic form, *haiku*, 'the great leveller' (see Chapter 11).

This last point is also particularly relevant to English teaching in a multi-ethnic context. Here the teacher has to encounter, and to some extent to accept the need for new ways of handling English, deriving from the connection many of his or her pupils make between what James Berry calls 'straight English' (see p. 165) and 'establishment' or even xenophobic attitudes. On the more positive side, a good poetry teacher will want to capitalize on his or her immigrant pupils' readiness to adopt a 'persona' – as Kenneth Ajegbo puts it – to conceal their sense of insecurity, and will show them how directly this relates to the poetry experience. A mixed-race classroom could well provide one of the most stimulating and creative contexts for poetry, whether newly 'made' (and perhaps written down or taped), spoken and performed, or read privately for enjoyment.

In Chapter 2 Frank Auerbach's way of describing the dynamic behind creative work as the 'recalcitrant, inescapable "thereness" (*Haeccitas*) of everyday objects' should serve as a reminder to us that one cannot systematize poetry into a graded series of lessons, marking set 'stages' in our pupils' understanding or knowledge. You can live with an everyday object all your life, then one day, in a flash of revelation, experience it afresh with all the 'glory and the freshness of a dream'. A new environment, a new friendship, an exciting or harrowing event, can make you see familiar surroundings, hear accustomed sounds, in a new and deeper way.

Poetry teaching in school has to take account of this rather untidy, questing, repetitive, spasmodic, open-ended way we experience each other and the world around us. Instead of conceiving the process of poetry teaching as a linear one – a path with stages along it, as so many old-fashioned English course books liked to envisage it – we would do better to think of it as developing in concentric circles like water ripples from a thrown pebble. Each new step includes, expands on and is informed by what has gone before, but is also new and unique. The experience of poetry is like telling someone the time from a digital watch and from an analogue clock-face at the same time. We have to organize and plan our poetry teaching in the consciousness of this; we have to learn to be opportunists, to recognize the potential for poetry teaching in particular circumstances – special events or happenings, team-teaching experiments, topical or local news items, vivid personal experiences – but we also have to understand and make explicit to our pupils the pattern of the fabric within which such isolated phenomena take place.

How do we convert such recommendations, such far-reaching aims, into the practice of poetry teaching in our mundane classrooms? The first consideration is the actual presentation of poetry and stimuli leading to poetry. Chapters 5 and 6 give detailed suggestions as to the kinds of poems and poetry-related work we can use within different age ranges in a secondary school. Any teacher to whom poetry matters will ensure that his junior classes (11- and 12-year-olds) in particular always have ready access to poetry in the English classroom, either through a class- or English-room library or bookshelf, or by means of portable book-boxes or display units. In today's confused secondary school environment there are often split sites involving teachers carrying teaching materials anything up to three or four miles between lessons. Some form of transportable book-unit is invaluable here. The enthusiasm of younger children is quickly aroused but can die equally quickly if poems are not to hand to maintain interest.

A point teachers sometimes overlook, or find it difficult to adjust to, concerns the accessibility to pupils of particular ideas or themes in poems. It is so easy for a teacher to assume that a poem which evokes a strong response in him or her will do the same in the (perhaps quite bright and lively) class he or she is about to teach, only to meet with incomprehension and boredom. I have tried to show how this can be avoided by including, in Chapter 5, recommendations for three different and overlapping age ranges: 11–13, 13–15, 14–16+. Another safeguard against this is to provide a context of some kind so that pupils are, as it were, 'tuned in' to the ideas or emotions the poem is exploring. I am convinced that working within a carefully chosen *theme* is one of the most effective ways of doing this in school. In Chapter 6 I give substance to this need for a 'meaningful context' to our English teaching – a need that is as evident in poetry teaching as in other branches of English. In today's mixed-ability and/or multi-ethnic classes, theme work can be particularly productive as it can provide English work of so many kinds and at many different levels. Poetry then takes its place naturally within this wider framework.

Frequently one will find that once poetry is given its rightful place within English teaching this will involve the writing of it by pupils – perhaps in company with their teacher. There are many opportunities for incorporating writing into poetry lessons in the following chapters, but particularly in Chapters 7, 9 and 10, devoted to particular aspects of poetry. In Chapter 11 I then draw together ideas into a (not too arbitrary) *schema* for teaching poetry writing involving three stages: stimulus, form and revision. It is necessary often in the course of this work to stress the *sound* aspect of poetry – rhythm, metrical patterns and structures, rhyme and assonance; the prevalence nowadays of personal cassette recorders makes the poetry teacher's task easier here, even if his school is ill-equipped in this respect. We need to encourage our pupils, particularly those for whom English is a second language or whose handling of English is shaped by its use in other countries like the Caribbean islands, to compose poetry orally as freely as with pen and ink, and we need to convince them that we do not attach any greater status to a written poem than to a spoken one. One aspect of a written or printed poem, in any case, is that of 'musical score' – a set of signs for oral re-creation into an art 'thing'. Once our pupils understand this, they can be made to realize that the reader of a poem, like the musician who plays a piece of music, has a creative and not a passive role in the poetry process.

This is nowhere more evident than in poetic imagery, which, like rhythm, is important enough to deserve a chapter to itself (Chapter 10). Children soon come to realize to what extent we are all image-makers, or 'proto-poets', to use Auden's expression, and this can be a good way of combating what I called, in Chapter 3, the 'so what?' syndrome – the assumed cynicism towards any kind of English for which a 'use' cannot immediately be seen. Another way to counter this attitude is through the oral 'performance' of poetry because one never needs to justify any public performance or display which has entertainment value in these days of ample (often enforced) leisure. Hence, in Chapter 8, considerable stress is placed on the performing 'by heart' of poetry as an end product of the poetry lesson. This may often have a special appeal with multi-ethnic classes where the countries of origin of many pupils may have much more live and strongly developed oral poetry traditions than remain in Britain.

Poetry teaching and learning is bound to involve the practice of poetry criticism, even if it is only evident in the way one selects poems for study, or books for the English stock. In a sense, therefore, much of what has already been reviewed in this chapter is concerned with 'critical appreciation', whether by teacher or pupils. A child who is really *engaged* by the writing of a poem soon shows him- or herself to be an acute self-critic, as Sandy Brownjohn has shown us clearly in her work and books on poetry in primary schools. In Chapter 11 I have tried to show how, in choosing and developing appropriate *forms*, and in revising his or her work, a secondary pupil can be encouraged towards an equally productive self-critical approach. A critical awareness of forms such as the sonnet is also touched on in Chapter 7, and Chapter 5 is concerned with the teacher's criteria in choosing poetry for study at various levels in the secondary school.

Most specialist English teachers think of 'critical appreciation' as particularly appropriate for senior students, probably those who have already jumped (or stumbled over) the 'O' level/CSE hurdles. In Chapter 13 I try to show that it is more productive to see such work as developing naturally out of critical work lower down the age range, even down to 13-year-old pupils. The important thing is not to isolate the criticism of poetry from other aspects of the poetry experience in schools; it may be that in the past there has been an over-emphasis on criticism at the expense of creation. I hope that the chapters that follow may do something to correct that balance.

5
CHOOSING POEMS

Teachers who take poetry seriously in school – which obviously includes all who are using this book – know just how difficult it is to find poems the children can relate to while still giving them some idea of the full range and potential of poetry in English. The temptation is ever-present to plump for 'immediate' poetry – ideas, images, feelings that are familiar and accessible, attitudes that are 'common sense', robust, unsentimental, and all couched in language having the simplicity and often even the syntax of straight prose. Much good poetry, including a high proportion of that appearing in the most familiar school anthologies, can be described in these terms; but to allow our pupils to leave school at sixteen or later with the established belief that that is what constitutes 'English poetry' is, I believe, to fail in our responsibility to them and to poetry as a whole, which, of course, includes much good – even inspired – writing that could never be described in such a way. Nevertheless, to be realistic, we must recognize that our range of choice is bound to be arbitrary to some extent, bearing in mind the inescapable constraints of time, English department stocks, cash allocations for new purchases and what is offered by educational publishers. In Part Three, pp.218–25 there is more specific guidance on what schools use at present and what publishers make available to them. Here I want merely to suggest, with some illustrations from actual practice, what criteria we might apply in choosing poems for English teaching purposes.

One problem that we have to face straight away is that of the range of maturity, both in the control and understanding of language and in mental and emotional development, in any single class; poetry in the classroom yields more surprises for English teachers than almost any other branch of their work. As an illustration of this, here is a poem written in the classroom:

Candlelight
A flutter of light came from the flame of the candle.
I watched as the candle was lit,
The way it hurt.
And as I remembered each second of its dying light
A tear rolled down its melting body.
The light of the candle stuck in my head
Like drying wax.

(Catriona Ferguson)

A talented sixth-former? Or at least an unusually sensitive and fluent fourth-year girl? Those would be my conjectures as I registered the rhythmic control here (notice how that first line almost depicts the candle flame it is describing – 'a flutter of light'), the identification of subject with object, starting with that surprising short third line, which lifts the commonplace image of the tear in line five to a significance that is sustained by the final transference '… stuck in my head/Like drying wax'. Not great poetry, of course, but by any standards an unusual achievement for a schoolgirl. It was actually written by one of Sandy Brownjohn's primary school pupils – the work of a 10- or 11-year-old working with others on the way metaphors act in poetry. So, while accepting the need for some kind of categorizing, we must always be on the alert for exceptions. Whatever poems we choose, a few pupils in a class may find them unapproachable, while for others they may seem childish or obvious.

The other point here concerns the relation between poetry reading and writing. It may have seemed odd that I should illustrate one of the problems of choosing suitable poetry for *reading* by referring to a poem *written* in the classroom. It is a part of the purpose of this book to show that once we accept the teaching of poetry as a central responsibility of English teachers we cannot separate and isolate from one another the twin (perhaps 'Siamese twin' would be a better term) activities of reading and writing it. Study of the poetry of others, whether our pupils' peers or established writers, constantly leads to or stems from their own writing; what is being demonstrated and encouraged is the poetic mode of apprehension, what C. Day Lewis called 'the poet's way of knowledge'.

Another general point about choosing poems concerns the question of types or *genres*. One needs to recognize that it is inappropriate to think of all poetry as falling into a simple scale graduated from 'excellent' or 'first-rate' through 'mediocre' to 'downright bad'. I hope I may be excused for pointing out this rather obvious fact. My justification for doing so is that teachers are so frequently asked to participate in the similarly unrealistic exercise of classifying their pupils in this kind of way. I refer, of course, to the writing of school reports. In teaching poetry it is helpful to have some broad categories in one's mind, so that one can first decide what kind of poem is needed for the work envisaged, then select within that category the best poem or poems available. No such classification can ever be final; as soon as one starts 'placing' poems in this way one recognizes the limitations of whatever set of categories is adopted. I put forward the following suggestions with some timidity: at the least, it may encourage poetry teachers to devise and adopt categories of their own, perhaps more suited to their particular circumstances, or to their perception of the range and scope of poetry.

The range of poetry: a suggested framework

(Note: withing each category poems can be classified as: *a*) serious, *b*) light, *c*) popular/'instant'. Teachers can then place any poem *before* deciding whether it is a good or bad example of the particular genre.)

  i)   Poems concerned with subjective or individual response/ feelings/state of mind/reflection/contemplation.

 ii)   Descriptive, without personal involvement – *a*) of things, landscapes, etc., *b*) of people.

iii)   Story poems: *a*) particular incident or episode, *b*) sequence of events.

 iv)   Dramatic poems – concentrating on interplay or interaction of characters.

  v)   'Adopted voice' poems, e.g. MacNeice, 'Prayer before Birth'.

It may sometimes be helpful to place in a separate category 'pattern' poems, i.e., where formal features like metre, refrain, stanza-form or visual appearance (e.g. concrete poetry) are to some extent an end in themselves. This category might also include song lyrics and words which depend for their effect on non-verbal elements.

Having, so to speak, cleared the decks, let us now study this question of choice in relation to classroom work. It is convenient to consider it within three broad age bands: 11–13, 13–15, 14–16+. The larger overlap between the second and third bands is to accommodate the widening of variations in poetic sensibility as children mature.

11- TO 13-YEAR OLD PUPILS

When the Cambridge Resources for English Teaching (CRET) team started work on themes (see Chapter 6) they quickly decided, as many other educationalists have urged, to ignore the artificial demarcation line established by the 1944 Act at 11 plus, and aim their materials at children aged 10–13, with an indication that bright 9-year olds would be able to respond to most of it. The growth of middle schools has tried to overcome the conventional break at 11 altogether, as have independent preparatory schools, but they cater for a tiny minority of the total school population, so we still need to come to terms with the Procrustean reality of a 'secondary' education starting abruptly at 11 plus for most children. English teachers often find the answer in a more flexible resource-based first-form classroom or teaching area – often shared by more than one teacher, in various kinds of team or project work. Some of the most productive first-form classrooms in secondary schools are often indistinguishable from primary school senior class-rooms. And in both you will tend to find similar or identical poetry collections – Geoffrey Summerfield's *Voices* and/or *Junior Voices*, the Bentons' *Poetry Workshop*, various Puffin collections and so on. The importance of having poetry within reach in such classrooms cannot be overstated. The more freedom first- and second-year pupils have to follow up their own interests and ideas, the more they are encouraged to look for what they want in poetry collections as naturally as in encyclopaedias or dictionaries, the better. Habits thus estab-lished can lead to more positive attitudes towards poetry throughout the school.

The teacher's choice of poems will often depend on the nature of the work in hand. I have given specific guidance related to themes, verse techniques, oral poetry, imagery and rhythm, in the five chapters following this one. The suggestions and ideas that follow are therefore more general.

Eleven- and 12-year olds respond strongly to rhythmic and

patterned elements in poetry, so that it is useful to pinpoint poems one knows from experience will get this initial response, even before the subject-matter impinges. The following five examples and the others for this age-range are drawn from the *New Dragon Book of Verse*, edited by M. Harrison and C. Stuart-Clark.

'There was a Naughty Boy' – Keats
'Roman Wall Blues' – Auden
'Daniel Jazz' – Vachell Lindsay
'Macavity' – T. S. Eliot
'Timothy Winters' – Charles Causley

The Auden and Causley poems point the way to an extension of the simple chant-like appeal into more serious subject-matter. The visual clarity of the portrait of the ragged pauper Timothy Winters and his background could lead into many different kinds of English work, both practical and creative, as could the context of Auden's Roman soldier – given a new relevance since the Falklands war.

Simple story-poems, as we see elsewhere (e.g. Chapter 9), have a strong appeal as long as interest is caught from the beginning. It is partly this that T. S. Eliot is working on in 'Macavity'. There are other well-established favourites that still have plenty to offer, some of which appear in the following list:

'The Pied Piper of Hamelin' – Robert Browning
'By St Thomas Water' – Charles Causley
'We are Going to See the Rabbit' – Alan Brownjohn
'The Highwayman' – Alfred Noyes
'The Jackdaw of Rheims' – R. H. Barham
'Diary of a Church Mouse' – John Betjeman

The criterion for story-poems, as for more reflective or descriptive ones, must always be the accessibility of the concepts to 11- and 12-year-olds. Can they understand someone (or – often – some animal) thinking or feeling like this, *without* needing the interposition of a teacher's 'explanation'? The following poems pass this test well:

'Sheep' – Ted Hughes
'The Eagle' – Tennyson
'Cynddylan on a Tractor' – R. S. Thomas
'Village Schoolmaster' – Goldsmith
'The Donkey' – G. K. Chesterton

Finally for this age band one can reckon on a strong response to suitably vivid or dramatic images – appealing strongly to one sense or more. Here are three poems that meet this requirement:

'Shepherd's Hut' – Edward Thomas
'The Listeners' – Walter de la Mare
'A Small Dragon' – Brian Patten

13- TO 15-YEAR OLD PUPILS

We all recognize this as the difficult age, when children are at their most truculent, unpredictable and awkward. When adults say that they were 'put off poetry for life' while they were at school, they are often referring to unfortunate or insensitive attempts at poetry teaching in these middle years of secondary schooling. One source of such unfortunate experiences is the tendency of exasperated, hard-pressed or over-worked teachers to use Draconian and indiscriminate punishments in their attempts to impose 'discipline' on unruly third- and fourth-year classes. I have known these to take the form of writing out (maybe several times) or even learning by heart a poem being studied – hardly the way to encourage a favourable response to the poem thus condemned or to the poetry lesson in general. It is as necessary as ever to maintain an open, enquiring and exploratory attitude in approaching poetry with this age range, and to forgo any temptation to present the work with any kind of authoritarian dogmatism. Partly for this reason I have always found it best to choose the work of contemporary, or at least twentieth-century poets. There is less temptation to lay down the law about a poem's or a poet's quality when it – or he or she – has not had to 'stand the test of time', and this in turn makes it easier to convince your pupils that their opinions matter. Furthermore, it is a risky enterprise to lay down the law about the work of a living poet, who may turn up one day and confound your theories. Another reason for concentrating on poetry of our own times with this age range concerns language. Many of the tensions associated with puberty are linked with inarticulateness; there are not words enough under their control for them to be able to formulate or express most of what they are feeling so intensely, so chaotically. Poetry of the past is often too remote in its language forms for its ideas to come over at all, so that it merely sets up another bar to expression; whereas poetry of their own age often illuminates their own feelings, and therefore releases energies that can find a controlled outlet in the English classroom. Here are two passages dealing with the same subject – a woman looking in her mirror:

> First, robed in white, the nymph intent adores
> With head uncovered, the cosmetic powers.
> A heavenly image in the glass appears,
> To that she bends, to that her eyes she rears;
> The inferior priestess, at her altar's side,
> Trembling, begins the sacred rites of pride.

> Now I am a lake. A woman bends over me,
> Searching my reaches for what she really is.
> Then she turns to those liars, the candles or the moon.
> I see her back, and reflect it faithfully.
> She rewards me with tears and an agitation of hands.
> I am important to her. She comes and goes.
> Each morning it is her face that replaces the darkness.
> In me she has drowned a young girl, and in me an old
>   woman
> Rises towards her day after day, like a terrible fish.

It may be argued that the comparison is an unfair one. To be sure, Pope's lines depend more on the context provided by the rest of the poem and rely on the reader sharing the classical 'conceit' of the priestess at her altar but Plath is also employing a conceit by speaking as if she were the mirror. The point is that Pope's whole social context is remote, and without some grasp of it by his reader the poem remains almost a foreign language text, to be construed rather than read. There is a strong case to be made out for introducing older and more mature students to such poetry, even before the sixth form, but it is a rare 13- or 14-year-old who can make the necessary adjustments that must precede any real *reading* of poetry of the past. George Steiner has set out the difficulty well in his essay on translating poetry prefaced to the *Penguin Book of Modern Verse Translation* :

> We translate perpetually – this is often overlooked – when we read a classic in our own tongue, a poem written in the sixteenth century or a novel published in 1780. We seek to recapture, to revitalise in our consciousness the meaning of words used as we no longer use them, of imaginings that have behind them a contour of history, of manners, of religious or philosophic presumptions radically different from ours. Anyone reading Donne or Jane Austen today, or almost any poem or fiction composed before 1915 (at about which date the old order seems to recede from the immediate grasp of our sensibility), is trying to recreate by exercise of historical, linguistic response; he is, in the full sense, translating.

Most modern anthologies compiled for use in third and fourth forms recognize this, and their editors rarely include more than a sprinkling of older poems. I shall use Michael and Peter Benton's popular *Poetry Workshop* as my main source and of the 143 poems included in it, only seven were not written in this century; the great majority have appeared during the last forty years. This is designed as a teaching anthology and I shall not duplicate here its admirable aims and methods. Those interested in organizing English work thematically, along the lines suggested in the next chapter, will find the arrangement of *Poetry Workshop* well adapted to the purpose, the poems in the first half of the book being grouped in three broad themes, of which the third, 'The World Around You', links up neatly with the two themes I have used as examples. Another section takes five particular poets and gives a representative group of poems from each of them – an idea I shall return to later in this chapter.

As a straightforward introduction to some of the central aspects of poetic expression, Ted Hughes' 'The Warm and the Cold' (*P.W.*, p. 72) is a very useful poem, with its wealth of similes, each one of which is sufficiently teasingly unusual or odd to arouse pupils' curiosity and encourage their emulation. I propose now to suggest three groupings of poems particularly appropriate for this age range.

Looking back to childhood

13 and 14-year-olds often enjoy studying poems about younger children; it reinforces their new sense of growing into the adult world, from where one looks back at childhood with a certain detachment and at the same time permits them to indulge their nostalgic feelings for their own so recent childhood without betraying themselves. The perceptiveness and honesty with which good poets can write about young children can provide an important means of directing both self-awareness and sympathy in teenagers. The following poems are particularly suited to this age range:

'A Child Half-asleep' – Tony Connor (*P.W.*, 28)
'At Seven a Son' – Elaine Feinstein (*P.W.*, 30)
'My Parents Kept Me' – Stephen Spender (*P.W.*, 31)
'How to Catch Tiddlers' – Brian Jones (*P.W.*, 32)
'The Rule' – Stephen Tunnicliffe (*see* p. 263)

Tony Connor's vignette of parent and small sleepy child is particularly approachable with its arresting final line ' "a wolf dreamed me", he says.' and should evoke personal recollections in the class. Elaine Feinstein's swinging boy is less subtle but vivid and memorable. Spender's poem is a school anthology favourite for obvious reasons, and introduces the perennial problem of class divisions not by any means exorcized even in comprehensive schools. Another popular school anthology poem that could join this group but is not in this particular collection is Roethke's 'Child on top of a Greenhouse'. The familiar setting of Brian Jones' poem makes it a good one to study for its language and the way it relates to the activity – in particular in the repetitions of 'hand' and 'net'. I include in this group a poem of my own, published some years ago, because it employs a variety of techniques to portray its subject-matter – a little boy watching the carpenter at work.

Relations with animals

Children of this age are often inhibited from exposing their feelings directly and therefore from responding directly to poems. Animals can often be mediators, allowing them to express feeling more openly. There is a wealth of animal poems, of course; but one needs to choose with some care. Mere descriptions of animals may be useful in connection with a theme but on the whole are more suited to younger, or older children (depending on the sophistication with which they are described). For this age range it is helpful to have a strong relationship established or explored in the poem between animal and human. Some appropriate poems from *Poetry Workshop* are:

'The Meadow Mouse' – Theodore Roethke (p. 12)
'The Arrival of the Bee Box' – Sylvia Plath (p. 20)
'Snake' – Emily Dickinson (p. 22)

Roethke's eye for detail 'now he's eaten his three kinds of cheese and drunk from his bottle-cap watering-trough' is likely to touch off valuable personal reminiscences in the class. Sylvia Plath's father was a distinguished natural scientist and a specialist on bees. Her poem gives a surprising dimension to the relationship between the beekeeper and his or her charges. In spite of belonging to an earlier age, Emily Dickinson has a freshness and directness of both language and sensation that makes her poem a good one to study. Questions of instinctive fear or revulsion to some animals can be usefully discussed and explored through poetry.

Symbolic images

This title may seem a little obscure. I believe it is possible to introduce children in third and fourth forms to an important function of literature that only poetry can fulfil properly, i.e. the presenting of memorable images which resonate beyond themselves and set off ever-widening ripples of feeling and consciousness. The important thing is to ensure that the subject-matter is familiar and immediate, so that it can be responded to directly and thus allow the ripples to spread. Poems in *Poetry Workshop* that seem to meet this requirement are:

'The Road not Taken' – Robert Frost (p. 86)
'The Bonfire' – Anthony Thwaite (p. 59)
'Digging' – Seamus Heaney (p. 82)

Robert Frost's is probably the clearest example of the way a matter-of-fact experience, an item from the trivia of daily life, can be isolated in a poem in such a way as to sound deeper chords. Many children will have helped to make garden bonfires; some find their first real interest in growing things, gardening or farming, in their early teens. Thwaite's poem has the necessary detail to make the symbol real before he explores the further vistas suggested by 'Gehenna', 'beacon', and 'hiding deep inside'. Seamus Heaney's poem is justly well-known. It is particularly useful because it establishes for the writing of poems a down-to-earth practicality that needs to be stressed to pupils of this age.

Third- and fourth-year pupils are sufficiently mature to begin to appreciate individual poetic styles. For this reason it is a good idea from time to time to study a particular poet's work a bit more fully. This can then be taken up and developed, perhaps throughout most of a school year, in individual or group work. Children can be encouraged to make their own choice of a single poet, and to seek out more of his or her poems or books, the end-product being a folio or file, or merely a personal selection. Some poets whose work – or some of it – is particularly appropriate at this level are: Dannie Abse, Ruth Bidgood, Charles Causley, Seamus Heaney, Ted Hughes, John Ormond; see p. 210 for references.

Hughes and Heaney are well represented in *Poetry Workshop*. A longer selection of poems can be found in Geoffrey Summerfield's *Worlds* which also includes some good photographs and background information about the writers. This book also features the work and personality of Charles Causley, whose use of simple and traditional poetic forms, though never facile, makes his work immediately accessible to children. John Ormond's poetic output has been relatively small, but his work has a rare clarity and directness and appeals strongly to adolescents. He is particularly good at poetic portraits – 'The Piano Tuner' (which I have compared usefully with Heaney's 'Thatcher' in another book), 'Organist', 'Cathedral Builders', 'Full Length Portrait of a Short Man' – all are lively, entertaining and approachable.

The much-needed movement towards greater sexual equality sometimes carries with it an assumption that no general statements can ever be made about what boys respond to more than girls, and *vice versa*. Any teacher knows this is not true. At the risk of being accused of sexism, therefore, I recommend the other two poets, Ruth Bidgood and Dannie Abse, for study with girls and boys respectively. Ruth Bidgood's is a modest and quiet talent and her tactile, sensitive vision appeals strongly to girls of 14 and older. I have included a particularly good example – 'Swallows' – in the appendix because her work is not as commonly to be found in schools as it deserves to be. Dannie Abse is better known. His down-to-earth – even earthy – comments on life as he sees it, through the eyes of a Welshman who is also a busy and successful London doctor, evoke a ready response in teenage boys. Particularly noteworthy are 'The Game' (rugby of course!), 'The French Master' – a cruel, but finally compassionate portrait easily recognizable to boys – the rather gruesome 'Pathology of Colours' and 'Chalk' – deriving from a similarly scientific starting point. 'Red Balloon' draws on Abse's personal experience of anti-Semitism in post-war London.

14- TO 16-YEAR OLDS

Much of what has been said in the previous section also applies here, as the overlap in ages suggests. Nevertheless, in teaching 15–16-year-olds and more mature younger ones, one is aware of differences that need to be catered for in choice of poems. There is much more choice here for teachers and most schools have a wide range of available material. Indeed, it is partly because of this *embarras de richesse* that I want to make some attempts here, however sketchy, at mapping the ground. I shall refer mainly to poems in the third volume of Geoffrey Summerfield's popular *Voices*. Although, having been published fifteen years ago, it is not as representative of today's poetry as one would like, it is still unique in its wide range, its catholicity and its freshness of approach both to poetry and to illustration. Because it has been around some time it is also available in many English stocks.

Self-consciousness

At this age, as we know, many pupils are just beginning to develop self-awareness. Ted Hughes once said in a radio talk: 'At about fifteen my life grew more complicated and my attitude to animals changed. I accused myself of disturbing their lives. I began to look at them, you see, from their own point of view.' There are many similar observations, whose truth echoes the experience of most of us. Much poetry relates to this, and it is good to give pupils grappling with their own problems of self-identity, with all the associated feelings of isolation, the chance to read it. There are many appropriate poems in *Voices 3* from which I choose two groups, the first dealing with identity:

'As Others See Us' – Basil Dowling (p. 22)
'What is He?' – D. H. Lawrence (p. 48)
'Leader of Men' – Norman MacCaig (p. 58)
'Birds' – Judith Wright (p. 147)

Lawrence's poem, with its interrogatory form, is intriguing to teenagers and helps them both to ask similar questions and to recognize the limitations of putting people into categories. Dowling again asks questions but from a more egocentric base. With MacCaig's brilliant piece of observation, we probe behind a public mask – a peculiarly relevant poem for today's world. 'Birds' does not, at first, seem to be on the same wavelength; but Judith Wright's third stanza with its transition from 'all these are as birds are' to 'But I am torn and beleaguered' shows the real purpose of the poem, a beautifully crafted piece like almost all her poetry.

The second group is concerned with the most intense personal emotion, love:

'Strawberries' – Edwin Morgan (p. 70)
'The Picnic' – John Logan (p. 71)
'The Clod and the Pebble' – William Blake (p. 97)
'The Garden of Love' – William Blake (p. 97)

'The Secret' – Denise Levertov (p. 172)

I know of no more accurate or sensitive portrayal of first love than Logan's gentle description, which is excellent for private, silent reading as befits its tone. Edwin Morgan's poem makes a good transition into more adult emotion, as do other love lyrics of his. (Two other poets worth studying in this connection are Peter Dale and the Welsh poet Anthony Conran.) The obliqueness of Denise Levertov's poem catches something of the glancing, transitory sweetness of school friendships; Blake's two poems open out the topic into a more universal significance.

The world and society

This is the necessary counterpart to the enclosed intimacy in the first group – although this topic is referred to in MacCaig's poem, which could well serve as a transition from the one to the other:

'Merritt Parkway' – Denise Levertov (p. 28)
'What Were They Like' – Denise Levertov (p. 108)
'Nationality' – Mary Gilmore (p. 113)
'Anthem for Doomed Youth' – Wilfred Owen (p. 125)
'Defence' – Jon Silkin (p. 130)

The point here is to help our pupils to think about how the modern world impinges on our private worlds, and focuses certain patterns of behaviour. Obviously there is a vast body of poetry devoted to this, from which the above list is a tiny fragment. Once again, I think Geoffrey Summerfield's instinct was right in choosing Denise Levertov's work for this age range. Both these poems look at their themes – the automobile society, and Vietnam – with critical, questioning compassion, and can arouse very positive responses in teenagers. Mary Gilmore's poem, almost aphoristic in its brevity and economy, speaks, to girls particularly, about the human realities behind such abstracts as nationalism. Geoffrey Summerfield includes a good selection of Wilfrid Owen's war poems – which again stress the human element. Jon Silkin's poem brings the war theme closer to our times, with a more sardonic emphasis.

The numinous

We should not try to dodge this topic, though it probably concerns the top of the age range being considered here:

'Ballad of the Bread Man' – Charles Causley (p. 63)
'Paradise' – George Herbert (p. 66)
'The Sick Rose' – William Blake (p. 76)
'The Parable of the Old Men and the Young' – Wilfrid Owen (p. 127)
'God's Grandeur' – G. M. Hopkins (p. 149)
'Juggler' – Richard Wilbur (p. 161)

Wilfrid Owen's telling version of the story of Abraham and Isaac serves as a link between the last group and this one. It is an excellent starter for a discussion. As a contrast, there is the joyous certainty behind Gerard Manley Hopkins's sonnet, and George Herbert's puzzle-like poem. On a lighter note Charles Causley's ballad is always a winner with classes – though it has been known to offend R. E. teachers. William Blake and Richard Wilbur use their poetic images of rose and juggler to explore the mystery behind appearances.

Finally – and also to conclude the chapter – I want to suggest five other directions in which one might look when choosing poems for this older age group, some of which have already been touched on.

First, it is important to open the field more deliberately to poetry of former times. There are two good reasons for this. One is that the children's accumulating experience of the different modes and registers of language means that they can engage with more confidence in the 'translation' process George Steiner referred to (p. 41). That being so, poetry of former times is more accessible to them, and provides new dimensions to their experience of literature. A similar inclusiveness should be encouraged towards actual translations. Geoffrey Summerfield gives a good lead on both these scores in *Voices 3*, with his inclusion of poems by Blake, Anne Bradstreet, Herrick, and so on, and by Villon, de Brébeuf, Wu-Ti and others.

Secondly, one needs to look in the other direction, i.e. to actually contemporary poetry, in the latest publications from firms like Carcanet and Anvil Press as well as the mainstream publishers with poetry lists and in poetry magazines. (Part Three gives some guidance on where to look.) Our pupils should always be conscious that we are aware of the actual practice of writing poetry today, and not teaching it as a dead or moribund or peripheral use of English.

Thirdly, with this age group useful work can be done by concentrating on poetry relating to a particular country or region – perhaps over several weeks of work. The obvious choices here are the different countries of the United Kingdom. There are good anthologies of contemporary and older Welsh, Scottish and Irish poetry. One of the best I have come across in this genre is an anthology of contemporary Ulster poetry; *The Wearing of the Black*, edited by Padraic Fiacc (Blackstaff Press, Belfast, 1974); there are many others. Choice will depend on where your school is as well as on your own and your pupils' particular interests, and perhaps also on what opportunities there are for inter-subject collaboration (e.g. history, geography, contemporary studies).

My remaining two suggestions are on rather different lines and concern the *sort* of poem one might be on the lookout for rather than the sources of the poems. One is well illustrated in *Voices*, and may be summed up in the phrase 'take them by surprise!' Over-played, this can lead to a pursuit of gimmickry for its own sake, but it is worth remembering the effectiveness, in a classroom context that may often seem a bit dreary or monotonous, of the unexpected twist, the touch of humour, the element of fun or play. Causley's 'Ballad of the Breadman' (and other poems of his not in *Voices*) makes its impact partly through this. Others are the word-puzzle content of George Herbert's 'Paradise' already referred to, and the intriguing mystery of 'The Clock Winder' by Thomas Hardy (p. 77).

The last point concerns a well-trained and proven way of bringing out the qualities of a poem, by putting it next to another on a similar theme. A good pair in *Voices* is 'Judgements' by William Stafford (p. 43) and Dylan Thomas's 'In my Craft or Sullen Art' (p. 78) where the similarity of theme is not immediately apparent and each poem makes its separate impact. Two collections compiled along these lines which I have found useful are

A. F. Bolt (ed.), *Double Take*, Harrap, 1976.
Raymond Wilson (ed.), *Poems to Compare*, Macmillan, 1966.

6

POETRY IN
THEMATIC WORK

During the last fifteen to twenty years English teachers have increasingly come to recognize how helpful it can be to organize their class work within a thematic frame. The first significant specialist work on this was Geoffrey Summerfield's *Topics in English*, a seminal work for many of today's English teachers. In it he writes:

> the theme may be what I choose to call 'archetypal'; that is, it may be concerned with some fundamental and universal experience such as a sense of isolation or the impulse to rebel, or it may be less general, more specific: even when most specific, in appearance, it will still ideally tap certain deeper roots. Nothing, perhaps, could be more specific than, say, the Eddystone Lighthouse: a boy with an interest in civil engineering or architecture might well become involved in such a topic; but the project, as I conceive of it, would be seriously limited if it did not carry the pupil into an exploration, through the imagination, of such things as loneliness, the violence and terror of natural forces, the

calamities and sorrows of shipwreck and the ingenuity and pertinacity of man.

Six years later the symposium that Geoffrey Summerfield and I edited, *English in Practice*, in which six heads of English describe their work, provided concrete evidence of the way themes were contributing to more focused English teaching, and in particular were helping to provide that meaningful context which is the necessary prerequisite for growth in children's language. The increasing popularity of thematic English has not been without its abuses. Geoffrey Summerfield warned us right from the start: 'we should be prepared to let literature *be*, rather than reduce it to a subsidiary role of stimulus' (*Topics in English*, p. 14); and more recently David Allen has pointed out that 'the material, selected by the teacher and truncated to fit the theme, conveys the *teacher's* values. The teacher becomes a block on the plurality of voices instead of offering real choice.' 'Truncated to fit the theme.' There lies the danger, and most English teachers are well aware of it. Nevertheless, as Allen himself says later on in his book, 'it is possible to collect poems and short stories together that do deal with an important aspect of human experience and to plan all the English work around an exploration of that aspect without doing violence to the poems and stories. Theme work needs to be more carefully thought out' (*English Teaching since 1965*).

As general editor of the *Cambridge Resources for English Teaching*, I have been involved over a number of years in the publication of English resource material on thematic lines. Some of what follows draws on this experience, which led to the production of three 'theme kits' under the titles of *Stone, Wood, Metal, Plastic, Friends and Enemies, Extra-ordinary*. These were produced collaboratively by the team of six English teachers, with a different team member taking chief editorial responsibility for each one. For the first theme, *Stone, Wood, Metal, Plastic*, that responsibility was mine. I quote from the introduction to the Teacher's Book:

The purpose of this theme is to encourage children first to look intelligently and sensitively at material aspects of their physical environment; secondly to think about the effects these materials have on the way we live – our dependence on them, our estimation of their value, and so on. In other words, the theme is both outward- and inward-looking. We shape and are shaped by these materials; we are aware of their qualities and their potentialities and these in turn determine the pattern of our daily lives and behaviour in many ways – often very pervasive and far-reaching ones.

The four materials are not linked arbitrarily. Stone and wood are the two basic 'permanent' natural substances, primary and ubiquitous constructional material, as well as forming the major features in any natural landscape. Metal, extracted from stone by means of the stored energy of wood, became the first manufactured material of any permanence. And now those products of modern scientific technology, the polymers, are demonstrating, both in their variety and in the versatility of their application, a new ubiquity that affects our life on all sides and is already being reflected in our literature.

A study and exploration of these four together should help children to articulate and to define their relationship with their immediate daily environment. In order to do this, language, as always, is the essential instrument. The material assembled in this set of resources will involve – indeed, will demand – a versatile control of language both in talk and in the written word.

The theme has been chosen with the special needs of ten- to thirteen-year-olds in mind. At this age children are endlessly curious about their world, yet in the society of their peers alone do not acquire the language tools necessary to explore it with full perceptiveness. If they are not given the opportunity to focus their attention on different aspects of their surroundings, to express themselves, first orally then in writing about them, and to link the phenomena they experience with the experiences of others through reading as well as directed discussion and drama, the frustration engendered by their inarticulateness will lead to boredom and indifference. English lessons give them a unique chance to explore these four materials and their relationship, with no practical or academic strings attached, so that their imaginative and creative faculties are given full play.

I believe what I said in that passage provides sufficient justification for giving below a reasonable sample of the work included in the theme kit *Stone, Wood, Metal, Plastic*. Just because theme work so effectively provides meaningful contexts and opportunities for many different kinds of productive activities, there are often no clear dividing lines in the work between different modes of English – prose fiction, factual or descriptive prose, drama, poetry and so on. Often children can be given a choice of between, say, writing a poem or a description; often the reading of an apposite poem in the course of work grouped round a theme may start off non-'poetic' responses. This fact means that thematic English does not lend itself to neat or exclusive categorizing as 'poetry teaching'; however, it can be a great ally to the English teacher who recognizes the essential unity of all written forms of English, and believes, as I do, that one needs to encourage children to accept poetry as as natural a form of expression as any other. Another particular advantage of thematic English, made clear in the work-suggestions given below, is that it lends itself to mixed-ability teaching, especially when group work is adopted.

The following selection of questions related to the theme *Stone, Wood, Metal, Plastic* come from over one hundred such work-suggestions, covering every kind of response and activity, that appear in the Work Cards accompanying the Theme Book. All of them have been used or devised by classroom teachers of English, with the needs of first- and second-year pupils of all abilities in mind. A few questions were devised particularly for more able or less able pupils. These are indicated. All the poems referred to appear in the Theme Book

(Cambridge, 1975). The references to the slides and tape forming part of the thematic 'kit' are explained in the notes. The boy's poem 'Dreams of a Stone' in Chapter 14 (p. 198) relates to this theme.

Poem-based work

POEMS: *'Gravel Paths' by Patricia Hubbell;
'The Pebble' by Francis Le Fevre (aged 12) (see
Appendix, p. 265)*

1 What do you hear and feel when you walk on shingle? or on a wooden bridge? or on a metal ladder or catwalk? Describe a walk over any of the four materials. Make sure you say what you are wearing on your feet or whether you are bare-footed (see slide A4) (Note *i*).

2 Read the poems 'Gravel Paths' and 'The Pebble'. The second was written by a boy of twelve. Try to *be* any other familiar substance or thing made of stone, wood, metal or plastic, and write a poem or story saying what it feels like. For instance, you could be the piece of sycamore being shaped for the harp's neck on the tape. (Note *ii*).

POEM: *'Wild Iron' by Allen Curnow*

3 Write a poem about any *repeated* noises by any of the four materials, e.g. plastic sheet flapping, waves on shingle. Listen to tape B3 (Note *iii*).

POEM: *'I like that stuff' by Adrian Mitchell*

4 Work out a group reading of this poem. Add verses of your own if you can, and find suitable background music for it.

POEM: *'The Grindstone' by Robert Frost*

5 Read the poem. Think carefully about the lines 'for months it hasn't known the taste of steel,/Washed down with rusty water in a tin'. Write about 'knowing the taste of steel' as if you were the grindstone. Do you like or dislike the man who turns you? If you can, get a tape recording of a grindstone to go with your writing.

POEM: *'The Carpenter' by Clifford Dyment*

6 (for less academic pupils) In the fifth verse of 'The Carpenter' the oak tree is said to be like a strong man, a weightlifter. See if you can think of suitable comparisons for other kinds of tree (e.g. willow, aspen, hawthorn, lilac). Make a list and do drawings to go with them.

POEMS: *'The Secret of the Machines' by Rudyard Kipling; 'Excavator' by Michaela Edridge; 'Things Made by Iron' by D. H. Lawrence.*

7 (for more able pupils) In the 'Secret of the Machines', Kipling makes the machines say 'we can neither love nor pity nor forgive'. Compare this with the description of the excavator and D. H. Lawrence's short poem. Is there any tool or machine you feel friendly towards and which seems friendly towards you? If there is (e.g. a family car) describe it – in a poem if you like.

POEM: *'The Ship' by John Masefield*

8 Read the poem. Work out a group reading, giving a separate voice to each part. Discuss how many different materials make up a car, or a bike, or a pram. How many 'wisdoms' were needed?

POEM: '*Autumn in Wales*' *by Tom Earley*

9 (for more able pupils) Read the poem together, then work out a group description of another season. The groups should, between them, cover the three remaining seasons. Include in your description as many comparisons as you can, like Tom Earley's 'metal' comparisons. Try to use stone, wood and plastic as well – or other materials if you think they are more suitable.

POEM: '*The Pigeon*' *by Richard Church*

10 (for less able pupils) Read the poem together. What are the noisiest places you have ever been in? Make a list of them, with notes about how the loud noises are made. Look at slides A2 and 17. Listen to tape B4 (Note *iv*).

Work not based on a particular text

11 Use a piece of music as a basis for a 'dream sequence' involving one or two of the materials. Discuss it together, each person in the group contributing part of the sequence. You will need to listen to the music several times (Note *v*).

12 Write a poem called 'Hands' (Note *vi*).

13 Have any big trees been felled near your school or home? Have you ever been there when a tree was cut down? Talk about the effect it would have on the animals, birds, insects, etc. that make their homes in trees. Find pieces of writing that describe tree-felling and its results.

14 Work out together suitable epitaphs to be inscribed on gravestones for a carpenter, for a farmer, for a bus conductor, for a housewife, for a shop assistant. Design a suitable tombstone to inscribe it on (see slides A7, 22) (Note *vii*).

15 Each member of the group prepare a riddle like an Anglo-Saxon riddle, dividing up the four materials between you.

Decide which are the best ones in your group by trying them on one another, then use the best with the rest of the class. The winner is the riddle that is a true description of the object, but takes the longest to guess (Note *viii*).

NOTES

i)   The slide is of a pebble beach.

ii)   The tape includes an interview with a maker of harps.

iii)   The tape includes a visit to a blacksmith in his forge. He makes a horseshoe.

iv)   The tape includes a short sample of the noise inside a steelworks. The slides are of a house being demolished and a steel ingot being cast.

v)   I have used very successfully for this work parts of Bartok's music for strings, percussion and celeste.

vi)   A number of references in the theme kit concern the craftmanship involved in shaping and using the four materials.

vii)   The Theme Book includes an anonymous eighteenth-century epitaph. The slides are of an old gravestone with a painted inscription/epitaph and an unusual inscribed memorial obelisk. In Chapter 9 I have drawn attention to the way *In Memoriam* verses can be used (see p. 126). Teachers wanting to pursue the idea of writing amusing epitaphs will find a wealth of material in *A Small Book of Grave Humour* ed. Fritz Spiegl (Pan) and *Seen Grandad Lately?* by Roy Fuller (Faber).

viii)   This work is based on an Anglo-Saxon riddle given in the Theme Book. Riddles are a rich source of materials and provide good models. They are included in many anthologies.

As is clear from the work-suggestions above, thematic English needs to be very open-ended and teachers choosing to follow a theme have to be resourceful enough – in two senses i.e. in their personal flexibility and readiness to adapt, and in being able to provide adequate resources for class use, e.g. along the lines of *Cambridge Resources for English Teaching* – to shift from one mode of expression to another, as the theme develops, or, at worst, to abandon the topic altogether if it becomes evident that the pupils' interest and energies are not being engaged by it.

Much of the resistance by some teachers to thematic English stems from unhappy experiences of the too relentless pursuit of a theme, possibly in an inter-disciplinary context, where in any case one's freedom of action is restricted by the exigencies of team-work.

One of the most interesting – and, with care, usable – series of thematic poetry collections is *Themes*, edited by Rhodri Jones. The seven themes explored, each through a separate (inexpensive) anthology with an accompanying book, are 'Men and Beasts', 'Imagination', 'Conflict', 'Generations', 'Sport and Leisure', 'Men at Work' and 'Town and Country'. Jones has also edited a junior (10–13) series of four thematic poetry anthologies: 'Families', 'Work and Play', 'Weathers' and 'Five Senses', with a teacher's book for the whole series. My chief reservation about these well-produced and lively collections is their rather ill-defined concept of what constitutes a 'theme'. Can one really meaningfully group within a common category such various ideas as are represented by 'generations' 'town and country', 'men and beasts'? Can one really separate 'conflict' from 'sport', or 'imagination' from any other thematic group? The danger is that thematic work defined as loosely as this may cease to mean anything to pupils, in which case it loses its chief value, that of providing context and motivation for English. However, samples of the series are well worth including in any school's English resources.

Surroundings – a theme for exploration through poems

I end this chapter with a suggested theme for third-year pupils. In some ways it is linked with the one already described for first- and second-formers, as once again it aims to concentrate attention on the children's immediate environment. However, a different emphasis is appropriate here, both because of the more sophisticated approach needed for third-year pupils, uneasily torn between childhood and adolescence and because one can explore the effect of environment on behaviour and personality more critically. It is possible to explore this theme chiefly through poetry – leaving the pupils to make such other connections and correspondences as will naturally arise, with novels, plays, pictures or their own prose writing. There is a wealth of suitable poetry, and most schools will yield plenty from their current stock, which judicious use of the photo-copier can turn into a theme collection for the duration of the work.

A good way to introduce the theme is to choose a poem in which both the environment and its occupant or occupants have equal prominence, as is implied in the title of the theme. Here is a short poem by Pamela Beattie, ideal for the purpose;

Alone
Yesterday you found
that on the 49th square
third row up, on the left
above the mantelpiece
was a fly splat, that
wasn't there on Monday
or was it Tuesday?
You shouted 'look'.
No one came.

This should immediately make possible lively discussion of how modern housing/urban planning, etc. can isolate people, of the relative importance of the environment and personality in causing loneliness, and so on. The advantage poetry has over more explicit description is the space it leaves for the reader's imagination to participate.

The single introductory poem can be followed by a group dealing with individuals, e.g. R. S. Thomas's 'Country Child', Philip Hobsbaum's 'I Know It Was the Place's Fault', Seamus Heaney's 'Personal Helicon' (all of these poets have many poems well fitted to this theme). The familiar town/country contrast can be explored, the emphasis depending on where the school is. Edwin Morgan's 'Glasgow Sonnets' (referred to in Chapter 7) and Douglas Dunn's *Terry Street* (London, Faber, 1969) give vivid glimpses of city life. In 'A Removal from Terry Street', Dunn in fact provides in his final lines a good transition from town to country:

>   … Her husband
> Follows …/… pushing, of all things, a lawnmower.
> There is no grass in Terry Street. The worms
> Come up cracks in concrete yards in moonlight.
> That man I wish him well. I wish him grass.

R. S. Thomas again, or earlier poets – W. H. Davies, John Clare for instance – can provide contrasting poems of country life. An intriguing choice for study might be Chris Torrance's 'South London Prose Poem' which starts:

> Sunset over a waste of allotments tended by gnomes: rows of squat houses with lazily smoking chimneys. Small gnomish houses surrounded by a waste of decaying allotments tended by dwarfish men smoking pipes.
>
> Rows of painted brick houses and untidy back-gardens, cabbage plots and patches of weed-strewn earth narrowly bisected by wandering muddy paths. A slow dreamy sunset curling away over the dark rooves of dwarfish little houses inhabited by gnomes tending their decaying allotments.
>
> Cabbage patches and small fields of earth and stones divided by scrubby hedgerows and pipe-smoking gnomes

carefully tending their unkempt gardens....

And if you want light relief Adrian Mitchell provides it in many poems – one of which I can't resist including:

> *A Good Idea*
> It should be the kind which stiffens and grows a skin
> But the creamier kind will do.
> Anyway, the Royal Albert Hall must be filled with
>   custard.

Work related to this theme can take many forms. The important thing is to emphasize the way in which accurate description of people in their surroundings will tend also to comment on the way behaviour is shaped by environment. Other modern poets whose work is particularly useful for this theme are Ted Hughes (e.g. in *Remains of Elmet*), Glyn Hughes, Carl Sandburg (especially on industrial environments), Alan Brownjohn, Charles Causley.

7

PLAYING WITH WORDS

The title of this chapter is not frivolous. We all know the value of creative play during a child's early years. By 'playing' he or she is in fact learning to manipulate, control, understand the world around him or her, as well as to express feelings, to develop a uniqueness. Poetry, like other art-forms, is an extension of that exploratory urge, and any teaching of poetry must take this into account. There is a sense in which poetry always includes forms of 'playing with words' – whether through such well-worn devices as the ones we are considering in this chapter – rhyme, alliteration, assonance and metrical forms – or in the more extreme ways explored in 'concrete' and shape poems. I shall describe a number of actual poetry lessons in the course of the chapter, all of which stress the element of play. In the first year of secondary school it can be quite overt; 11-year-old children spend much of their waking life in play, and don't as a rule feel self-conscious at taking part in it even in the classroom. As our pupils grow older the play factor may be less openly acknowledged, but I hope users of this book will recognize it just as clearly, and present the material to their pupils in the same spirit. Once 'the poetry lesson' becomes synonymous with 'work' – even, as can happen, with drudgery, or boring, uninvolved work – it will cease to achieve even its most limited aims.

The purpose of the lessons outlined is to suggest various approaches by giving workable examples of them. I hope they will all serve as types or models rather than simply as one-off experiments. Together, with others in Part Two, they will demonstrate an approach to the teaching of poetry that is in line with the concept of poetry and the poetic process that informs Part One.

As we saw there, poems initially make their effect by appealing to (or assaulting!) the sense of hearing and sight. We don't, in general, directly feel, smell or taste poems, and experiments that try to impinge directly on those senses do not constitute a significant part of the experience of poetry. Hearing is still, as it always has been since the invention of language, the primary channel, and this means that the *sound* of words, both individually and in combinations, has an overriding importance. Because our most familiar and convenient means of preserving and 'repeating' poetry is print, sight also has a part to play in the totality of the poetry experience. The lessons that follow examine *a*) the techniques available for ordering sounds – rhyme, alliteration, assonance, metre; *b*) techniques particularly concerned with the appearance of poetry; then, amalgamating the two, *c*) verse-forms. As we shall find, it is not always in practice possible or even desirable to separate these three elements in actual lessons. Underlying them all come questions of syntax and grammar, and it is desirable to plan some poetry lessons simply as exploration into the children's already acquired – but for the most part only sub-consciously understood – knowledge of language. The first lesson shows what can be done with a junior form.

Establishing the patterns

An 11-year-old girl wrote this as the first verse of a poem on 'The Wind':

> The wind blows across my garden
> Taking with it leaves and flowers
> Birds are tossed and blown about
> Please stop blowing wind.

In its simplicity and economy this rivals Stanley Cook's little poem in Chapter 3 (p. 19). It would be possible to use it simply as an example of someone responding to a stimulus and to develop a traditional poetry lesson with this as a starting-point (What is the effect of the wind? Does the writer like it? Is it alive or dead? etc., etc.) I want to suggest another way of using it.

First get the children to cut out twenty-two leaf shapes in paper, eight smaller (say 3 inches long), the rest larger. This may be done at the end of a lesson or in an odd five or ten minutes. If there is time, each can be coloured in a suitable autumn colour, or they can be cut from different coloured paper. Before the lesson in which you are to use them, write in capitals, with felt pen, the words in this verse, one to a 'leaf', using the smaller ones for the/across/my/with/it/and/are/and/. Write on both sides. These, with board and chalk, and scribbling pads for the children, are all the equipment needed. The aim will be to establish by demonstration and experiment the irrevocability of syntactical word-order, and the contribution of syntax to poetic expression. The way you start the lesson depends on your relationship with and control of the class. Assuming these are both adequate, why not try shock tactics?

Stage 1: throw all the 'leaves' in the air in a clear space, and let them flutter to the ground. Rescue any that have gone too far, and ask the children to look without touching and jot down any combinations of two words they see together that 'make sense'. There will be some discussion of this, e.g. noting that three of the words (wind, blows, leaves) have two quite separate meanings. They do not yet know the poem, so don't know the *context* that will enable them to select the appropriate one – a useful small point to draw to their attention. One or two stirrings of the leaves will yield more word pairs.

Stage 2: Collect them up, and sort them into four bundles for the four lines of the verse. Don't at this stage show the children the verse. It is useful at this point however to rule out of order the 'wrong' meanings of the three ambiguous words. Divide the class into four groups and give each line to a different group. Ask them to compile a list of pairs of words from those they now have (they can consult their notes to see if they've already got any) that make sense, either complete or partial. It will help to ask them to draw an arrow either before or after the pair if it seems to need extra words with it. A simple example will help them to see what you mean; Sentence: *She practises often*. Six possible pairs, one meaningless, thus:

she practises	she often	practises often
practises she	often she	often practises

Ask them to put in brackets pairs they are not sure about. The result for line 1 should look something like this:

the wind	blows the	across my
the garden	(blows wind)	across the
(wind across)	blows my	(across garden)
wind garden	(blows garden)	my garden
	blows across	my wind
		garden wind

Once this stage is reached – and you need to be prepared for much talk, discussion and questioning before it is so – have a report-back session from the groups. Doing this will establish a consensus of what constitutes a meaningful pair of words, which words need or imply others, and so on. It is useful to ask which pairs could act as *titles* (e.g. in line 1 *the wind, the garden*, *my wind*, *my garden*, and perhaps *wind garden* – an evocative phrase).

At this stage – which may also be the conclusion of the lesson, or of the first part – you can ask each group to make a line of poetry out of their words. Having checked each line with the original (which may occasion some instructive discussion about differences between their line and the original), the class as a whole can decide the order of the four lines. Again, the comparison with the original order will be useful, in demonstrating the inevitability of certain sequences once one has crystallized out one's ideas in language.

What has the lesson achieved? First, it has shown that few if any words can take us far as isolated 'things' – like dead leaves. They gain their real meaning in word patterns or groups. An alert pupil may at some stage have asked why some leaves are smaller than others, which could lead to discussion about which words or kinds of words are individually meaningful, which depend totally on context for meaning. Secondly, it has brought the children into some awareness of their own considerable grasp of syntactical forms. Thirdly, it has enabled the children to participate in the mechanics of the poem, so to speak, and therefore to recognize more clearly something of the range of linguistic choices open to anyone who sets out to make a poem. Finally, it has demonstrated visually something of what the poem is about. This may seem a small point, even an over-simplified one. I do not think we can too readily discount the contribution to poetry learning of sensory impressions – visual, aural and tactile stimuli. In this instance it may act as a corrective to the rather artificial way we have fragmented the original verse. It can help to remind us and the children we are teaching that the girl who wrote the poem was not just stringing words together according to known patterns, but applying her unconsciously acquired knowledge in order to make something new out of her experience of the wind. We have not, in fact, discussed at all the subject-matter or the imaginative response of the writer. This reminds us that such lessons need to take their place alongside ones concerned more with the imaginative and emotive aspects of poetry. Such lessons are to be found in Chapters 6, 9 and 10.

The kind of lesson outlined above may take many forms, depending partly on the size, age- and ability-range of the learning group, partly on the aspect of syntax that you wish to be concerned with. It may, for instance, be used in the course of a more extended plan linked with poetry writing, or group anthology compilation. Let us now turn to that most basic of poetic processes, the ordering, arranging and patterning of *sounds*. In one sense this is as wide as poetry itself, but in practical terms we can approach the topic more modestly. (The concept of *rhythm*, which is the basis of all sound patterns, needs separate treatment, so will be discussed in Chapter 9, after we have looked more closely at heard and spoken poetry in Chapter 8.)

Matching sounds (alliteration, assonance, rhyme)

One of the recurrent problems in English teaching is to cope with our pupils' already acquired language habits. In a representative class of thirty there are always seven or eight or more sharply different sets of assumptions about what constitutes acceptable or appropriate language in a given situation. While we should, especially in poetry teaching, be able to turn this very variety to practical use, it is helpful sometimes to demonstrate certain shared elements. Delight in repeated sounds is one basic one, and is justification for spending poetry teaching time on a technique like the use of rhyme, in spite of the warnings from the 'creative writing' lobby. Some of those warnings stem from the alacrity with which children, especially if they have had prolonged exposure to nursery rhymes before coming to us, can use this kind of word-play as a refuge from emotional involvement. That gifted poetry teacher Sandy Brownjohn seems to be taking an extreme position when she says: 'I make no apology for deliberately banning the use of rhyme when teaching a group of children for the first time – unless the rhymes occur naturally' (*Does It Have To Rhyme?* p. 72). But she is talking about primary school children, and she goes on to explain and demonstrate usefully how she 'starts the children off again' on using rhyme as one resource among many in the poetic control of language. Before following her lead, let me give a telling example of the way rhyme, even in the secondary school, can inhibit an able pupil. Both the following pieces were imaginary, i.e. not based directly on first-hand experience. The second was written in response to a vivid newspaper report of a military coup in a foreign country. Both are by the same 13-year-old girl; it is interesting to see how her emotional response to the event led her to take up the idea previously played with in rhyme. Because her sympathies were engaged her need for greater emotional intensity forced her to abandon rhyme, which she had not yet learned to handle. In doing so, she also abandoned the trite metrical scheme she had chosen as appropriate to rhyme:

I

Walking, walking, walking miles,
Over fields and over stiles,
No family, no friends,
Only the road which twists and bends,
Every day I go trampling on,
Under rain and under sun,
But my life is the life I love
With the ground below, the sky above.
So on, on, on I go
Till death parts me and the beloved land I know.

II

Walk, walk, walk is all I seem to do.
Now and again I look back
To a destroyed country,
Black, grey and dismal.

A shattered house,
A littered street, broken windows,
Doors, papers with anti-slogans
Upon their crumpled surface.

This is a warning, but it is not the whole of the story. Given proper guidance and encouragement, and an understanding of what is being aimed at, rhymed poetry of high order can come from children, even young children. Consider this, for instance, from an 11-year-old-boy. He uses the first two lines of each stanza as a refrain, with significant variations. The opening lines, for instance, had been:

They sent us off to Ireland, that green and pleasant
  island,
They sent us off to Ireland, across the Irish sea.

The poem tells a story, ballad-style, of a young soldier hurt by a bomb explosion. Here are the last two (i.e. the fifth and sixth) stanzas:

They sent me back from Ireland, that dark
  unpleasant island,
They sent me back to my land, across the Irish sea.
While my friends drive round in cars,
Go to discos, go to bars,
Is there anyone who'll change their place with me?

Oh, the government did their best, pinned a medal
  on my chest,
They have done everything that they can do;
But when the fighting's done,
Does it matter who has won,
When you're crippled, blind and only twenty-two?
(Marcus Natten in E. Lowbury (ed.), *Night Ride and
            Sunrise*, Aberystwyth, Celtion, 1978.)

Some attention of the right sort paid to *sound* patterns in verse can pay dividends, both in children's own writing, and in their enjoyment and appreciation of the poetry they read.

This is a lesson for 11- and 12-year-old pupils. A good way to start this investigation of rhyme is through examples that will be familiar to most of them. Cockney rhyming slang is one of the best-known (plates of meat – feet/apples and pears – stairs/tit for tat – hat, etc.). General discussion will probably throw up plenty of examples, including some new inventions. Point out, if they do not know, how by abbreviating the rhymed expression (hat becoming 'titfer', etc.) one enhances the enjoyment of the sound-matching by making it a shared secret. If this catches on in the class, they can develop a secret rhyming slang of their own and use it to one another around school. The collection of rhymes thus acquired will make it easy to introduce the idea of making lists of rhyming words. Rather than leaving this as a free-for-all, it is helpful to use a short rhymed poem as a starting-point, such as Elizabeth Jennings's 'Rhyme for Children'

> I am the seed that slept last night;
> This morning I have grown upright.
>
> Within my dream there was a king.
> Now he is gone in the wide morning.
>
> He had a queen, also a throne.
> Waking, I find myself alone.
>
> If I could have that dream again,
> The seed should grow into a queen
>
> And she should find at her right hand
> A king to rule her heart and land:
>
> And I would be the spring which burst
> Beside their love and quenched their thirst.
>
> (From *The Secret Brother*)

Take the first rhyming word of each pair (night, king, throne, again, hand, burst) without revealing to the class the whole poem, and allocate one each to a group of four or five children. Their job is, first, simply to collect rhyming words. It can be made into a contest, using as a reward the order in which groups report back, either this activity or a later one. You will probably have to discuss the equivocally pronounced word 'again' with the group concerned (it is interesting to see what the poet did with it). The exercise of making a list will itself draw the children's attention to a number of points about rhyming. They can be led to formulate the 'true rhyme' rule of changed initial consonant, identical vowel and final consonant, and to discuss the possibility of variations from this. The question of rhyming single- with poly-syllabled words will inevitably come up, and this will lead to discussion of stress – if 'night' can rhyme with 'right' and 'delight' does it also rhyme with 'wheelwright' and 'insight'? Which rhymes are stronger? (When the poem is divulged, the rhyme king/morning, and its effect on the way one feels the rhythm of the line – and why the poet wanted it this way – should lead to productive discussion.) Another point that should come up spontaneously, but could be prompted if necessary, is the question of local or dialect pronunciations. These words, for instance, may elicit such 'rhymes' as night/wait, throne/down, again/line, hand/end, etc., regarded by most of the children as 'true' rhymes. When this stage is completed – which could well take more than one English period – the original poem could be read and written out, and its rhymes commented on in relation to meaning. At once this will lead to new discoveries about the way rhyme works. Notice how the 'hinge' of the poem is that teasingly half-rhymed fourth couplet. Once the children's attention is drawn to this someone will notice the more insistent assonance in this verse – dream/seed/queen – and begin to appreciate the poet's skill in thus subtly drawing attention to the way this part focuses the poem, and how it expands from the desolation of 'find myself alone' to the consummation of the final couplet. When that is grasped, even in part, a question to the class about the meaning of 'I am the seed that slept' should yield rich results, both in discussion and in writing of their own. This is a poem that might well stick in children's minds, so that it could serve later as a point of reference in other lessons on rhyme.

Let us now tackle the question of metre. This is a vast subject, and it is quite outside the scope and the intention of this book to try to present any exhaustive catalogue of metres, or examination of the range of metrical patterns. A workable summary of the commonest English traditional metrical feet is given in the excellent school anthology *Poems* (Harrison and Stuart-Clark). Our task is to open our pupil's minds to the possibilities and advantages of metrically ordered language in poetry. I want to set out now two complementary lessons, the first relating to 'free' or unmetrical verse, the other to metre. Both lessons are for more senior pupils than we have considered so far in this chapter – they are pitched at the level of 14- to 16-year-olds. They assume, therefore, that by this time the children have had a fair grounding in reading, listening to and writing poetry. They will have made discoveries of their own about how best to set out their poems on the page as well as about the way this relates to how one reads or hears them.

Free verse – eye or ear?

(It is essential to have one or more tape-recorders (preferably cassette recorders) for this and the next lesson.)

Stage 1: Start by recording an immediate spoken response in not more than twenty words to a visual or aural stimulus. Examples of the first might be: a picture, the view from the classroom window, a sculpture (felt as well as seen if possible), an animal, a treasured object – coin, ring, brooch – or personal possession, or an article of clothing. If you prefer aural stimuli (and they can sometimes carry the advantage of surprise or unfamiliarity), it is worth experimenting with collecting sounds on tape: remarkable effects can be caught from walking on different surfaces; many kitchen sounds – soup bubbling, washing up etc.; mechanical or animal noises; a fire burning, etc. (Some such sounds are included in the *Cambridge Resources for English Teaching* kit referred to in Chapter 6.) It is important at this stage *not* to write anything down, but to record the response direct, as soon as possible after the stimulus that gives rise to it. If there is more than one recorder this is best done in groups. Here is one such response, from a fourth-year girl in a West Riding school: 'Tarnished brown hillsides seen from the deep valley burn in the sun.' The groups can now exchange recorders and transcribe each other's descriptions, or if done on a class basis you play back the recordings and get the whole class to transcribe them; the only stipulation is that they start a fresh line after each natural pause of the speaker. Our example came out as:

> tarnished brown hillsides
> seen from the deep valley
> burn in the sun

This activity will establish the way language takes on 'sound shapes'. A selection of the most successful pieces should be written up on the board or added to the classroom wall display. *Stage 2*: R. S. Thomas's poem '*Ffynnon Fair*' (St Mary's Well) from his *Laboratories of the Spirit* can now be introduced. It is useful to have a copy for each pupil, or at least one between two. Ask them not to read it aloud yet, but first to compare its line changes with those in the pieces just transcribed, and comment on any differences. It is likely that this will lead to some surprise at the apparent arbitrariness of Thomas's lineation, and some discussion as to his reasons. Now ask them to listen to the poet reading his poem (on Oriel Records OR 004). Ask the pupils to put a pencil line at each pause as the poet reads, then transcribe his poem in its spoken form. The result should be as follows:

They did not divine it,
but they bequeathed it to us:
clear water, brackish at times,
complicated by the white frosts of the sea,
but thawing quickly.

Ignoring my image,
I peer down to the quiet roots of it,
where the coins lie,
the tarnished offerings of the people
to the pure spirit that lives there,
that has lived there always,
giving itself up to the thirsty,
withholding itself
from the superstition of others,
who ask for more.

Only one of the printed lines survives. Before going further it may be useful to give a few background details. The 'St Mary's Well' (or spring – the words mean the same in Welsh) of the poem is right by the sea at the tip of the Lleyn peninsula, opposite the ruined St Mary's Priory on Bardsey Island, and near where the poet, a retired Welsh country clergyman, now lives. His economy of language should be appreciated by most pupils: the way the pronouns 'they' and 'us' are totally adequate, suggesting the continuity of a tradition; the way the title is taken up by the word 'it'; the just opposition of 'tarnished' with 'pure', and the way the overtones of 'tarnished' are transferred to those who are superstitious enough to use this holy place as a wishing well, instead of accepting simply what it offers – pure water. Some may go further, recognizing how 'giving itself up to the thirsty' takes on a symbolic significance with its biblical echo, in keeping with the well's origin and the observer's occupation.

If the pupils now compare the poet's actual 'lines' as he speaks them with their own descriptive pieces, they will find that in both the words are grouping naturally into forms determined by language structure. The coincidence of the same word in both makes this very obvious in our description:

> tarnished brown hillsides
> the tarnished offerings of the people
>
> seen from the deep valley
> complicated by the white frosts of the sea
>
> burn in the sun
> (I) peer down to the quiet roots of it

We now return to the printed version. Why is it set out like this? This raises the question of how we *read* poetry on the page, and how also we respond to the page's orderliness. We shall come back to this in Chapter 8 (p. 101). In the printed version the lines are regularized to an average length of 7 or 8 syllables. Only one line (the second) falls below. The three longest lines all come in the second stanza or section, giving it an appearance of more substance, befitting the shift from the general description to poet's personal response. One might describe the use of the printed lines as a kind of intellectual guide to the silent reader rather than any indication of its spoken tempo or shape. Thus we can appreciate, for instance, the juxtaposition in print of the two phrases 'the coins lie, the tarnished offerings', even though when speaking the line the poet attaches them respectively to the relative 'where' and the qualifying 'of the people'.

This lesson has tackled the question of the relationship between form and substance in poetry. In fact it has been concerned with questions about the *shapes* of language similar to those dealt with more simply in the first lesson described in this chapter. Taken on its own it should stimulate a greater awareness of what the children are achieving in their own attempts at free verse. However, I believe it is of more value if linked to a follow-up lesson concentrating on metrical verse.

Metre and rhyme – reins or shackles?

For this let us take a more familiar poem, W. B. Yeats's 'An Irish Airman Foresees His Death'. I find it easier to lead up to this poem *via* a general discussion of the loss of friends through bereavement. Another approach is through the present Irish question, its toll in human terms and its history in Yeats's time. That fine elegy 'In Memory of Major Robert Gregory' should really be read with the other, but is probably too mature for fourth-year classes. When the subject has been opened up in general discussion the poem 'An Irish Airman ...' should be handed round on duplicated sheets which pupils can write on. I favour group work again here. Ask them which of the repeated words in the poem – there are five, and one repeated phrase, a significantly high proportion in so short a poem – catches most closely the pattern and the tone of the poem as a whole. It should not take long for them to decide on 'balance(d)'. At this point, particularly if the class has boys in it, it is helpful to show pictures of First World War planes of the kind flown by Robert Gregory – ideally a slide projected on to a daylight screen, so that it can remain there while the poem is under discussion. The extent to which the pilot actually does 'balance' the plane with his own weight, and must have the sense of 'riding' the air almost as one rides a surf-board, is much more clearly grasped once the pupils have seen pictures. The eighth stanza of 'In Memory ...' provides an apt commentary:

> When with the Galway foxhounds he would ride
> From Castle Taylor to the Roxborough side
> Or Esserkelly plain, few kept his pace;
> At Mooneen he had leaped a place
> So perilous that half the astonished meet
> Had shut their eyes; and where was it
> He rode a race without a bit?
> And yet his mind outran the horses' feet.

This is a good point at which to ask one or two groups to prepare a reading of the poem. Each should choose its reader (or commandeer one from another group if necessary), get him or her to record a first reading, listen to it critically, and help the reader to prepare his or her final reading. If two groups have done this the better one should be decided by popular consent.

The next stage is to examine the line structure, comparing it with R. S. Thomas's spoken and printed versions and with the pupils' own original transcribed descriptions. It will soon be seen that syntactically Yeats's poem is closer to the spoken versions in spite of its very regular metre – every line a regular octosyllabic, and most of them iambic. (The only variations, lines 2, 3, 4 and 12, transfer the initial stress to the first syllable with telling effect, especially in the powerful twelfth line.) The readings will have established how the poem falls naturally into couplets, and how the idea of 'balance' is made an integral part of the actual structure, with its repetitions, its tightly controlled rhyme scheme and its antithetical syntax. This very control imitating the control the airman must have gives added intensity to the rhythmically disturbed couplet 'A lonely ... clouds', and the assonance of impulse/tumult concentrates our response to this central statement with extraordinary effect. The airman's 'balance' has led to 'tumult', but he remains poised and triumphant.

By this time the students will be sharply conscious of the different ways the two poems – Yeats's and R. S. Thomas's - work. They may try to dismiss Thomas's more intimate, small-scale one as inferior. The best way to counter this, and to draw together the various points covered in this exploration of the two poems, is to draw their attention to the most notable feature they have in common, the first person/narrator/actor. A comparison between their respective attitudes to the experience they are recounting and between the nature and the settings of those experiences (one, of course, is really the poet's imaginary construct of the experience) will soon establish how appropriate the form of each poem is to its subject-matter. The

Welsh clergyman, solitary and detached, musing first on the history of this small shrine, then – 'ignoring my image' – on others who have come to it from time to time, and on its continuing 'life' and potency for those prepared to accept it on its own terms, not theirs; the airman, again detached, indeed fatalistic, but arriving at his truth through balance and masterly control, and so manipulating the event as to make death a triumph.

Measure and form

The next two suggested lessons are planned with second- and third-year pupils in mind. They are both concerned with word patterning, but in rather different ways. The first derives from my own experience of original writing for music, i.e. libretti and song lyrics. This is a fascinating but complex kind of writing, and it would fall outside the scope of this chapter – indeed of this book – to talk about it in any detail. One aspect of the disciplines imposed on verse writing by music can serve our purpose, and that is practice in recognizing and matching clear rhythm patterns. Chapter 9 will take this matter further when it deals more fully with language rhythm. Here I am suggesting using the music as an aural aid in helping children to recognize and respond to the verbal potential of metred language. A piece of music I have found particularly effective for this exercise is the Tijuana Brass version of Jankowski's 'Walk in the Black Forest' (on Music for Pleasure record 1202, and on CRET cassette for *Stone, Wood, Metal, Plastic*) (I shall describe the lessons in terms of this; the method is of course applicable to many other kinds and pieces of music.) It is a strongly rhythmical, jazzy piece with a clearly defined sequence of musical episodes. Play it through two or three times. The whole sequence is repeated, so you may find it simpler to use just the first statement of it. If the pupils are alert and lively and have some musical children amongst them they should easily pick up the sequential pattern of four 'lines' of rhythm: A A B^1 B^2 A. Now play just the A pattern two or three times, getting them (you won't have much difficulty!) to whistle, sing or clap with it. Their next job is – as quickly as possible – to write words that could be said or sung to the same rhythm. A few can be tried out with the music and adjustments made before you go on to the B pattern. This is simpler because although the tune changes the two halves follow the same rhythm. The re-statement of A with its extra 'foot' can use the same words as before, unless they feel like changing bits of them. Our best version came out like this:

A {
O I'm the man who mends the roads
I ride on the fuming asphalt loads I do,
                              Oh yes I do!

B {
I like it, it's just the life I like to lead;
I'm happy, there's not a single thing I need.

Once the pattern is clearly grasped children often want to go on to write other stanzas and to develop it into a ballad or song of their own. It is sometimes a good idea to follow the intial hearings of the tune you are using with a discussion about its mood, the feelings it arouses or suggests, before the children start matching their words to the musical shapes. Our words obviously owe a lot to the mood of the Tijuana Brass music as well as to the rhythmical shape of it – which is also, in any case, related to mood as we see in Chapter 9. The fact that the lines are rhymed makes clear the close relationship between rhyme and metre.

It would be pointless to suggest other music for this kind of exercise; it is all around us, and easily taped as required by anyone with an alert ear and a cassette recorder or deck. Traditional jazz is often the best source, and is unfamiliar enough to most children these days to come freshly to them.

What does this lesson achieve? The first point is that it isolates and draws attention to the musical aspect of metrical, repetitive verse. The poet Adrian Henri has said: 'I regard the printed page as the equivalent of sheet-music, and bearing the same relationship to the song/poem as printed music would to someone who can sight-read.' Lessons like this can also relate tempo to subject-matter, and lead to discussion about appropriateness of the one to the other.

Haiku and *cinquain* sequences

Many English teaching books have accepted the value of the miniature Japanese verse-form of the *haiku* – 17 syllables in 3 lines, divided 5/7/5 – as a starting-point for children's writing. Sandy Brownjohn also suggests using the extended forms of *tanka* – 31 syllables, divided 5/7/5/7/7 – and the analogous American verse-form of the *cinquain* – 5 lines, of 2,4,6,8 and 2 syllables. I think one can overstress this kind of exercise; it can easily become a rather barren syllable-counting process. However, it does have the advantage of stressing that regular measures in verse do not always depend on end-rhymed lines – a fallacy it is hard to expunge after some children's primary school indoctrination into 'poetry', i.e. nursery rhymes and facile versifying. Children quickly grasp the *haiku* form, especially if one allows a certain latitude over the syllable count. After everyone in the class (including the teacher) has produced at least one it is possible to establish what constitutes an effective *haiku* – the quality of a vignette or epigram. It is a good idea to get hold of some copies of the pictures in illuminated manuscripts or even old broadsheets. Most museums and art galleries have coloured cards and one can soon build up a useful collection. These can be passed around without comment; the children will quickly catch the point of the comparison. One of the *haiku* produced by Sandy Brownjohn's 10- and 11-year-olds is worth giving here as a remarkable example of what can be achieved:

> A kingdom of birds,
> The voice of wings fluttering,
> A tune gathering.
> (Andrew Hall)

I do not myself favour the *tanka* form; but the American *cinquain* does usefully extend the syllabic principle, and with its neat final line can often be fun to play with. Here is another of Sandy Brownjohn's examples:

> News Flash
> An elephant
> Was seen walking over
> The queen at Buckingham Palace.
> She died.
> (Anthony Wakefield)

Once pupils have mastered this effect those who have enjoyed it can be encouraged to try their hand at the much better known limerick form. *Poems 2* (Harrison/Stuart-Clark) begins with a lively selection of them which make good models.

It is possible to achieve something useful, then, merely by practising these forms in isolation. I prefer to use them in *sequence*, because it counters the slightly unsatisfactory one-off fragmentariness of the verses. A good example is Anthony Thwaite's 'A Haiku Yearbook'. Here are four of the twelve *haiku* that compose the whole poem:

> February evening:
> A cold puddle of petrol
> Makes its own rainbow.

> Morning in June:
> On the sea's horizon
> A white island, alone.

> September chestnuts:
> Falling too early,
> Split white before birth.

> Sun in December:
> In his box of straw
> The tortoise wakes.

Michael and Peter Benton's *Poetry Workshop* anthology prints
it with the signs of the zodiac on one side and a set of old
woodcuts depicting the seasons' activities on the other – a
useful combination for class discussion stimulus. With this
poem as an example you can set the children off on their own
sequences by suggesting other possibilities, such as: the four
seasons; growing up (baby, primary school, secondary school,
dole!); speeds – human, animal, mechanical (many possibilities
here up to interstellar travel and down to slugs, road-rollers,
etc.); travel on water, land, air; dwellings – cave, hut, cottage,
house, mansion, palace. As a variant on the second of these you
can use Jaques's 'Seven ages of man' speech from *As You Like
It*, which has the advantage of demonstrating how to vary the
language from 'age' to 'age'. This sequence-building is often
valuably done in groups, each group member contributing his
or her own *haiku* or *cinquain*. The best sequences – or all of
them – could be illustrated with a view to class or school
display, perhaps as an art project in integrated studies.

The value of this lesson or series of lessons is self-evident.
Children have achieved something of their own, and have
begun to recognize the cumulative effect of regular stanzas as
well as the visual attractiveness of verse patterns. The principles thus established will inform their further study or reading
of stanzaic poems, and encourage them to use the discipline of
metre, as was done so succesfully by Marcus Natten in 'Soldier
Boy'. (p. 71).

More elaborate forms

There have always been English poets ready to play with more
elaborate verse-forms, but it would be foolish to attempt any
detailed study of these before sixth form or college. Interested
individual pupils can always be shown where to find examples
– the *ottava rima* of Byron's *Don Juan*, for instance, or the
many variants of more elaborate rhyme patterns like triolet
and rondeau. I want to end this chapter by suggesting that the

best known of them all, the sonnet, can be profitably studied by 15- and 16-year-olds, and can provide a useful challenge as a writing exercise which may sometimes achieve quite remarkable results. The hold that this poetic form has maintained in English poetry is itself remarkable. One of the reasons derives from its 14-line length, which still seems peculiarly apt for us, the best contemporary example being Robert Lowell's booksful of 14-liners (they are too loose in structure to be called sonnets), *Notebook*, *History*, *The Dolphin*, *For Lizzie and Harriet*. There have been a few examples of 16-line so-called sonnets, the most notable being Meredith's *Modern Love* sequence, imitated recently by Anthony Thwaite and Roy Fuller. The other technical features that combine to make the sonnet form are: lines consisting of iambic pentameters rhymed in a regular pattern, and a division of meaning – often reinforced by the rhyme scheme – between the first eight lines (octave) and the remaining six (sestet). Another frequent but not invariable feature – perfected by Shakespeare – is the closing rhymed couplet summing up the 'message' of the poem, or giving it a wry or unexpected twist.

The best approach, since we are considering work with senior forms, is to allow plenty of preparatory reading, making sure that books containing most of the well-known sonnet collections are to hand: Shakespeare, Donne (the 'holy sonnets'), Milton, Wordsworth, Elizabeth Barrett Browning ('Sonnets from the Portuguese'), Gerard Manley Hopkins, and some twentieth-century examples – C. Day Lewis, W. H. Auden, Dylan Thomas ('Altarwise by Owl-light') are the most accessible of pre-war sonneteers; among more recent practitioners are Geoffrey Hill (in his 1978 book *Tenebrae*), Peter Dale, and Edwin Morgan ('Glasgow Sonnets'). As a stimulus to reading one can ask pupils to choose not more than two favourite ones on different, widely contrasting topics, and to prepare either a taped reading or notes of use to someone else who is to read it aloud. Versions can be brought to class or group discussion. During the time sonnets are being studied it is helpful to have on display in the classroom a large-scale charted pair of examples, on the following lines (but probably hand-written in script):

GLASGOW SONNETS I

structure		rhyme
	A mean wind wanders through the backcourt trash	A
	Hackles on puddles rise, old mattresses	B
	puff briefly and subside. Play fortresses	B
	of brick and bric-à-brac spill out some ash.	A
OCTAVE	Four storeys have no windows left to smash,	A
	but in the fifth a chipped sill buttresses	B
	mother and daughter the last mistresses	B
	of that black block condemned to stand, not crash	A
	Around them the cracks deepen, the rats crawl.	C
	The kettle whimpers on a crazy hob.	D
	Roses of mould grow from ceiling to wall.	C
SESTET	The man lies late since he has lost his job,	D
	smokes on one elbow, letting his coughs fall	C
	thinly into an air too poor to rob.	D

(Edwin Morgan)

SONNET 81

structure   *rhyme*

OCTAVE

Or I shall live your epitaph to make,　A
Or you survive when I in earth am
　rotten,　B
From hence your memory death cannot
　take,　A
Although in me each part will be
　forgotten:　B
Your name from hence immortal life
　shall have,　C
Though I, once gone, to all the world
　must die;　D
The earth can yield me but a common
　grave,　C
When you entombed in men's eyes shall
　lie:　D

SESTET

Your monument shall be my gentle
　verse,　E
Which eyes not yet created shall o'er-
　read;　F
And tongues to be your being shall
　rehearse　E
When all the breathers of this world are
　dead:　F
You still shall live – such virtue
　hath my pen –　G
Where breath most breathes, even
　in the mouths of men.　G

(William Shakespeare)

Or (line 1) – whether
From hence (line 3) – from this world
From hence (line 5) – from henceforth
to be (line 10) – in the future

As a result of the students' preparatory explorations there should be a growing common understanding of the nature and scope of sonnets, the way they tend to catch, preserve and/or assess a significant thought, moment, scene or event rather than 'tell a story'. There may be some discussion of the relation between a sonnet sequence and a contemplative or descriptive poem in stanzas, like Keats's 'Ode to a Nightingale', or C. Day Lewis's nostalgic 'The Whispering Roots':

> Roots are for holding on, and holding dear.
> Mine, like a child's milk teeth, came gently away
> From Ireland at the close of my second year.
> Is it second childhood now – that I overhear
> Them whisper across a lifetime as if from yesterday?

At some point in the series of lessons – for as will already be clear, I do not believe it possible to tackle something as far-reaching as this in a mere one or two – you will need to move into a discussion of appropriate subjects for sonnets. A carefully crafted poem like this one can be a useful means of switching from the content of the sonnet to its form. It should not be hard to find one of the students who can point out that, although we still have ten-syllabled, five-stress lines in the C. Day Lewis poem (except for the extended last line of the stanza), the rhythm has quite a different quality. If we then isolate the recurrent anapaests, e.g.

> are   for   hold/ing
> like   a   child's
> at   the   close   of   my   sec/ond,   etc.

this will show up clearly, by contrast, the iambic 'foundation' metre, so to speak, of sonnets.

The two poems I have suggested as examples for display indicate well the freedom which poets can exercise even within the iambic decasyllabic norm. Taking Shakespeare's first, we find that in the opening quatrain he adds a syllable to the second and fourth lines. The two words thus picked out for attention, which are also rhyming words, emphasize the poet's insignificance at the beginning of his offering to his friend – 'rotten' 'forgotten'. If we now read the poem in natural speech rhythms the nearest to iambic pentameters are lines 5 and 13, each, significantly, a direct address to the friend – 'Your name' 'You still shall live'. The flexibility of decasyllabics is well demonstrated by this sonnet. It is worth getting the students to decide where the caesura falls in each line (after 'live', 'survive', 'memory' and 'me' in the first quatrain). The frequency with which it comes after the fourth syllable may surprise them. But this regularity throws into sharp focus the departures from it, notably line 8 – where the remarkable image 'entombed in men's eyes' pushes it nearly to the end of the line, and line 12, which scarcely has a caesura at all. If there is one it is again after the tenth syllable, or more accurately before the final iambic foot 'are dead'. This sonnet demonstrates well the way a regular metrical pattern skilfully used can enhance the variety of natural speech rhythms and point the meaning behind them. The other technical feature well shown here is the aptness of the rhyme scheme to the shape and progress of the thought. The first quatrain, as we have seen, states the contrast between the poor poet and his rich and famous patron. The second quatrain develops and even exaggerates this – 'immortal life' 'entombed in men's eyes' is the lot of the patron, the latter phrase suggesting an ornate, grandiose sepulchre, while the poet is lost to the world in 'but a common grave'. This makes the claim in the ninth line all the more surprising: the monumental tomb is to be 'my gentle verse', because this can claim immortality 'When all the breathers of this world are dead'. The poem seems to have ended on that heavily accented 'dead'. But no: the 'breathers' of future generations will confer this immortality on you, my patron, because through my verse you shall breathe again.

Why does the rhythm of the Morgan sonnet seem so much more fluid when it is read after Shakespeare's? You will need to lead the students to discovering this for themselves, perhaps by suggesting that they compare the punctuation of the two poems. They will soon detect the end-stopped regularity of the Shakespeare contrasting with the run-on lines of Morgan's sonnet. Then point out the disposition of the run-on-lines: 2–3 and 3–4: 6–7 and 7–8; 13–14. This will demonstrate to them the cunning use of the sonnet structure, the quatrains being units of meaning as well as of rhyme and metre. None of the run-on lines violates the taut structure of quatrains and couplets. When they look for a regular iambic pattern, however, they will recognize how speech rhythms have moved away from the iamb since Shakespeare's day. Every line is a regular decasyllabic, but the only one clearly recognizable as an iambic pentameter is line 8, and this, with I think deliberate irony, describes the dour, superannuated slum tenement block 'condemned to stand, not crash' – though it is evident that it has little to recommend its apparent permanence. There is much more to be discovered in this rich and subtle poem, in particular the brilliant handling of the exacting rhyme scheme – look at the cumulative effect of the harsh A rhymes for instance; trash/ash/smash/crash.

The Edwin Morgan sonnet above might well be compared with one of Peter Dale's from *One Another* to demonstrate the amazing range of the sonnet, its suitability for both public and private utterances. When this leads, as it should, to the students' trying their hand at writing them, it will need stressing that the only attempts likely to be worth anything will involve many revisions and re-writes. I find it best to set as work the writing of a sonnet as an alternative to a rather less exacting piece of writing, such as the following:

a)   Choose one of Edwin Morgan's 'Glasgow Sonnets' and write *either* a news item as it might appear in a Glasgow evening paper about an event that occurred in the same setting he has described; *or* a short story set in it.

b)   Write a letter to a close friend of your own sex, telling him/ her about a sonnet (any of the love sonnets you have read will do) that you have received from an admirer, and commenting on it.

It is also a good idea to offer some incentive to your potential or aspiring sonneteers – a guarantee of acceptance for the school/house magazine or poetry journal (under a pen-name if desired) of a satisfactorily completed poem, or even exemption from another piece of written work. Dylan Thomas's worksheets can provide excellent and arresting examples of the need for re-writing and revision. For instance, the British Museum possesses one of his worksheets for his *Author's Prologue* to the *Collected Poems* (Add. MS 52903). Harvard University library possesses a further *ninety-four* such worksheets of the same poem!

In this chapter I have tried to show that it is possible to engage children's interest, at many different ages and levels, in questions of verse technique, and to isolate these questions to some extent from content – or 'creative writing' – without in any way devaluing the central importance of 'having something to say' when you write poetry. Saying it, in fact, involves you in technique whether you like it or not. In the course of the investigation I have touched on many other aspects of poetry. Some of these are dealt with more fully in the remaining chapters of Part Two, notably Chapters 10 and 13. Chapter 11 draws together points on pupils' own writing from Chapters 6 and 9 as well as this one. Let me conclude with a few warnings on the dangers of allowing any study of technique to depart too far from the muse it serves, from some prominent poets of our own time. They are drawn from the results of a fascinating investigation into the actual practices of working poets carried out by the magazine *Agenda*:

Basil Bunting Once people wrote their poems out right across the page: there was too little paper to waste. I don't think readers found themselves much handicapped by it. Dividing the thing up into lines suited prosodists and similar parasites of literature, and of course it must have pleased those poets who were vain of their agility in various meters and didn't want readers to miss it. Now it's convention, leading, if anything, in the direction of singsong inattention.

Donald Davie   Some of the sloppiest verse one encounters has been perpetrated by people who thought they were writing free verse when in fact they were writing for instance loose pentameters.

And on syllabics (i.e. determining line length by the number of syllables):
John Heath-Stubbs   I regard the theory of syllabic verse as totally spurious as far as English is concerned. It is a device whereby incompetent poetasters can set something down on the page which looks like verse but isn't.

Michael Hamburger   The ear doesn't count syllables, but takes in rhythms, cadences, echoes, repetitions and variations of cadence. Syllabic verse strikes me as free verse with a bad conscience.

Peter Dale   I don't write syllabics. You don't need anything but ten or eleven fingers and cloth ears. If your only way to escape iambics is finger-counting, you are in the wrong trade.

And finally a hopeful note ...
Thom Gunn   It is nonsense to say that meter is dead. It was never alive, it is an unbodied abstraction: it's the poem that has to be alive, and if a metrical poem *is* alive then the meter is the muscle of that living thing as much in 1972 [or 1982!] as in 1600.

8

ORAL POETRY

There is a curious and remarkable mismatch between oral and written poetry in schools, and many teachers – including English teachers – are instrumental in perpetuating it. Because they come to their professional life through the filter of the academic world – sixth form, college or university, education institute – such experience of poetry as they have is inescapably a bookish one. Hence what they think when they hear the word 'poetry' is radically different from what their pupils think. At its lowest level the latter is reflected in the casual comments of media people like the television commentators and the disc jockeys on Radios 1 and 2. A 'poem' or 'poetry' to them is always rhymed, usually in more or less crude ballad metre and frequently accidental rather than deliberately composed. It is easy for teachers to shrug these off as superficial; but we need to recognize their affinity to our pupils' own experience if we are to take seriously – as I believe we should – the whole idea of oral poetry, and its relationship with the more permanent *corpus* of literary poetry which is necessarily the main concern of this book.

The first important point is the quite different function of *memory* in oral poetry. When we read a poem in a book, even if we read it aloud, our memory is occupied first in supplying recollections of similar words and word patterns and their contexts, analogous ideas, and recognized rhythms, so that we can make sense of what we are reading by relating it to our past literary experience. Secondly, the ideas, images and moods of the poem will touch off memories that help to determine our response. This can sometimes be a snare because a strong personal recollection may even push aside or distort the intentions of the poet. Compare all this with the much more direct and utilitarian use of memory in oral poetry. When someone recites a poem or a verse narrative 'by heart' a part of our attention is held by the actual feat of memory. Before cheap print, memory was a prime means of learning at every stage and a good memory was prized and cultivated. The bulk of Shakespeare's education almost certainly consisted of learning by rote, or by heart, and right up to our own day we find people with large chunks of the Bible, *Pilgrim's Progress* or the Koran stored away in their memories. Ours is an age of instant mechanical (or electronic) accessibility, so that memory, whether for phone numbers, recipes, formulae or poems, has come to be held in low esteem. Perhaps the only profession, apart from that of acting, which still values it is that of the serious musician. We expect a concerto to be played by heart, and most musicians take such apparently daunting tasks in their stride. An important reason why they do so is relevant to our theme. It is because they have already worked closely, repeatedly and intelligently, over and over again, at every part of the concerto, every note and phrase and its relation with every other. They have made the music their own first by these means, shaping it and giving it life before passing it on to us. Any tradition of spoken poetry developed amongst its practitioners – and still develops – a similarly close understanding and feeling for words. Most of us have to go back to early childhood for any first-hand knowledge of memory functioning in this way. It is no accident that Iona and Peter Opie refer to memory ten times in the three short pages of their introduction to *The Puffin Book of Nursery Rhymes*. 'Oral rhymes', they write,

> are the true waifs of our literature in that their original wordings, as well as their authors, are usually unknown. But this does not mean that they are necessarily sickly strays to whom only an indulgent and undiscriminating nursery will give shelter. Rather it is true that having to fend for themselves, without the benefit of sponsor or sheepskin binding, they have had to be wonderfully fit to have survived. If Auden and Garrett's definition of poetry, that it is 'memorable speech', contains no more than a tincture of truth, it is yet enough to dye the rhymes with the tints of poetry. They owe their present existence to this one quality of memorability.

If we look to other cultures we can see oral, *remembered* poetry still at work – in the vigorous Maori traditions (with regular poetry contests like the Welsh *Eisteddfodau*), in Somali culture (which can boast the invention in 1954 of a new poetic form, the *balwo*, by Adbi Deeqsi, a lorry driver), amongst Eskimos, Australian aborigines, even the 'hairy' Ainu of northern Japan before they became integrated into Japanese society and their unique language lost. A six-thousand-line unwritten 'epic' was recorded from them sixty years ago. I think there is a good case to be made out, once again, for encouraging children to learn some poetry by heart and for including this in poetry teaching, especially to first- and second-year classes, as a regular feature. In more senior classes it is often worth setting a learning by heart task as an alternative to written work. It is a pity if the memory faculty in school is used solely to 'mug up' scientific or historical facts. Anyone who has a retentive memory for verse knows how much pleasure it gives to recall a loved poem, the words seeming to gain a sonority and richness of association that one experiences nowhere else. I like to think of Field Marshal Lord Wavell, who compiled his whole anthology *Other Men's Flowers* from the poems he held in his memory, 'declaiming out loud' as he rode on horseback. 'One can never properly appreciate a poem,' he said, 'until one has got it by heart; memory stumbles over a word or a line and so wonders why the poet wrote it so, and then savours it slowly that its meaning and relish may stay.'

Lord Wavell's remark, however, points to a distinctive difference between written poetry committed to memory and a living oral poetry, and we need to keep these separate although they both indicate the true source of all poetry in the spoken word. A performer of traditional oral poetry may know neither title nor author of what he or she recites. To some extent, as performers, they may take some part in composing the poems as well, may vary details, omit or add verses, according to circumstances and audience. Here indeed 'the letter killeth, but the spirit giveth life'.

The oral tradition, by and large, because it is not literary, has been connected with ordinary people, their life patterns and their work. It is the same tradition that produces folk song and ballad. Nowadays it is as easy to record, store and reproduce oral performances (on disc or tape) as it is to print poetry; and though they can never be quite as accessible as books, cassette recorders make it very easy to use such recordings when teaching oral poetry. The problem is that so much in this direct kind of entertainment depends on performance and the sympathy set up between performer and audience. When we hear a traditional song or popular ballad recited in the flesh, we accept the rhythmic regularity and the rigid rhyme schemes that are the almost indispensable mnemonics of oral performers but when coldly reproduced on a disc they can sound crude and monotonous. For this reason I do not recommend too frequent recourse in the poetry classroom to the wealth of excellent recorded folk song now available, especially on the Topic label. (Some interesting records are listed in Part Three.)

It is better, too, when you do decide to use traditional songs of this kind, to tape a particular track or two for the purpose rather than submit the class to the whole side of an L.P.

So far I have pointed to two aspects of oral poetry: that which depends solely on *memory*, and on tradition (which is no more than the memory of a community or society), and often handed down, changed and adapted, by word of mouth – perhaps without ever taking on a more permanent or 'literary' form; and *written* poetry, possibly committed to memory, spoken or performed orally. Looking now from the point of view of the classroom, we need to consider another question: the function of the written word – whether printed, typed or handwritten – in oral poetry teaching. And here, as I hinted at the beginning of this chapter, we need to be on our guard, so that we do not imagine we are teaching oral poetry, while really thinking of it as merely another way of 'getting them to *read* poetry'. Ears and mouths are our chosen organs for the oral poetry lesson. We must resist the temptation to start the lesson with 'get out your notebooks' or even 'have rough paper and pencil ready'. It is surprising how often we assume that the printed word *automatically* leads to close attention by pupils. A book for English teachers in Avon, for instance, *Guidelines for English 13–16* states categorically under the heading *Listening*:'effective listening is more likely to occur if pupils have a copy of the poem or story to follow.' For the kind of oral poetry teaching I am suggesting in this chapter, we could well substitute 'less' for 'more'. We should *at all costs* avoid writing up the text of an oral poem on the board, or pinning it on a notice board. Tape recorders rather than notebooks, music rather than displayed words. The nearest one can reasonably get to a visual aid might be a slide or picture to back up the subject matter – such as Roy Palmer uses so skilfully in his collections like *The Painful Plough*. I would even extend this embargo to the reading aloud of written poems within the context of most oral poetry lessons. Obviously, as is evident elsewhere in this book, reading poetry aloud from a text rather than reciting it by heart is a frequent and necessary practice in other kinds of poetry lesson. As I shall show it can lead to good oral work with senior classes.

'The Oily Rig' (first-year class)

Bob Roberts, who wrote and recorded this tall story in verse, is one of the dying race of sailing barge skippers, who is also a fine folk musician with a big repertoire. I choose the only spoken piece on his record more as an example of what can be done with this kind of material than as a 'poem' – though it is a successful story as told by Bob Roberts. (*Songs from the Sailing Barges*, Topic 12TS361). For the benefit of those without easy access to the record it may be useful to summarize briefly the 'yarn'. Its seventeen traditional four-line ballad verses, rhymed *abcb*, relate in the first person a story of a fisherman who takes a job on an oil rig because fishing is poor and good wages are offered. The drill makes a 'bloody great 'ole' in the North Sea bottom, through which the North Sea, surprisingly, pours like a bath running out through the plughole. The unexpected conclusion is that the Devil pokes his head through the hole and berates the oil men for dousing all his fires. The story is cunningly handled and has many authentic touches that come over well in Bob Roberts's recitation – the fact that he doesn't like being idle, but is nevertheless suspicious of being offered so unfamiliar a job even though it promises big money; his eventually being persuaded by 'the missus' who is glad to get him earning again. His graphic account of the drill at work lies at the centre of the narrative, verse 8, and this is followed by the disturbing revelation that all the ships are aground, and the sea shrinking as it swirls down the 'plug 'ole' leaving the fish floundering. The Devil's appearance and words sound remarkably like an aggrieved stoker's. 'I'll never get 'ell 'ot again, I've lost me bloody job' (Bob Roberts now skippers a 300-ton coaster, *Vectis Isle*) – and his discomfiture is made more comic and more authentic by the narrator's laughing response and his satisfactory conclusion: 'So now, if you die, there's only Heaven, So no more need to worry.'

I am not putting this forward as 'poetry' in any deep literary sense. It *is* a good example of its genre designed to entertain at a first hearing and not be studied as literature. Children like repetition and you can let the class hear the story two or three times without spoiling it, but probably not more. What is useful about it is:

a) the authentic tones of Bob Roberts's voice and manner – not labouring the metre or rhyme unduly and with turns of phrase that ring true:

> 'But I couldn't see no good could come
> Of drillin' these 'oles off shore.'

> 'You'll earn more money out there in a week
> Than a whole bloody year wi' your net,'

> 'Hey, Dad! our tug's aground:'

b) The structure of the story is effective and economical: four verses describing the stranger's proposal of work, three verses on the wife's response, then the centre verse describing the drill at work. This is followed by four verses on the surprising outcome of the sea drained dry, three on the Devil's appearance and remonstrances and two to round off the story.

c) The refreshing naiveté that humanizes the world of oil rigs and high technology, and to some extent deflates the pretentions of that world by seeing it in such common-sense terms, while at the same time laughing gently at the kind of ignorant speculating that might assume that when you drill a hole in the bottom of the sea the water will run out through it.

This is best tackled as a group enterprise. When the groups are arranged and settled (no paper or writing implements permitted) start one or two ideas on North Sea explorations for oil and gas. Compare it with fishing from the sea. Which do they like the idea of more? Can *all* the fish ever be caught? There are plenty of ideas associated with sea harvesting: international fishing disputes keep the topic in the public eye. The lesson could well fit into the context of a 'sea' theme (see Chapter 6). At an appropriate time play the Bob Roberts track through once – and again, straight away, if the class ask for it. After the hearing tell the class you want each group to think up a similar story to do with a job. They can follow the sea ideas already discussed, or if this doesn't yield enough possibilities (e.g. in a factory or farming district) use an idea connected with local work. The starting-point of 'The Oily Rig' – out of work and an apparently easy way of earning money offered – can well be taken almost wholesale. At first the class may seem a bit distressed by the 'no paper' rule. Present the task as a contest if it helps; each group is to make its own ballad story and the prize goes to the group with the most entertaining story, in deciding which length is an important factor. (You can point out how all seventeen verses of Bob Roberts's tale are necessary, and how they contribute to the total effect.) *Tape recorders* are helpful but not essential for such a lesson. If there is one to a group they can be used as 'oral notemakers', and will help towards longer verse narratives than might have been possible. It is important, however, to stress the need for knowing the story by heart before the group can consider it complete. They may choose one person as reciter or may arrange their 'poem' so as to have two or more speakers, perhaps in a semi-dramatic way.

The purpose of the lesson (or sequence of lessons) will have been achieved by actually doing it; and the children will gain a sense of achievement by the end-product of a performance of each ballad, even if only to the rest of the class. If anything worth wider attention is achieved, rehearsed versions can be tape recorded, perhaps with sound effects – the sea, ship sounds, etc. – or with background music. Another way might be to develop one or more of the stories dramatically and have a proper performance in costume. Such a lesson may spark off many things: if there is a local 'performer' like Bob Roberts, he might be visited by a team with a tape recorder or be invited into a lesson. A child may recall a parent or acquaintance who used to tell such stories. And it leads usefully back to written ballads and stories in verse like 'John Gilpin' (see Chapter 9). The value of memory as a useful way of making poetry their own will have been stressed and enhanced.

Making choices

The suggestions that follow are made with fourth-form classes in mind, but the ideas could also be used with intelligent and receptive third formers and with older students. We shall see, in the next chapter, that as soon as one takes on the job of reading a poem aloud one is confronted with a series of choices. These are presented by rhyme, metre and syntax, by the *tone* implied in the form of words, even by the poem's layout and appearance on the printed page: where the lines end in relation to the sense and grammatical structure. When we add to all that the relation of speaker to audience, quality and volume of the individual voice-instrument (including peculiarities of dialect, intonation and perhaps even speech defect), and the general context of the reading (e.g. classrooms, assembly hall, drama studio, pub), we can recognize that spoken poetry is a fairly complex operation, needing careful thought and preparation if it is to be an effective teaching process. In a BBC Reith lecture on 15 December 1982 Professor Denis Donoghue gave an eloquent description of what is involved:

> We read [the poem] first with the eye and the mind in conjunction. If we try we can probably hear some of the phrases, as a musician, by looking at the score, can hear, at least to some extent, how it goes. But mostly, the reading is still silent. Normally we go through the whole poem, taking it as it seems to want to be taken, stopping if the going gets hard, puzzling it out. Parts of it may be ambiguous; we don't

know exactly what goes with what, or where the syntax is taking us. Sometimes it seems simple enough, but there are more choices of meaning than we want.... As long as we are reading the poem silently, taking the words on the page, we can mull over these questions, and if we like, leave them undecided. But if we read the poem aloud ... we have to settle for one interpretation rather than another. Our voices insist on speaking with particular emphasis upon some words rather than others. Whatever reading you decide on, there is always misgiving. You are aware of the other meanings that are possible. But in a convincing reading, you have to convince yourself that one interpretation is, on balance, richer than another. Even then you have to lean and hearken to the words, trying to catch the sound of their sense, then the mind settles upon one interpretation and the voice steadies itself in its favour.

Much poetry-speaking in English lessons does not, if we are to be honest, come anywhere near meeting these stringent standards; but if we take the teaching of poetry seriously I believe we must at least aspire to them. One way of doing so is to work, over a series of lessons, towards a special poetry-speaking session, when a number of speakers, either solo or in conjunction, present their prepared 'performances' or poems they have learned by heart. To give this focus I have chosen three pairs of fairly well-known poems. All but one are included in one or both of two useful school anthologies, Norman Hidden's *Say It Aloud* and *The New Dragon Book of Verse*, but all are easily accessible elsewhere. The extract from Wordsworth's ode 'There was a Time' is included in the Appendix, where I have stated my reason for recommending such an 'edited' excerpt. For such an extended piece of work it is vital that the poems should be chosen with great care. Many good poems do not lend themselves to such intensive work by immature readers/speakers and one needs to feel sure, and if possible convince one's pupils, that the poems being committed to memory ('for life' in many cases, no doubt) in this way are intrinsically worth the effort involved.

Pair 1   'Wind' – Ted Hughes
       'Look, Stranger' – W. H. Auden

Pair 2   'Ozymandias' – P. B. Shelley
       'At the Round Earth's Imagined Corners' – John
         Donne

Pair 3   'Ode: There was a Time' – William Wordsworth
       'Fern Hill' – Dylan Thomas

Stage one: getting to know the poems

For this initial stage it is necessary that all the class have copies of all the poems to be included. It is very helpful if most pupils have access to a tape recorder. Do not read the poems aloud: in this work the reading and interpretation need to be arrived at by the pupils themselves and a teacher's reading may have the effect of imposing one particular interpretation on them. The first aim of this session is for pupils to choose which poem they respond to most, and would feel happiest committing to memory. Since it is virtually impossible to offer a sufficiently wide choice while restricting the range to poems of the same length and complexity, the teacher needs to devise some way of ensuring that there are 'rewards' for choosing longer or more difficult poems, e.g. extra homework time allocated or special opportunities for 'performing' the harder poems. Ensure that pupils base their choice on genuine preference, not on a perceived 'soft option'. The teacher's job throughout this stage, which may extend over two teaching periods, is to explain particular obscurities (but not on any account to 'explain the meaning of the poem') and as the pupils start making their choices and working on their performances, to clear up obvious mis-readings and mis-pronunciations. This should not involve 'correcting' any local dialectal forms unless these interfere seriously with the poem's rhyme-scheme or rhythmic patterns. It is very helpful at this stage for the pupils to work in groups; this also has the advantage that five or six tape recorders are enough for a whole class (one to a group). The notes that follow indicate the kind of information likely to be needed by the pupils; the teacher needs to prepare his or her ground in this way whatever poems are chosen, before starting on the project.

Why pairs?   It is obviously not essential to offer choices in this way. However, I have found it very useful in drawing out meanings to give pupils the chance of working together on different poems with similar themes. Often the mere juxtaposition may lead to ideas on how to speak the poems – contrasts of tone, mood, pace and so on. It also makes choosing easier; pupils can first decide which of the themes interests them, then, after reading the two (or more) poems grouped within it, decide on the particular poem. It also offers opportunities for collaborative choices – useful with longer poems and for those with a potentially dramatic presentation.

Pair 1
Pupils should respond immediately to the mood of each poem – Hughes's violent, vivid words and images and the active involvement of the poet, in contrast with the stillness and poise of Auden's poem, its static quality determined with the very first word 'Look!' If two choose to work in partnership, the stronger or louder voice should be chosen for the Hughes poem.

'Wind'   Point out how the stanza divisions help to shape the meanings as you read it. Even the run-on verses 1–2, 4–5, make sense, the first indicating the transition from night to day, the second pointing the word 'rang' usefully to a speaker. Make sure the speaker appreciates the need for bringing out the contrast between indoors and outside.

'*Look, Stranger*' (Check the accuracy of the printing of this poem against the author's approved version in W. H. Auden, *Collected Shorter Poems*, London, Faber, 1950. Both the anthologies mentioned earlier have serious misprints.) Make sure that any pupil choosing this poem regulates the pace of his or her reading to make the most of the many subtle sound effects, often pointed by the lineation, e.g. line 8 'pause', line 9, assonance of -a- sounds, last line, 'water saunter'. Make them think about the final stanza, especially the paradox, 'urgent voluntary' and the meaning of 'the full view'.

Pair 2

The sonnet lends itself to speaking aloud. The self-consciousness of the form makes it a good vehicle for declamatory public verse, even – as in both these cases – when the statement provides a basis for deep reflection. It is good to have pupils working together, comparing the structures and discovering for themselves how the verse form is used to strengthen the total meaning and impact.

'*Ozymandias*' The pupil choosing this will need to decide on the purpose and dramatic effect of its being narrated to the poet, who is the first speaker, but who is audience to the 'traveller'. There are four 'characters' involved altogether, in fact, because the traveller's story involves both the tyrant Ozymandias and the sculptor who understood him so well.

'*At the Round Earth's*' As with the previous pair, this poem offers a marked tonal contrast with the reflectiveness of its partner, being dramatic rhetorical monologue. A medieval print of the earth (or 'mappa mundi') decorated with trumpeting seraphim would add point to the opening image. Its elemental quality is emphasized by the four 'elements' all referred to within the first five lines.

Pair 3

I have deliberately included two longer pieces, for a number of reasons: it is beneficial sometimes to get away from the short lyric in poetry lessons, just because it is so tempting to choose poems that fit into a single lesson and this can be very unsatisfying. It is important for pupils to realize that there are poems that depend on amplitude rather than compression where the rhythms set up over several stanzas or even pages can have an important cumulative effect. Pupils gifted with quick memories often like the challenge of learning a more substantial poem, though it must be acknowledged that anyone tackling the learning by heart of either of these deserves special encouragement by way of revised work-loads in other directions, or other incentives.

'There was a Time'   (Three stanzas of the same passage are included in Hidden's anthology.) The performance of this passage learned by heart could well form the prelude to a full reading of the poem at a later occasion perhaps by a professional on disc or tape, or in the flesh. (For further notes on my edited version, see Appendix.)

'Fern Hill'   Dylan Thomas's vision of childhood is as resonant as Wordsworth's and, though more complex in language, is more accessible to this age range as spoken poetry, because of the sensuous directness of its imagery, sustained by a rapid, almost galloping rhythm, until the final six lines.

Stage two: committing them to memory

This follows on from the explorations of Stage One. Pupils have now made their choices with some judicious guidance to ensure that a reasonable proportion choose each poem if you have selected them as a group. It is useful to choose more poems than you actually need for the project – perhaps allow for two out of eight to be rejected or remain unchosen. At this stage, the process of learning really starts. Warn the pupils that after the end of such and such a lesson printed copies will be collected in. From then on any references should be to their own taped versions, which should have been done sufficiently carefully to serve as required. Much of the committing to memory can be done by simple repetition. It is best done in stages over several lessons and homeworks and subject to correction and discussion. Discourage pupils from having recourse to writing down even as much as a complete line. Make it clear this is an *oral* exercise, practice in handling the spoken not the written language. During this stage the teacher can be helping by pointing out structural features like rhyme schemes, e.g. Shelley's cunning use of the rhyme across from the second quatrain (line 7) to the first triplet (line 10) in 'Ozymandias', the rhyme itself diminishing 'king' to 'thing' as the poem does.

Stage three: rehearsal

An element of stage managing needs to come in at this point. Pupils can be encouraged to include sound and visual effects – pictures, posters, projected slides, background music or sound effects. Try to discourage over-obvious effects, though the suggested fanfare at the beginning of Donne's poem can be very effective in performance, especially if there is a good trumpeter in school. Where groups are working together on a poem or poems, it is helpful to be able to send them to a sound studio, or simply a small room (English store?) with a tape recorder, while the rest of the class is engaged on something else. Monitoring can be sustained by insisting on their handing in the rehearsal tape for checking at the end of such a session.

Stage four: performance

It should be clear from the outset of the work that this is the end-product aimed at. It may not be possible to include all the poems learned by heart and certainly will not involve every pupil, unless a short poem is learned chorally as a curtain-raiser, perhaps a few verses written within the class specially for the occasion. During Stage Three the teacher will have found which pupils show the best grasp of each of the poems chosen and can select accordingly. A performance such as this can often provide an interlude during some other school production or concert. If school funds, or a collection, will run to it, the best performers can be given copies of the anthology or poems recited. A tape recording of the final performance makes a useful addition to the English department's sound resources and can stimulate more work of the same kind.

The emphasis throughout this chapter has been on oral performance – the speaking of poetry so that not only its meaning comes across but the performer's understanding and sympathy with the poet's ideas and feelings. I believe that all our secondary school pupils should, at some stage, have the opportunity of committing poetry to memory then speaking it aloud. It adds a valuable dimension to the experience of poetry in school and may bestow on our pupils something that will last them a lifetime.

9

RHYTHM

It is important at the outset to know what we are talking about.
For our purposes there is no such thing as pure rhythm separate
from the language it inhabits, any more than in the world of
music one can isolate pure sound. (A physicist might define
white sound as 'pure' but it has little to offer to musicians.) In
poetry rhythm involves and indeed gets its life from tensions set
up by the intermeshing of three things – word patterns and
syntax, metre, and meaning, the last including what might be
called scientific or objective sense at one end, and emotion or
feeling at the other, with all the gradations between the two.

There are two immediate problems to be faced as soon as one
attempts to deal with this phenomenon. The first is that its
effect is 'synthetic' to poetry, and that if and as soon as it
becomes a consciously recognizable separate element in a
poem, it can lose some of the synthesizing power, as though in
quantum physics one were trying to observe the effect of
particles and wave movements at the same time. The other
difficulty is that because it is so involved with the way we grow
into full consciousness – and then into self-consciousness –

there is a very wide variation in our capacity to respond to rhythm. As a teacher of music, I was sharply aware of this variability in rhythmic perception. A piece of music – perhaps a simple melody – could remain for one player a succession of arbitrary long and short notes, while for another, responding instinctively to the rhythmic 'message', it would take shape as the flowing melodic line the composer intended.

Another way to describe it is by analogy with certain kinds of paintings. Most people have at some time had the experience of 'seeing' a picture, first as a jumbled and meaningless chiaroscuro of colour, light and shade, then – in a flash, as it were – as an ordered and significant pattern, possibly representing a figure, a still life or a landscape. Once the true significance of the picture has been seen, it is only by a conscious effort of withdrawal and assumed 'blindness' that one can recapture the first chaotic impression of the picture. It is not surprising that art critics and teachers so frequently talk about the 'rhythm' of a painting, even of the rhythmic line of a creative draughtsman, such as Picasso. So we have to reconcile ourselves to the fact that some children, and for that matter some teachers, will always find it harder than others to move from the first 'seeing' to the second, i.e. to respond creatively, sympathetically, or 'synthetically' to rhythmic elements in poetry; and for some, the richness and subtlety imparted through rhythm may always remain almost entirely inaccessible.

This may seem a pessimistic approach to the subject. It is intended more as a warning. As teachers, we need to be aware of the central role rhythm plays in poetry, but we need also to recognize that it can never be as clearly demonstrable as the more formal aspects dealt with in Chapter 7. Often we must merely suggest that there are rhythmic discoveries to be made, point our pupils in the general direction and hope for the best.

With those *caveats* let us now look a little more closely at this strange and powerful element. Rhythm, as we said in Chapter 7, is the basis of all sound patterns. In its simplest linguistic forms it can be described as consisting of sound patterns in time. At the very simplest level we tend to group successive sounds while hearing them, and to derive pleasure from doing so. A clock may tick at a uniform pace and loudness, but we hear it as *tick*-tock, with as it were a dominant and a subservient sound. A train's wheels may drum over the rails in repeated groups of four; we hear them as ⌣ ⌣ ⌣ ', with a stress on the final sound. Speech similarly falls into *stress patterns*; one only has to hear a foreigner – an Indian, for instance, whose language is relatively unaccented – speaking English to realize how much we depend on recognizing them for our understanding of language.

The placing of stresses, and their relative weights, determine rhythm patterns. In language these patterns tend to form short rhythmic units separated by *pauses*. Sometimes – more frequently in prose than in poetry – the pauses are diminished or even overridden in the interest of a continuous rhythmic flow; but they are always felt by speaker or reader, and contribute importantly to the meaning. As in music, sound is defined by silence. The length, frequency and position of pauses form the other important element in rhythm. In writing we sometimes need punctuation to ensure that our readers place the pauses correctly: I have just used it thus after the word 'music'. In poetry line-endings can (though they do not invariably do so) – serve the same purpose. Let us consider a little more closely how such an organically oral and aural element in language as rhythm can be conveyed through the written word. When we read we 'hear' the words. Less practised readers can often be seen mouthing the words silently as they read. So we meet the writer half-way over rhythm. Nevertheless, there is often a large area of choice. In ordinary discourse, and in unengaged or merely utilitarian prose, this doesn't matter, so long as the rhythm is not left so uncertain as to distort or conceal the sense. The context of each rhythmic unit within the passage provides guidance enough. In more urgent or more imaginative writing rhythm becomes increasingly important, and our awareness of and response to it can affect our total understanding as well as our enjoyment to a considerable degree.

Rhythm in our daily speech

The purpose of this lesson (or to be more realistic this series of lessons) is to encourage a greater awareness of the links between rhythm and meaning in all language and thereby to show that poets are talking 'the same language' as the rest of us. It can also lead children to appreciate more fully the dependence of poets on shared rhythmic perceptions with their readers or listeners. It may indeed come as something of a surprise to some students that the poets whose work they read – not always willingly at first – *do* depend on them as readers in the same way as a composer depends on the performers of his music. As readers of poetry we are both performers and audience.

This lesson is planned for third- or fourth-year pupils. The first step is to draw their attention to the importance of intonation and stress in determining meaning in ordinary discourse, and especially that important part of meaning that involves emotional colouring or weighting. I have found it best to approach this indirectly by introducing for class or group discussion a topic that bears on the poem to be studied at a later stage. The poem here is Philip Larkin's 'Toads' so the topic would naturally be *work* or *jobs*. It is likely, in any case, that this or an associated theme would crop up in the course of English work with this age group.

STAGE 1

Here are some possible 'starters':

i) Given the choice between a secure job with a pension after a number of years' service and occasional work or no regular job at all, which would you prefer and why?

ii) Two people take the parts of a mother or father and son or daughter. The child assumes that his or her parent will provide something after school age – a home, pocket money, etc. – while the parent resents his or her child taking it for granted.

iii) Is it right that there should be gypsies and other vagrants drawing money from State social security funds?

(Nos *i*) and *iii*) could be approached through role play on the same lines as *ii*) if this was preferred.)

If this preliminary stage is set up in discussion groups the teacher may be able to go from group to group and collect short examples of the conversations. With a little judicious pushing, it should be possible to find phrases and expressions close to the following:

a) Why should I let you
$$\begin{cases} \text{wear me out?} \\ \text{live at my expense?} \\ \text{be a parasite?} \end{cases}$$

b) $\begin{cases} \text{No one actually said so} \\ \text{No one actually asked me about it} \end{cases}$

c) I'm not saying I don't deserve it,
I don't say it's not right,
but I do say it's
$\begin{cases} \text{hard} \\ \text{rough} \end{cases}$ on me

(I have included a few alternatives to show one can catch the right general emphasis in intonation without insisting on exact wording.)

It may be advisable to edit the recordings and use them in a separate lesson. The discussions could well lead to, or be a part of, quite different work – extended essays or dramatic exercises, a debate, a theme on work, etc.

STAGE 2

This stage starts with a closer look at the extracts you have taped, together with the sentences given above. It is worth spending time on practising different emphases (e.g. in *a*) emphasizing each of the pronouns in turn, I, you, me, and noting how this changes the meaning.) This should lead to discussion of how, in written English, one can ensure that a particular emphasis is chosen, i.e. the importance of *context* and *tone*. For *b*) the stress is likely to be placed on 'actually' in a normal reading, and a few questions may elicit the suggestion that to make sure a different word is stressed you may have to underline it (i.e. print it in italics).

After establishing these points (perhaps half a lesson, perhaps more) it is time to introduce the poem. Probably it is best to read it through first *without* the pupils having copies. Ask them to look out for expressions like the ones they have been talking about. If you have read it with the intended wry and colloquial tone, making little or nothing of line endings where lines are run on, you might ask, after the reading, whether they think it is rhymed or unrhymed, free verse or in regular stanzas. Most are likely to be surprised when they see the actual poem on the page. This leads to a valuable point about the relation between *form* and *rhythm*. Once they have the copies in front of them, a slightly more emphatic reading will show how the natural speech emphases are disciplined by the rhyme scheme (*abab*, but with false or half-rhymes in all but one instance) and the stanza form. You can also show how once a verse pattern has been set up it helps the poet direct his readers to a particular one among a choice of rhythmic emphases. A good stanza to study for this is the fourth one:

> Lots of folk live up lanes
>   With fires in a bucket,
> Eat windfalls and tinned sardines –
>   They seem to like it.

The stress pattern of 3 2 3 2 is helped by alliteration in line one. When we come to line four we know there should be two strong stresses, so we get the right ironic emphasis on 'seem' and 'like', where without such guidance we might stress 'they' instead of 'seem'.

It has become clear as this lesson has progressed, that in English rhythm is often set up and its shape determined by the natural stress and intonation of the spoken language. A craftsmanlike poet will harness this hidden sort of rhythm, and guide it towards fulfilling his poetic intentions, recognizing always that, as D. W. Harding puts it in his valuable study *Words into Rhythm*:

> Whether the metrical scheme or the sense of the words determines our choice between alternative rhythms in verse, the one chosen must be acceptable in ordinary speech; the established rhythm of the spoken language is basic and inviolable.

Elsewhere he says:

> The rhythms of natural speech are an intrinsic part of the language. Verse, especially metrical verse, can indicate which among possible rhythms is intended, but it must always be a rhythm possible in natural speech.

STAGE 3

We have not up to now devoted any time to discussing this poem's meaning or message; and this may be a useful corrective to the tendency for English teachers to regard every poem they study as a text for exegesis rather than an art 'thing' (*res*). Here we have looked first at the verbal pattern and its dependence upon our familiar speech habits. Before going on to the more creative part of this investigation into rhythm (which I shall call Stage 4) it may be worth clearing up one or two points of meaning. The most difficult one has already had the pupil's attention drawn to it, so will probably have prompted some questions: I refer to the clinching final stanza with its deliberately ambiguous syntax in the run-on lines 1–2 (does he intend 'the other one's' or 'the other, one's ...'?) and its fatalistic assertion that the two 'toads' are interdependent and therefore inescapable. Many children will reject the poet's pessimism that accepts the existence of 'something sufficiently toadlike' in himself, but this could generate an interesting discussion and perhaps some useful introspection.

Another point concerns the 'hinge' stanza 6 with its wry realism and its literary echo (from Prospero's final speech). This allusion is far more than just a clever piece of literary one-upmanship but without the fuller context of *The Tempest* and Prospero's part in it, there is probably little to be gained by trying to explain it further than to point out the pun on 'stuff' – underlined, as we have already seen, by its distinction of being the only 'true' rhyme in the poem. Finally in this stage we might ask who is being addressed in the poem. By posing the question thus we should be able to stimulate the pupils to recognize it for the reflective monologue that it is: the poet talking to himself, so that we are eavesdroppers, as it were, on his private thoughts. It is this form that enables the poet to reveal something of his own personality without prompting the charge of egotism. And this also brings us back to our starting-point, the speech rhythms that give authenticity to the poet's voice, even within the constraints of metre and rhyme that he has imposed on himself.

I have not suggested a specific classroom method for dealing with the points raised in this section, partly because this will depend on the individual teacher and his or her relationship with the class. It could be dealt with by class or group discussion, by silent individual work directed by written questions or more obliquely through such questions as: What sort of a person do you think the writer is? Do you know anyone like him? What job might he have? I would not extend this to private study or homework because I think this is best left to the next and final stage.

STAGE 4

If a good classroom anthology is available, it is helpful to start this stage by looking for poems using similar resources, i.e. the private monologue with idiomatic colloquial language to provide an authentic tone. This is an excellent opportunity for group work, particularly if there are small sets of poetry collections. The choice is obviously far too wide for me to include any comprehensive list of suggestions here. The following choice of ten poems gives some indication of the kind of poems that could easily be found in fairly well-known general anthologies.

Poetry Workshop, ed. M. and P. Benton
1 D. H. Lawrence, 'Old People'
2 Alan Brownjohn, 'Parrot'
A Flock of Words, ed. D. Mackay
3 James Stevens, 'The Shell'
4 Laurie Lee, 'April Rise'
5 Edward Thomas, 'Adlestrop'
6 Robert Frost, 'Stopping by Woods on a Snowy Evening'
(Poems 3 – 6 will be found in many other school anthologies, e.g. 3 and 4 are also in the *New Dragon Book of Verse*, ed. Harrison and Stuart-Clark.)
Voices Book 3, ed., G. Summerfield
7 Edwin Morgan, 'Strawberries'
Voices of Today, ed. F. E. S. Finn
8 Philip Larkin, 'Going, going'
9 Norman MacCaig, 'Sparrow'
Poems 2, ed. Harrison and Stuart-Clark
10 Patricia Beer, 'Abbey Tomb'

There are many ways in which the pupil's choices can be shared and made use of; prepared group or individual readings aloud; the compilation of small class or group anthologies, perhaps on a dominant theme, or under a general title like 'monologues' or 'musings'; the selection perhaps by class vote of favourites for inclusion in a wall display or for more detailed study along the lines already suggested in Stages 2 and 3. Whatever option is favoured, this investigation needs to be focused from time to time on the rhythmic aspects of poetic language that we have been exploring. Its purpose is to set a more extended piece of writing to widen pupils' experience of poetry in general as well as to direct their critical attention to this form, preparatory to producing something of their own.

At this point it is useful to point out briefly the thought structure of the poem, roughly along the following lines:

Question: Stanzas 1–5 inclusive	Idea – why be a slave to the work 'ethic' when many other people live happily without working?
Answer: Stanza 6	Because I haven't the courage to abandon the security of a steady job and pension.
Reflection: Stanzas 7–9	In any case the imposed discipline – regimentation of 'the job', with all its limitations, is reflected within my own personality, so that the two depend on each other.

This should not become a detailed investigation into the poem's 'significance' (which would in any case bore most pupils), but merely provide a pattern for a piece of their own writing. Pupils could be given the option of writing in prose or verse but whichever they choose, they should be asked to indicate three sentences or expressions, at the beginning, the end and somewhere in the middle, where the tone and rhythm of the speaker's voice is apparent. A follow-up to this might involve the exchange of what has been written, in pairs. Each pupil would then have to attempt a version of the three marked parts in the other form – verse or prose. Another way to do this is to pair the pupils before setting the first written essay and let them decide, at that point, which of the two writes in prose, which in verse. An advantage of this method may be that both partners can, if they wish, take the same topic.

What has this scheme of work achieved? It may seem that we have departed a long way from our initial purpose of investigating rhythm. My justification for it is that it inderlines the *central* importance of recognizing how all rhythm in poetry derives from language *as we use it*. It can never be imposed externally. It is especially necessary to impress this on pupils today, because the term 'rhythm' is misused so often in the world of popular music to be synonymous with 'beat', or indeed almost any regularly repeated sound. (Electronic organs often have a 'rhythm section' which imposes a pre-programmed beat pattern on whatever tune is being played.) As a corrective to this grossly limited and over-simplified concept of rhythm, we have shown that a true sense of rhythm, founded on an alert perception of the speed, pace and tone of the spoken language, helps to make us aware of much in poetry that might otherwise elude us. Moreover, since the way we express ourselves in speech is so vital an indication of our feelings and attitudes, rhythm in poetry is inextricably linked with the sort of value judgements we need to bring to what we read, when we refer to such things as 'sincerity', 'sham', 'condescension', 'friendliness', 'remoteness' and so on. Often a mismatch between the subject-matter, or the apparent meaning or significance of a poem, and its rhythm is the clearest indication of a weakness that may not be definable in any other way.

Repetition (a lesson for first and second years)

Rhythm, or at any rate our capacity to respond to it, has evolved from simple repetition – perhaps even from the repeated movements of heart and lungs – and involves recurring patterns of sound in time. We know the compulsive force of repeated lines in nursery rhymes and repeated groups of words for little children. The use of a refrain can draw on this power at almost any level, from 'Ring a ring a roses' to 'This ay nicht' ('The Lykewake Dirge') or Yeats's magical

> Like a long-legged fly upon the stream
> His mind moves upon silence.

Here is a 12-year-old girl's use of it, in a convincingly heart-felt little poem in free verse:

Show-off
I wish I had a new dress,
It's her very best,
It's orange with a big thick belt,
I wish I had a new dress.

She shows off in her new dress,
I would not I think,
I hope I do not,
I wish I had a new dress.

She walks down the road making the boys look at
  her,
I wish they would look at me,
I would not make the boys look at me,
'Oh' she shows off in that dress.

She's got an orange handbag to go with her dress,
And orange shoes,
She's got an orange hair-band,
'Oh' she shows off.

I wish I had all the things she's got.

(Kim, aged 12)

There is no doubt that the effectiveness of this derives in large part from repetition but two or three readings aloud, perhaps by volunteers from the class, will soon establish that the rhythm follows the feelings of the speaker very closely, even within the repeated lines. The first line demands a strong stress on the second 'I' but on its repetition at the end of the stanza the stress is transferred to, or at least shared with, 'wish'. By the end of the second stanza it is more strongly on 'wish', the 'I' having had plenty of emphasis in the two previous lines. Another instructive bit of repetition is 'orange'. It is an artless enough poem, particularly in the revealing honesty of its final line, but it provides a clear example of the way the stress patterns of colloquial speech are paramount, even in repeated refrains.

The first ten or fifteen minutes of a lesson should provide ample time to deal with this. It could usefully generate more 'I wish . . .' poems. Some of the children may bring in jingles or nursery rhymes starting this way, but should be discouraged from using the ballad metre of alternate four and three stress (generally iambic) lines, because of its tendency to force the stress towards 'wish' and thereby destroy the variety that makes Kim's poem so effective. It is a good idea to give a selection of 'starters' so that children can try two or three before they decide on an idea to build into a poem of their own. Here are some suggestions; the children themselves will probably provide others:

> Can't I go?
> What a rotten idea!
> Does it matter?
> I am the lucky one.
> That's twice he's $\left.{\text{done} \atop \text{said}}\right\}$ it.
> You have all the luck!

In setting the work, stipulate that the refrain they choose must come at least three times, and twice in the first stanza or group of lines, with at least one important change of emphasis. It should be possible to make a selection of the best ones for preservation in some form – wall display, form magazine or anthology, etc. One of the simplest methods is to keep a clip file in the classroom for such things, which then becomes a sort of portmanteau anthology, and can be accessible for the children to browse through. (A volunteer can usually be found to act as 'editor', who can also be prompted to decorate the cover and put the agreed title on it – an opportunity for careful lettering.)

Metre and rhythm

The suggestions that follow involve a two-stage sequence, first, at first- or possibly second-form level, then at fourth- or fifth-form level. Ideally this is with the same class and teacher, so that the two approaches are closely linked and pupils at the second stage can be reminded of what they did two or three years before. Teachers who have experienced the advantages of this kind of continuity in their English teaching will testify to its value. However, each stage is valid in its own right, and can be regarded as an independent unit of study.

STAGE I   'JOHN GILPIN'

In 1953 Penguin Books issued a delightful edition of this ballad in their King Penguin series with superb illustrations by Ronald Searle – I do not know if these have ever been reissued, but if an epidiascope or projector can be used to display them they form a most valuable visual aid to any reading, catching the spirit without in any way belittling Cowper's light-hearted story. Searle's humour makes its own independent contribution, and by small details, especially in facial expressions, provides an amusing running commentary on the farce as it develops.

It would be almost presumptuous to suggest ways of presenting such a straightforward story in verse. It lends itself to mime, prepared (perhaps taped) reading, semi-dramatizing – the cast being Mr and Mrs Gilpin (it may be instructive who, on the evidence of the opening conversation, is 'the boss' in this partnership), Betty the maid, the Calender (best described as a cloth processor), and the post boy, with a chorus of turnpikemen, children and bystanders. The important thing is not to labour it, but convey something of the spirit in which it was written – thrown off by Cowper in a day's writing as an antidote to his persistent melancholia in later life.

Once the class is familiar with it from the first reading or performance, encourage them to practise the verse form by beginning a story of their own about a journey, just to feel at home in the ballad metre, then return to the poem and draw their attention to two characteristics: first the padding lines or expressions in some verses, put in more to sustain the jog-trot of the ballad metre and rhyme than to carry the story foward. One way is to point to one obvious rhyme (e.g. 'so gay' in verse 34) and ask them to find similar examples of the rhyme determining the choice or order of words (e.g. stanzas 1, 6, 10, 20, 25, 26, 27, 32, 35, 39, 41, 45, 60, 62). The second feature is the remarkable faithfulness to the iambic metre. Almost the only variation is an occasional anapaest formed by reversing an iambus (usually the first one of a line). It is instructive to look at the four clearest examples of this in stanzas 11, 28, 32 and 39, and show – or preferably let the pupils discover – how the metrical device is used to emphasize a dramatic moment in the story. The point being made by drawing attention to these deliberate crudities in the verse form is that they are appropriate to the style and intention of the piece. Speed, and a reassuringly regular jingle, serve to maintain the level of light-hearted entertainment where narrative line is all-important. Such artificiality, especially in the direct speech (this can be demonstrated by asking pupils to rewrite verses like stanza 16 in more natural speech), allow us to enjoy the story more readily, by keeping it in the world of make-believe.

So far, this lesson might equally well have taken its place in Chapter 7. What is its relevance to any study of rhythm? I believe that to develop an understanding of what rhythm is in poetry it is necessary to make clear the distinction between it and metre at an early stage, and to ensure that pupils don't confuse the two. By demonstrating, as we have done, the way a strongly marked, even exaggerated metre, tends to override the natural rhythms of the language, this difference becomes clear.

So pervasive is the metre in this poem that it is almost impossible to allow speech rhythms precedence when there is a strong clash. Cowper has in fact helped us to accept the dominance of iambic metre by deliberately setting up some small clashes of this kind in the opening stanzas; the stress falls on 'was', 'and', 'eke' in the first verse and 'to' in the second verse, against the sense.

STAGE II   BALLAD METRE TRANSFORMED: A. E. HOUSMAN

A. E. Housman's poetry has run the gamut from extreme – almost 'cult' – popularity to dismissal as mawkish sentimentality. We are now far enough from him, and can more readily recognize and respond to his particular achievements within the restricted modes he chose to use. In *A Shropshire Lad*, his first and still most popular collection, forty-five of the sixty-three poems are in four-line stanzas of ballad type (4–3–4–3) rhyming second and fourth lines. For this lesson with fourth- or fifth-year pupils, I have chosen one of these; many others could be used in the same way. The poem is the poignant lyric 'White in the Moon' (no. XXXVI). It is worth taking some trouble to present this so as to achieve maximum emotional effect at a first hearing. (I am not one of those teachers who believe that children of this age are too immature or too brash to respond to such personal emotions as this lyric contains; but if the idea of it embarrasses you, it is probably best avoided.) Choose your time well – maybe a last lesson or a time when the atmosphere is relaxed and untense – and use a piece of music to establish the tone of the lesson. I have found the slow movement of Ravel's Piano Concerto good in such a context. There are many recordings – mine is by Eva Bernathoba with the Prague Symphony Orchestra under Smetacek, on Supraphon SUAST 10602. Another good piece is Alan Rawsthorne's *Elegy* for solo guitar of which there is a fine and eloquent performance on disc by its dedicatee Julian Bream (RCA SP 6876). The first, slow section, is ideal for setting the right atmosphere. A pre-recording of the poem on tape may be preferable to a live reading. One can then time the transition from music to voice better, starting the words over the fade-out, if it can be done smoothly and without clicks.

Only when the poem has had time to sink in in its own right should you start to look more closely at how it gains its almost magical effect of despair and loneliness. This may be – perhaps *should* be – in another lesson, rather than trying to cram both emotional response and critical appraisal into the same session. Here one can draw on recollections of 'John Gilpin', with its quite different aims for the same metre. It is useful to jog memories by quoting again the opening stanzas, and a selection of others. If the first reading of the Housman poem was successful, many pupils will have memorized the opening stanza. One can contrast the effect of the opening anapaest 'Whĭte ĭn thĕ moōn . . .' with 'smack went the whip . . .', etc. in Cowper's stanza 11, to emphasize the danger of too readily making assumptions about the effects of metre. Again, the repetition of the opening line is far removed from any kind of ballad 'refrain', and needs to be looked at as part of the almost drugging hopelessness conveyed by the repetitions throughout the poem – 'the moon' (three times in the first verse alone), 'still' in stanza 2, the prosaic callousness of 'trudge on, trudge on' in stanza 3, and 'far, far' in stanza 4, before returning to the opening lines.

The next point is the way Housman has succeeded in enhancing rather than destroying or overriding the natural rhythm of the language. The metre is an obedient servant here, coming forward as needed by the mood and emotional pressure. Thus, in the first two lines in stanza 2 it is almost submerged:

Stĭll hangs the hed̄ge   withoūt a gūst,
Stĭll, stĭll the shādows   stāy.

This gives the appropriate stress pattern, but is far too crude an analysis of the rhythm. In particular, the alliteration of 'hangs the hedge' makes one linger on 'hangs', so that the rhythmic weight of the line all comes before the caesura, and the qualifying phrase 'without a gust' is merely a gloss on it, faster and almost weightless, pushing us on to the insistent heavy double stress of 'still, still', so that we are momentarily surprised that it is only 'shadows' that stay so still. (Notice the effect in this line of the repeated sounds st, st, sh, st.) An interesting comparison, if one needs it, is with the opening lines of Keats's *Hyperion* using similar means for a similar effect. Verse 3 strikes a deliberately prosaic note, cutting across the intense loneliness and isolation with its home-spun wisdom. Consequently the mundane ballad metre can be given its head, with the additional stresses of the third line, 'trudge on, trudge on' adding a note of almost jocular insensitivity.

There are other details that comparison with 'John Gilpin' might bring out – the use of archaisms like 'ere', 'hie' (c.f. 'eke' in verse 1 of 'John Gilpin') for instance, or the use of inversions like 'straight though reached the track'. One interesting contrast concerns references to the road – almost obsessive in Housman's static poem ('road' three times, 'way' twice, 'track' once – all in four verses), compared with hardly any reference in all sixty-three verses of Cowper's story. Actually he uses 'way' once only, and 'road' three times, but always merely for referential purposes.

This lesson does not lend itself to the setting of any associated writing work. It could lead to further reading of Housman and perhaps to a search for similar deceptively simple lyrics capable of conveying deep feeling. As a contrast and as material for further discussion of the relation between rhythm and sincerity, one could ask pupils to seek out examples of *In Memoriam* verses in their local paper. The well-known fact that these are often drawn from stock by the undertaker or even the newspaper rather than being individual submissions by the bereaved should help to neutralize any feeling that to examine such products is in poor taste. A few are included in the Appendix (pp.269–70).

One point that will have become clear from this first part of the chapter is that one cannot isolate and study – let alone *teach* – rhythm in poetry. Just because it is so central to the art form, it is bound up with almost every other feature capable of being discussed about poems, particularly those concerned with sound and pace. Thus we have found ourselves considering metre and rhyme again, as well as other things discussed in Chapter 7. In its practical aspects, i.e. in relation to poetry as performance, Chapter 8 has already also been concerned with rhythm, especially when considering how to use recorded spoken poetry. I have advocated fairly oblique approaches. In practice it is likely that English teachers will not wish in any case to give 'a lesson on rhythm'; I hope I have made my lesson suggestions in such a way that they can be used as a source of ideas for other kinds of English work. My aim in giving the topic this central place in the book has been to try to remind my readers of the key role of rhythm in poetry, arising directly from its key role in language itself. It is the universal pervasiveness of rhythm that Lorenzo celebrates in his contemplative words to Jessica (in which his concept of 'music' or 'harmony' includes all aspects of rhythm):

> There's not the smallest orb which thou behold'st
> But in his motion like an angel sings,
> Still quiring to the young-ey'd cherubins;
> Such harmony is in immortal souls....

And

> The man that hath no music in himself,
> Nor is not moved with concord of sweet sounds,
> Is fit for treasons, stratagems, and spoils,
> The motions of his spirit are dull as night,
> And his affections dark as Erebus;
> Let no such man be trusted.

10

IMAGERY

'In free-verse and in Dylan Thomas's complicated metrical stanzas the articulation and spacing of images is done by rhythm instead of by syntax.' I start with this suggestive statement from Donald Davie's book *Articulate Energy* because it indicates the link between this and the previous chapter. Much poetry can be described as 'the articulation and spacing of images'. We have spent some time on looking at the way rhythm helps the poet 'articulate' his material, where by 'articulate' we mean both to join together and to 'speak' or divide into a sequence of separate sound-sense utterances. Let us now turn our attention to the images themselves. At the beginning of the last chapter (p.109) I made an analogy with quantum physics. We might use this again now; rhythm can be described as the wave-like movement of poetry: imagery as the particles that constitute a poem. Like all analogies this can't be pushed too far, nor does it cover all kinds of poetry. Much narrative poetry, in particular, is relatively sparing in its use of imagery. Where the analogy is valuable is in identifying imagery to be as central a 'building material' for poetry as rhythm. This is not the place to define imagery. (For those who need it, a useful general description can be found in D. Thompson and S. Tunnicliffe, *Reading and Discrimination*, pp.49–54.)

Our purpose is to develop an awareness in our pupils of image-making as a poetic activity. I put it in this way because I believe that, more than any other aspect of poetry teaching, an understanding of the way imagery works involves active participation. This is because the basic units of language – even down to the separate written symbols we call the alphabet – are all grounded in imagery. When we converse, we make images all the time and the words we use – however prosaically – are themselves soil composted from the fallen leaves of the image-tree. Our job when we come to concentrate on this aspect of poetry is to bring forward into conscious recognition what our pupils know already – know in their bones, so to speak.

Finding and making images

This approach is described in terms of a lesson or lessons for first- and second-year pupils. Teachers will readily recognize that it can be adapted for other levels.

1 By means of class discussion, establish the value of *comparison* as an essential of clear expression. The old 'chestnut' about a spiral staircase gives a lead as to how this can be done. You ask 'What is a spiral staircase?' and when your partner starts gesticulating in his or her reply, say that you are blind. Here language is inevitably clumsier than gesture. By depriving your answerer of the visual medium of communication you have forced him or her to intellectualize. Now put some such question or exercise as:

Describe: Velvet
A calm sea
Wind in trees

without comparing it with anything else. Again the answering is deprived of a 'sense' as it were.

2   This is a good point to introduce some images made by poets. Your choice will depend on what is available to you; it is a good idea to be able to refer children to the complete poem so that they can see the image later in context. The following small selection indicates the range of possible effects open to poets using images, and they have been chosen for their immediate sensuous appeal to children. I hope the reason for the groupings is self-evident. It is probably wise not to use more than one or two such groups in the course of a single lesson; mere multiplicity can confuse rather than clarify.

Group I

i   My fingers *tight as ivy* on her shoulders
From 'Singing School', Seamus Heaney, (*The Wearing of the Black*, ed. P. Fiacc)

ii   Bustling big as a *laundry bag*
With her hair in rubber bands
'Queen Whirligig', Cara Lockhart-Smith
(*The Magic Tree*, ed. D. Woolger)

iii   This December is cold, but the sweet
Orangeade *shrills* heavenly, up the waxy straw, a cool
Perfect *runnel* over his tongue.
'Representational', Alan Brownjohn,
(*A Night in the Gazebo*) (see Appendix)

(*see pp.210–11, 220 for full references to examples below*)

Group II

iv   White plates that write their Os across the dresser
'After a Death', John Ormond
(*Definition of a Waterfall*)

v   the bee is a merchant.
He trades among
Flower planets.
'The Bee', Peter Kelso (aged 12)
(*Junior Voices 2*)

vi   My roots burrow in rainclouds.
I grow down to earth at midnight.
I am the negative of a tree.
'Lightning Tree', Edwin Morgan
(*The New Divan*)

Group III

vii   She lies down, as if she were lowering
A great snake into the ground.
'Tigress', Ted Hughes
(*Moonbells and Other Poems*)

viii   In the grey evening
I see a long green serpent
With its tail in the dahlias

It lies in loops across the grass
And drinks softly at the faucet.

I can hear it swallow.
'The Garden Hose', Beatrice Janesco
(*Junior Voices 3*)

Group IV

ix   How did he steal them, whom will he bring
Loaves of blue heaven under each wing?
'The Crow', Russell Hoban
(*The Pedalling Man*)

x   The lamps grew plump with oily reliable light
Geoffrey Hill (from XXIII, *Mercian Hymns*)

Notes

Group I   The straightforward comparisons between *i* and *ii* could usefully be imitated: *iii* describes a small boy. The whole poem is worth coming back to, perhaps with older children (see Appendix).

Group II   Here again, the third example in the group is more complex than the other two, and older children – perhaps third- or fourth-year – would get a lot from the whole sequence *Three Trees*, the other two being 'Water Skier's Tree' (describing the transient wake-patterns of water-skiing) and the even more surprising 'Impacted Windscreen Tree'.

Group III   These are more conventional comparisons. It would be worthwhile to ask which of the two snake images is the more effective or to discuss the respective merits of comparing animal with animal in *vii* and animal with inanimate object in *viii*.

Group IV   These more subtle images are probably better used after work has been done on the simpler level. Number *ix* is an excellent example of the creative 'jump' a poet can make through imagery, and how instantaneous its effect can be for an alert reader. The crow flying, and the shopper carrying loaves home from the bakery or supermarket, are mundane sights enough but the combination is startlingly effective. Geoffrey Hill's prose poem (No. xxiii in the sequence of thirty) really needs its full context for one to appreciate the resonances it sets up; I have included it to show that the element of direct comparison in imagery, so evident in examples like *i* or *viii*, is not essential. Hill's 'animation' of the lamps – 'grew plump' – contributes strongly to the sensuous atmosphere of the poem to which the imitative assonance of 'oily reliable' also adds its own contribution.

3   The notes have already indicated the third stage of this lesson for first- and second-year pupils. If your examples are

carefully chosen, especially bearing in mind the need to relate them to the children's world of sensation (in Keats's sense), they will almost automatically lead to imitation or emulation. By trying it out the children are made much more alert, both to things and experiences they usually take for granted and to the pleasure to be derived from getting close to the sensation or experience, and giving it a degree of permanence, through words. Practising image-making in this way also helps them to be more alert to the effect of imagery in writing, whether prose or verse.

Abstract made concrete

This approach to imagery is for use with third-year pupils. It is concerned with making rather than reading or responding to imagery, and it links up with further ideas and suggestions in Chapter 11. As the title indicates, the idea is to encourage children to 'actualize' or express through images familiar emotions and sensations. However deeply felt, such feelings as loneliness, fear, excitement, etc. often remain inchoate and even (because of this) out of control, for lack of an adequate vehicle whereby they can be distanced and shared. I am not intending to claim that poetic image-making is psychologically therapeutic — though interesting work has been done along these lines by social psychologists. For our purposes we can be content if we alert our pupils to the ability of imagery to transmit feeling, often in unexpected ways.

1   The first step is to identify and list some of the commonest feelings that members of the class have recently experienced. This will involve a 'talk out', which can be initiated in various ways:

a)   Directly by the teacher through such questions as one hears on radio and TV interviews – how did you feel when you won your gold medal/you got clear of the blazing building?

b)   In discussion groups of four or five (say, six groups in a normal class of thirty), where each group is asked to choose a different emotion from a list (preferably of seven or eight), and find experiences they have had where they have felt the emotion. The list might include any of these:

aggression	excitement	nervousness
awe	fear	reverence
boredom	happiness	sympathy
delight	jealousy	tenderness
depression	loneliness	timidity
envy		

As an alternative to *a*) you might ask the children to collect (i.e. tape or make notes of) or collect yourself, in preparation for the lesson, examples of TV or radio interviewers asking such questions, and the replies given. Pupils can then discuss whether the replies helped them to understand or sympathize with the person asked. (It will be instructive to find out how far the interviewees' *manner* and *tone* conveyed their feelings, rather than or in addition to, what they actually said in their reply.)

2   For this stage present the pupils with a number of contrasted pairs of epithets like slow/fast, bright/dim, black/white, hard/soft, clear/dull, rough/smooth, open/secret, clean/dirty, stormy/calm. It is important to choose pairs that are normally associated with fairly concrete and specific things, and to avoid getting too close to abstracts like the ones considered in the first stage. A list can soon be compiled of all the suitable ones.

3   This is best done individually or in pairs. Ask the pupils each to choose one (or two, if in pairs) of the feelings discussed in stage 1. Try to get a variety chosen, though it is likely that some will prove more popular than others. From the list of contrasts ask them to compile a list of epithets more appropriate to their chosen emotion. Urge them to try and decide on one

of the two for as many as they can, even if it doesn't seem to make immediate sense. (There are no 'right' answers; it is quite likely that two different children will attach opposite epithets to the same emotion.) The result of this might be along these lines:

Depression is slow, dim, rough, secret, black. . . .

4 Finally ask them to look at their list of chosen epithets and decide on something that fits them all – e.g. an animal, a scene, an action or series of actions, etc. This will constitute their 'image' of the emotion they have chosen to make concrete. Pupils can be offered a choice of ways of getting this down – perhaps as a short poem (*haiku* for instance), an episode from a story, a short descriptive paragraph. For ideas on similar lines see Chapter 11 (pp.143–63).

Expanded images

This and the next lesson in the section are for fourth- and fifth-year pupils. They are simply explorations into the use of imagery by poets. This lesson need not lead to any particular piece of written work, other than to encourage pupils to find other similar examples. I have chosen three examples. The first is an extended simile, the well-known conclusion of Donne's 'Valediction Forbidding Mourning':

Our two soules therefore, which are one,
    Though I must goe, endure not yet
A breach, but an expansion,
    Like gold to ayery thinnesse beate.

If they be two, they are two so
    As stiffe twin compasses are two,
Thy soule the fixt foot, makes no show
    To move, but doth, if the 'other doe.

And though it in the center sit,

> Yet when the other far doth rome,
> It leanes, and hearkens after it,
>   And growes erect, as that comes home.
>
> Such wilt thou be to mee, who must
>   Like th' other foot obliquely runne;
> They firmnes makes my circle just,
>   And makes me end, where I begunne.

(I have given Donne's original spelling. In quoting bits to children it may be advisable to modernize it.) A reading of the whole poem will establish the sense of the poet striving for an exact counterpart to his feeling of the essential unity of the lovers in spite of separation. The gold beater image is beautiful in its almost tactile and sensuous quality of 'airy thinness', and this gives way to the image of 'the compasses' or navigator's dividers. It is worth spending a little time on making clear how through its precision and length the image sets up resonances (e.g. of exploration, adventures, discovery) that add richness to the whole poem. Attention can also be drawn to the way the language here consolidates the feeling of the whole poem – tenderness, solicitude, and trust between the lovers.

The second example of an expanded image, from the same period, is Sir Walter Raleigh's lyric 'What is Our Life?' The ideal way to approach this, in my view, is through the musical setting of it in the madrigal by Orlando Gibbons (see Appendix for an account of this). However, even without the music it is worth reading to see how a single image can be drawn out and in the process yield unexpected insights. 'Life is like a play' seems an unpromising image by itself. Raleigh gives it new validity by presenting the 'play' as a comedy for which we are first 'dressed' in our mother's wombs. Heaven sits as spectator, and our graves provide the final curtain, leading to the closing sardonic comment 'we die in earnest; that's no jest'.

Finally in this exploration I take a more recent poem. Here the expanded image once again forms the whole poem; but unlike the Raleigh lyric the comparison is not made explicit, although it is once again a comment on life. In 'The Combat' Edwin Muir has really written a parable in verse. Pupils find it puzzling, strange, intriguing. It does not lend itself to explanation, but is a good poem to leave in pupils' minds at the end of a lesson. If any student shows particular interest in Muir's poem, he or she could be referred to Kafka's short stories, e.g. 'Metamorphosis', or 'The Burrow'. There is no doubt that Muir was strongly influenced by Kafka's vision, having been his first translator.

Linked images; image sequences

In this final lesson or series of lessons, which is intended once again for fourth- and fifth-year pupils (though no. 3 can yield worthwhile results with third-year groups), we look at the effects that can be achieved by using linked images. We need to look at complete poems for this and I have chosen three short ones, two given here in full, and a more obscure and longer one by Dylan Thomas to complete this lesson and the whole chapter.

The first poem is about writing poems. I have chosen it because, coming from war-torn Ulster – a place not normally associated with poetry these days – it has an authentic ring that teenagers respond to and that may encourage some of them to use poetry as a medium for expression who might otherwise fight shy of it. The editor of the anthology it comes from describes the poems in the section including this one as 'dealing with the bitterness stemming from the results of violence: intimidation, frustration, the mass exodus of so many from the province, and the depression of those left behind'. Its author, Meta Mayne-Reid, is a well-known children's writer. This poem's title is also the title of her first collection published by Outposts Press.

No Ivory Tower
I do not envy those

who write in locked studies,
in Ivory Towers.
Give me the rub of circumstance,
the electricity which springs
from daily living.
I will not,
like puss in the midnight dark,
stalk my prey in a shuttered room,
will not entreat
honourable words to visit humble pages,
as I sit, insulated by silence.

I will write at the bus stop,
in the kitchen, between form-filling.
If my thoughts refuse
to clamour for words' clothing
let them die naked.
They must pierce through life
as infant's thrusting head
breaks the womb's waters,
before I will give them names,
and own them as my children.

A good way to open the lesson is to introduce the rather hackneyed image of the ivory tower and ask the pupils to say what it suggests to them. The discussion could be developed by then asking what kind of activity or event or behaviour would provide the biggest contrast to the notion of the ivory tower. If the discussion develops, it could form the basis of a piece of writing. Before this, and as a stimulus to it, introduce the poem.

Draw their attention to the way the first stanza develops the claustrophobic implications of the title through the images of static electricity, the cat (with the implied reduction of the poem to a mouse) and the word 'insulated'. Having established this, ask what is the dominant image in the second stanza. Girls will appreciate the force of the contrast between the deliberately locked ivory tower and the baby's head bursting open the womb's prison. A contrast is reinforced by the 'clamour' of thoughts to be clothed in words as opposed to the insulated silence of the shuttered room.

> *The Empty Church*
> They laid this stone trap
> for him, enticing him with candles,
> as though he would come like some huge moth
> out of the darkness to beat there.
> Ah, he had burned himself
> before in the human flame
> and escaped, leaving the reason
> torn. He will not come any more
>
> to our lure. Why, then, do I kneel still
> striking my prayers on a stone
> heart? Is it in hope one
> of them will ignite yet and throw
> on its illuminated walls the shadow
> of someone greater than I can understand?
> (R. S. Thomas)

The first poem concerned life and action. Yet not all life is clamorous and noisy. It may help in introducing this second poem to set the atmosphere by talking about big empty buildings. Who has been in one by himself? Where? Has anyone been inside an empty chapel or church? What time of day? What do they remember of it? More could be done by means of sound effects – an echo chamber and footsteps perhaps and whispered voices. (A group might be given this to prepare on tape before the lesson.) The second potent set of images concerns the candle and the moth. Some will, in any case, think of candles in association with churches. As with the Housman poem in the previous chapter, this poem is best heard at the end of the lesson, so that having prepared the ground by discussion of the main images, the poem can rest on its own merits.

Another response to this poem could be visual, perhaps in collaboration with the art teacher. There are many opportunities here – candle flames, 'some huge moth', 'the shadow of someone greater'. Teachers interested in following this up would do well to look at another volume of R. S. Thomas's poems, *The Way of It*. For this small collection he collaborated with an artist, Barry Hirst, and the result is both atmospheric and suggestive.

As an antidote to what might seem the rather rarefied atmosphere of R. S. Thomas's poem, I suggest now a rather different choice: Richard Murphy's 'Reading Lesson' from *High Island* (see Appendix). Because this deals with an easily recognizable school situation, that of a reluctant teenage reader – a farm lad, in this instance – it can be used successfully with less able groups of third- and fourth-year students. This time there is a positive advantage in making sure each pupil has a copy of the poem in front of him or her *before* you read it, the point being that they are put in a similar situation to the one being described. I find it best to run off copies on a duplicator with plenty of space around the text for notes or scribbles.

After the first reading, which should be carefully prepared, it should be easy to develop a general discussion. Don't go straight to the central question raised by the poem – summed up by the victim's words 'I'll be the same man whatever I do' – but aim first at making sure the pupils have a clear picture in their minds of the boy's rich outdoor life. Some might be encouraged to draw pictures of any of the creatures mentioned, at the appropriate place on their sheet. There are plenty to choose from: hares and greyhound, mule, goat, 'flushed snipe', piebald mare, bantam cock, wild duck, pheasants, wrens. Let the discussion bring out the *appropriateness* of the comparisons 'caught in a trap' (like the hare at the dog-races), 'as a mule baulks at a gap/from which a goat may hobble out and bleat', and 'his eyes jink from a sentence like flushed snipe/escaping shot'. After this it is profitable to have a spell of silent reading and thought, with the instruction to think about other ways used of describing the boy and his predicament. They should enjoy the final group of images but may miss, without judicious help, the significance of the contrast in it between what represents work to the lad, farming, ploughing, drilling – 'a field of tasks' – and what gives him real enjoyment, the open road, petty thieving, poaching pheasants. It is only after this that you can return to the point mentioned earlier: will he 'be the same man' if he has learned to read?

It would be a pity to relate any writing tasks for the class too closely to the poem and its method. If they have enjoyed its way of describing the boy they will have learned plenty about imagery. The more natural way to lead on from the poem would be to plan an open discussion or debate on the value of compulsory schooling to those destined for unacademic lives. The study of the poem should have helped them to recognize that 'even poetry' can say significant things about their lives and future work.

For the final part of this sequence I am suggesting a poem of Dylan Thomas's, 'Where Once the Waters of Your Face'. At the beginning of this chapter I quoted Donald Davie commenting on Dylan Thomas's poetry. Thomas, he said, relied on rhythm rather than syntax to hold his images together. Another poet, Malcolm Povey, puts it thus: 'By breaking the rules of informational uses of language, poetry makes the reader find new meaning.' You will remember that in Chapter 8 I referred to the way the reader of the poem was essential as interpreter as well as audience.

The best way to approach a poem as rich and confused in imagery as this is to introduce it almost as *incantation*. If you decide to do this, it is best actively to discourage questions about meaning at first. Tell the pupils not to worry if it doesn't make sense. Once they accept this, they will find that they can get some surprising results by approaching it as a pattern of word-sounds to be performed. More can be involved in this process if they are allowed to work on it in groups, preferably with cassette recorders. As they do so, the dominant images will emerge – the contrasts between wet and dry, death and life, and the sense of lost or frustrated love – 'the weeds of love's left dry'. In my experience, teenagers find it easy to approach poetry in this way, using the words as incantation, and responding to images in isolation first – as happens in much pop music, especially the more adventurous kind like Pink Floyd and their successors. Another reason for adopting this approach is that Thomas's poetry gains so much of its potency from his metrical craftmanship, a feature that would make this poem equally in place in Chapter 7. The poem is as much a pattern of sounds as a text, what one might call, with other poems of Dylan Thomas's, a 'word score'. The final 'performance' of the poem or, if more than one group has prepared one, the one voted the best, should be taped and listened to critically by the whole class and improved where it is voted necessary. This constitutes the end product of this lesson.

In this and the previous chapter I have tried to show how both rhythm and imagery spring from sources deep within language, and indeed from the roots of our consciousness, the source of language itself. We are not likely to make much progress towards conveying this to our pupils by speaking about it directly in such terms; but our knowledge of it should inform the way we present poetry to them.

11

WRITING POETRY

Students are much more likely to see the point of reading poetry in order to write it better, than they are to appreciate that one should write poetry in order to read it better.

(Rachel McAlpine, *Song in the Satchel*)

One thing I think all my classes profited from was the fact that the children had written a number of poems before, independently of the study of the adult works.... This was a great help to them in reading what other poets had written. They were close to poetry because it was something they created themselves.

(Kenneth Koch, *Rose, Where Did You Get That Red? Teaching Great Poetry to Children*)

Some years ago a widely-travelled English teacher, Brian Powell, attempted to systematize his experience of the classroom teaching of poetry writing in a book (still in print) called *English through Poetry Writing*. Unfortunately the book fails to live up to the promise of its title, in spite of some good ideas here and there. This is mainly because Mr Powell's classroom practice would seem to be fairly far removed from what goes on nowadays in productive English classrooms. There is an oddly old-fashioned ring to such advice as this, for instance: 'the pupil should write a prose comment after each of his poems, recording it below the poem itself on the right hand page of his special exercise book.' And we cannot take very seriously someone claiming to prescribe methods of teaching poetry who can solemnly say to his fellow teachers, 'a characteristic of poetry is that it usually has some basic rhythm. This is not to be confused with rhyme....' I mention this disappointing book not merely because of its weaknesses, but because its attempt to formalize the teaching of poetry writing in conventional 'English lesson' terms constitutes a useful warning. Mr Powell's rigid 'schema' of form ('gives the pupil a number of structures for the shaping of his writing'), content ('presents him with suggestions for subject-matter'), and evaluaton ('designed to help him improve his expression') becomes a straitjacket as he follows it relentlessly through six chapters, first at an 'introductory', then an 'advanced' level. To be effective, poetry teaching needs to be more flexible and more sensitive than this. Another danger to which the book alerts us is that of insisting too firmly on presenting students with 'models' for imitation. It is a hundred years since R. L. Stevenson 'played the sedulous ape to Hazlitt, to Lamb, to Wordsworth' and the rest, yet English teachers too often seem to advocate the sedulous aping by children of writers or of literary models regardless of their fitness as vehicles for these necessarily less mature, more groping and exploratory minds and sensibilities. An English teacher whose work I shall refer to later in this chapter, David Young, says quite bluntly, 'I am reluctant to stimulate written words by other written words.' This is a healthier attitude than Powell's insistence on the slavish imitation of Dylan Thomas, Ezra Pound or Ted Hughes, or his blunderbuss approach in such pieces of advice as: '[the teacher] should read several carefully chosen pieces of prose and poetry as an introduction to a writing session.'

After such strictures it may seem inconsistent for me to suggest a 'schema' of my own. I offer it not as a blueprint for poetry writing, but simply to clarify the actual process we have in mind. This process I believe has three natural stages.

Stage one: *stimuli*

There has to be some starting-point for any teaching process. In English it is frequently (some might say 'too frequently') a text of some kind. In geography it might be a country, in history an event and its context. The ideal stimulus for a poem is an experience that is seen as significant by the person making the poem. I would not exclude the reading of a poem as one such experience, but it should certainly not be the only or even the most usual kind of stimulus. Moreover, to consider the reading as *experience* rather than *model* does, I think, act as a useful corrective to the 'sedulous ape' syndrome. Experience capable of sparking off poems – or poetic writing to be more precise – can be as various as life itself, and may often be isolated or brought into full consciousness by means of exploratory discussion, perhaps on a theme, perhaps itself triggered by a reading. A shortcut may often be to provide the experience directly. Sandy Brownjohn's ideas for her primary school children give a good indication of possible approaches with first or second-year pupils:

> *Direct observation* is a tried and trusted way of encouraging children to write: bringing in objects; bottles containing cotton wool soaked in different solutions to hand round for writing about smell; looking at pictures, slides or films; listening to music or tape-recordings; taking children out to a park, a high street, market, or anywhere they can write while experiencing their surroundings. Any way that involves direct use of the five senses can lead to good poems.

Brian Powell, in the book already referred to, has some more elaborate suggestions, one of which it may be worthwhile to refer to, to redress the balance after my earlier criticisms of his book's shortcomings. He was in the practice of getting pupils to think up stimuli, and describes one such occasion:

> I vividly recall coming to class one day and having the boy in charge of the period tell us to put our heads on our desks and close our eyes. As soon as we did this, he pulled down the blinds so that the room was in almost total darkness. He then hung over the light above the blackboard a thick piece of hangman's rope, at the end of which was a large noose. As the light shone on it the rope stood out stark against the dark background. The boy then switched on a portable tape machine on which he had recorded twenty minutes of a grandfather clock ticking loudly. He then told us to open our eyes.

Stage two: *form*

Not until there is some impulse in the pupil to find a way of expressing his or her response to a stimulus, of recordng the feelings or ideas aroused, does he or she recognize the need for form. Some of the work in earlier chapters, particularly Chapter 4, has aimed at preparing the ground for this, so that there is more chance of the pupils' finding an appropriate vehicle or framework, a cage in which to trap the experience, or a pattern it can dance to. Another advantage of introducing separately some practical work on the *forms* of poetic expression is that by concentrating on the technical problems presented by them pupils are sometimes stimulated to discover in themselves the germ that makes a poem. This does not invalidate my first statement under this heading. An illustration may make this clearer. Let us suppose that a cabinet-maker, noticing the way the grain lies on the surface of some wood he is using to make a bureau, devises a secret compartment whose edge conforms with that grain so closely as to be virtually undetectable. As he does so, he realizes this would be the ideal hiding place for a document he needs to conceal – perhaps a Will or Deed. Until the technical feat of making the drawer suggested it he had been unable to secure the document. In such cases my stages 1 and 2 coalesce – another indication of the dangers of any kind of rigid plan of campaign in poetry teaching.

We have already seen how the *haiku* form can be used to advantage in the classroom (pp.82–4). In an article some years ago entitled 'Haiku: the great leveller' (*English in Education*, vol. 9, 2) Barrie Wade made a further point, arising from his own experience of teaching poetry writing. The use of a simple yet strict form such as the *haiku* can release pupils in some way from apparent language difficulties. Here are three out of the many *haiku* his own pupils produced:

> The pot of flowers
> Laughed strongly in summer light:
> I laugh in winter.
>
> > (Elaine)

> I thought of myself
> Under the cemetery mud
> And put flowers there.
>
> > (David)

> A young, naked girl
> Is combing out her long hair,
> Watched by the old moon.
>
> > (Julie)

After quoting many such examples, Barrie Wade pointed out that although each age and ability group is represented in the poems quoted there are no obvious pointers in the poems themselves, a fact which should make us wary of assuming any relationship between general ability and poetic achievement, and wary of placing our level of expectation too low for many children. Do we still assume our remedial classes should spend all their time on structured reading and comprehension schemes and do we still reserve for 'abler' pupils the luxury and satisfaction of writing verse? The last question is given poignancy by his revealing that 'David' was a second-year boy in a remedial class. It may be instructive to quote the final paragraph of Barrie Wade's interesting article:

> One fourth-year group wrote specifically for each other. They each wrote several haikus, then spent one period reading each other's which were displayed anonymously round the classroom. Each person selected one or two poems which appealed to him, discussed them informally then later read them to the class, sometimes with further discussion. I had written three poems each in a heavily-disguised hand. Throughout the lesson I waited for someone to choose one of my poems. No one did. Haiku is a great leveller.

The same point about the 'levelling' effect of concentrating on a particular verse form is made by Neil Powell (*Use of English*, 30, 2). He says unequivocally that 'if one is to teach people how to make poems at all, I think one should start with the fascination of what is difficult – the forms, the structures, the skills'. In pursuit of this he set as a class assignment the writing of a *villanelle*.

> Another colleague, Peter Scupham, wrote a villanelle for the occasion and I polished up an unfinished one of my own; then we showed these to our groups, together with villanelles by Auden and Dylan Thomas. . . . I explained the rules of the game briefly, but suggested that a close study of the examples was the best approach. The class contained some who are having one to one remedial English coaching and a couple who may be reading English at Oxbridge in three or four years' time – a wide range. I'd guess that about half of them found the exercise rewarding and surprising, while perhaps half a dozen produced unmistakably well-made, successful poems. That is as good a result as I could have expected from a comprehension or an essay assignment.

Powell sees as one advantage of such an exercise

> that it entices into creative writing, the pattern maker, the mathematician, the scientist, the pupil too easily and misleadingly called by Liam Hudson a 'converger'.... There is clearly in poetry, as in music, a strong convergent element which is shamefully ignored whenever English is loosely equated with 'imagination' or 'expression'; and this neglect is greater in schools or classes where the likeliest source of convergent compensation in the humanities – Latin – is least taught. The making of formal poems, like the playing of contrapuntal music or chess, is a vital bridge between arts and sciences: to ignore it is to invite muddle-headedness in the arts and aridity in the sciences.

Stage 3: *revision*

All writers know how important redrafting, word changing and revision are to effective writing. They have different ways of coping with this necessary fluidity from draft to draft until the final version emerges. One writer I know works with a soft pencil and a generous supply of india rubbers. This page on which I am writing has widely spaced lines, leaving room for crossings out, additions and changes of position. Every page of my manuscript is full of such alterations. In view of the obviousness of this, it is odd that English teachers so often insist on neatness and good handwriting in every draft of their pupils' work. For no kind of writing is this more harmful than for poetry. Sandy Brownjohn's advice cannot be too strongly emphasized:

> let the children have rough books to work in. They should not have to be bothered about spelling and neatness when they are writing. If you are encouraging them to rework their poems there will inevitably be things to cross out and words to add in. A writer's note book is often messy. The time to write out a fair copy in the English book is when the poem is

in its final version. Then spellings should be correct and handwriting neat. If the children have to think about that when first writing, it will interfere with their spontaneity.

In calling this stage 3 I do not wish to imply that it necessarily follows the other two after they are completed. The process of revision often begins to take place from the moment the first word is written, and when a student is really engaged with a particular *form* there are bound to be many versions and redrafts before it emerges. It is helpful, however, to be aware of the different stance of a writer involved in the revision process. The initial stimulus ideally leads to an unselfconscious involvement with the subject, often exciting or otherwise emotionally charged. The pursuit, first of an appropriate form, then of greater refinement and precision or even a more satisfactory shape on the page, involves moving towards greater self-consciousness, and at the same time 'stepping back' from the thing made so as to see it more objectively. For children such a process is very valuable, forcing them to recognize that the proper control of language involves a discipline of its own. Once they are engaged in the activity of poetry writing it is surprising at what an early age this can start. Anyone who has heard Ted Hughes talking with primary school poets about their work may need to revise accepted notions of leaving 'critical appreciation' to the senior forms.

David Young, an English teacher, took a class of 11-year-olds out to a pond in the school grounds, then encouraged them to try and capture in language something of what they had experienced. One of the class threw a stone in the pond. These are three successive drafts by one of the boys in that class:

1   Dead frog, weeds, tadpoles go in and out. Water ripples as a stone is thrown. Spread out. Leaves from the trees float on the pond. Grass.

2   Dead! as the frog
    Stretched out in the pond

Cold water
Tadpoles wriggle about
Ripples spread out as
far as they can.

3   Dead!
　　As the frog lying
　　　　　stretched
　　At the bottom surrounded by
　　　　　cold
　　dark water.
　　　　　Tadpoles
　　small weavings in and out
　　of the green moss
　　　　　bigger
　　and bigger still
　　ripples stretch as far as far.

It is interesting to see how the pursuit of a more effective shape
actually stimulates a clearer perception of what had been seen.
Notice, for instance, how the original 'tadpoles *go in and out*'
changes, first to 'wriggle about' then to the more metaphorical,
and much more powerful

　　　　　Tadpoles
　　small weavings in and out
　　of the green moss

The pursuit of form, coupled with the encouragement to revise
and refine the first impressions, has led the writer back to the
experience and made him respond more deeply to it. David
Young tells us that 'the revision of poems was a normal,
accepted part of English lessons and I am sure that, for the most
part, the revisions were made with a genuine desire to improve
the quality of what had gone before. To this extent, then, the
class were conscious of choosing, selecting, and rejecting'
(*English in Education*, vol 9, 3).

The poet Peter Abbs provides another good example of the beneficial effects of encouraging revision, this time from an 11-year-old girl (*The Use of English*, 26, 4). I include his comments, which are informed by his own engagement with the craft of poetry:

> *The Owl*
> I look around with my enormous eyes
> I listen carefully for every ~~scuffle~~ shuffle
> And then, a rustling sound in the grass
> ~~A mouse~~ I look down and see a mouse
> My supper
>
>   spread   soft
> I softly ~~open~~ my silk   wings
> And noiselessly, I fly above
> Suddenly I dive and then a squeak.
> I have caught my prey.
>
>   screeching bundle
> Climbing with my ~~prey mouse~~
> I perch on a high branch
> Out of all danger.
> My prey is teared to pieces
> By my strong curved beak and sharp talons.
>
>   catching
> I'm a clever one for ~~caching~~ mice
> It's very rare I miss
> And also I am agile
> With quick movements ~~and~~ good hearing and
>   penetrating eyesight.

It is revealing to notice how at the beginning of the second stanza the child first wrote: ' I softly open my silk wings'. Then as she quickly considered it, she must have deleted the verb 'open' and inserted the rhythmically more suggestive and perceptually more accurate 'spread'. The line then read: 'I softly spread my silk wings'. Then she considered the line, now revised, and responding to the new rhythm even so small a change had created (particularly in the run of soft sounds) she suddenly saw what the full line as a poetic movement had to be. Between 'silk' and 'wings' she inserted the word 'soft' and achieved the final line: 'I softly spread my silk soft wings'. It is a line that through its rhythm and alliteration beautifully enacts the owl's hushed movements.

Putting it into practice

What has already been said in this chapter has given some clear pointers to the class teaching of poetry writing, and most of the ideas can be readily adapted to different school situations. What follow now are two more fully worked-out schemes of work, one at a junior level, the other for more advanced students. The purpose of these is to show how the three elements of *stimulus*, *form* and *revision* all play their parts in the effective teaching of poetry writing. I do not claim any originality for the lessons; like most English teachers, I have over many years picked up and adapted to my circumstances, jackdaw-like, ideas from many sources. If anyone recognizes a jewel or feather of his own in the text here, perhaps he will return the compliment by borrowing from my store.

PICTURES INTO POEMS — A SEQUENCE OF WORK FOR A FIRST OR SECOND FORM

The emphasis here is on the first stage as outlined above, but the activities that follow will necessarily involve the children in stages 2 and 3 as they absorb the visual stimuli and make them their own. This method is more appropriate for a class familiar to the teacher, i.e. if a first-year class it should not be attempted before the spring or summer term; for a second-year class, it helps if the same teacher taught them in their first year.

Preparation

a)   This can take place over a considerable time – several weeks if necessary. It involves the teacher in gathering together two or three pictures for each child in the class from whatever sources are available – colour supplements, magazines, posters, advertising material, snapshots, handouts from museums or art galleries. A list of the children, with notes beside each name, recording particular interests or characteristics, can be very helpful – such things as 'just got a new bike', 'likes animals', 'shy with adults', 'junior first 11'. The aim is to keep a lookout for pictures likely to evoke strong responses from each particular pupil. As this may involve gathering anything from fifty to a hundred separate pictures it is a good idea to number each one as they accumulate and also to write the numbers against their respective names on your list. *Don't* write the pupil's name on the actual picture.

Note   It is obviously impossible to prescribe the subject-matter of your pictures. As an indication of the kind of range you might aim at I list below a few I have collected in the past:

i) Home
> A mother or older sister comforting a girl and wiping her tears.
>
> A grandmother playing 'hands across' (i.e. putting one hand in turn on top of your neighbour's) with two young children – all laughing.

ii) Street
> A street cleaner at work with shovel and handcart outside a pub.
>
> People outside shops, one of them with its sign in mirror writing.
>
> A group of teenage boys round a powerful motorbike.
>
> A soldier showing a young boy (about 8 or 9) how to work a machine gun (Northern Ireland).

iii) Work
> Docks: A ship unloading sacks of grain or foodstuff with black and white workers.
>
> An old bearded cobbler hand-sewing a sandal.

iv) Nature   The sun shining through the bare twigs of winter trees.
Strangely shaped piece of driftwood dramatically lit.
Snow in pine woods; one person in the empty landscape.
A lion, front face, lying down with paws forwards, yawning widely.

This is not a particularly lively set and I cannot give an adequate idea of colours. The main thing is variety. Often a picture with no immediate 'human interest' can spark off a child's imagination.

b)   Arrange groups of four, five or six children, and explain that once children have chosen their groups they must remain with them throughout this work. Sort the pictures into piles according to the groups whose numbers they have been chosen for. As this can't be done efficiently in the midst of a busy classroom, it is as well to do the grouping in a separate lesson.

Presentation of material (one teaching period)

a)   Hand over the piles of pictures to each group. Do *not* identify to the children which of them you had in mind for each picture. Tell them each must choose one picture only at first. Give them plenty of time to talk together about this and to make a choice they feel reasonably happy with. If your preparation was efficient many children should have picked the ones you chose for them. It is worth remembering, though, that they may have chosen their groups so as to be with children of similar interests.

b)   Rough books or paper and writing things needed. Ask the following four questions and allow at least four minutes of silence after the first one, two or three minutes after each of the others, during which they jot down words, ideas, phrases as quickly as possible – any order, in any way they like. There should be *no* group discussion for this stage. If necessary, separate the groups.

Question 1   What does your picture remind you of? (Suggest feelings, events, people met or known, dreams, etc.)

Question 2   A picture – especially a photograph – records one moment only. What do you think happened or was there *before* and *after* your picture?

Question 3   You have used only your eyesight so far. What other senses might be involved in your picture? (Smell, taste, feel or touch, hearing.) Jot down any words that occur to you.

Question 4   Try to jot down the main idea or ideas in your picture. What is the main theme of it?

Writing

They now have the 'bricks' for building their poems – the picture, and their jottings on it. Time for the actual writing is a matter of choice, depending on circumstances. It could be set as a homework. I have found that a second teaching period, after a break, on the same day as the presentation above, often helps concentration, as does a specific time-limit, if not too rigidly enforced. Perhaps half the period can be for silent individual work, half for comparing together in the groups, and/or final polishing and revision. It is often interesting to display the final versions separately from the pictures – or alternatively display all the pictures used and make an anthology of the poems – so that class members have the chance of matching poems to pictures. This encourages more careful and more directed reading. Often this exposure of the poems leads to further revisions by the writers themselves. A few children may prefer not to show their poems to anyone but the teacher; this should be respected.

A poem-sequence: model and workplan

This exercise in poetry writing is for the other end of the school, i.e. for senior pupils, with some experience of poetry reading and writing already behind them, as well as sufficient maturity to be able to look back over and assess their own lives to some extent. Obviously it would be quite unrealistic to expect any kind of total objectivity in such matters from pupils still at secondary school and not, in any case, desirable. I think, nevertheless, that it is worth trying to introduce senior students to ways of handling and shaping the richest source of material for poetry they and anyone can have, their own lives and experiences.

For this I want to present a model. The American Robert Lowell is often described as a 'confessional' poet, so intense and unremitting, and so devastatingly honest was his chronicling of his upbringing, family background and personal relationships. I had occasion to write to Mr Lowell in 1973, and asked him in particular for his advice and comments on the need for plan and structure in poetry. The whole of his reply was fascinating and very valuable to me at that time. Two short comments are worth quoting from the letter, couched in his characteristically diffident, questioning tone:

> I wonder if structure isn't in a way everything? I mean a subject, a way of saying it, a coherence that is controlled. A plot may seem a dry thing, but how much easier everything is if one has one. . . .
>
> Is there a way of saying anything, if one could find the form? Your questions seem to argue for plan, form, etc. These are such a good thing they at times seem everything. I think though structure ~~rises out of~~ follows matter and experience.

These comments form an appropriate prelude to the model I am proposing here: namely, a sequence of five poems from Robert Lowell's book *Life Studies*. The biggest part of the

book concerns Lowell's childhood and his parents – particularly his father. Part Two consists of a long prose autobiographical memoir subtitled '91 Revere Street' which was the house
in Boston where the Lowells lived for some years during
Robert's childhood. As an introduction to the plan of work, I
recommend reading to the class some excerpts from this
fascinating account. Many of the incidents are very funny and
evoke an immediate response: e.g. the almost successful
attempt to cheat his friend into swapping all his collection of
rare toy soldiers (pp. 22–3); the description of his father's den
(pp. 25–6); his quarrel with his best friend at school (pp. 29–
32); the unfortunate incident in class with the girl Elie Norton
(pp. 39–41) and his father's attempts at carving the joint
(pp. 45–6). The five poems all come from Part Four of the
volume, subtitled eponymously 'Life Studies'. In a sense it does
some violence to them to withdraw them from their context
and anyone tackling this workplan ought himself or herself to
read all the poems, so as to build up the richness of association
and particularity of which Robert Lowell is such a master.
However, the first poem in Part Four, the moving, masterly and
elegiac 'My Last Afternoon with Uncle Devereux Winslow', is
too long for class study, and it and the next two, 'Dunbarton'
and 'Grandparents' are more concerned with Robert's Winslow grandparents than his actual parents. The poems we are
concerned with are:

1 'Commander Lowell 1888–1949'
2 'Terminal Days at Beverley Farms'
3 'Father's Bedroom'
4 'For Sale'
5 'Sailing Home from Rapallo'

It may be impractical to have sufficient copies of all five for the
whole class, though this would be the ideal. As a minimum I
would suggest copies of 2, 3 and 4 complete (2 is reprinted in
the Appendix to this book and 4 appears in Geoffrey
Summerfield's *Voices 3*), and of the third and fourth sections

of 1 (from 'Anchors aweigh...' to 'sixty thousand dollars').
Number 5 refers to 'Dunbarton', which could be read to
illustrate it.

The poems can be introduced as a series with a clear sequence.
1 is a pen-portrait of his father, in which the viewpoint of the 7-
year-old forms an important element at first, but gives way to a
deceptively anecdotal description of the failed naval officer,
failed golfer, failed businessman, which nevertheless manages
to convey successfully the son's warm affection. The second
poem chronicles his father's death and deserves closer study,
which we can come back to. Poem 3 is less ambitious, a 23-line
description of the room after his father's death, each detail
contributing to the atmosphere of loss. Of the fourth poem,
Geoffrey Summerfield has this to say: 'pupils who by now are
interested in technique as a result of their own efforts, will be
fascinated by the deft organisation of this poem: the contrast
between the expansive confidence of line 2's twelve syllables
and the plain finality of line 3's monosyllables; and the way in
which the word "ready" serves as a transition between the
furniture and the mother, both superfluous.' Then comes
'Sailing Home from Rapallo' in which Lowell tells of his return
from Italy with his mother's coffined body. It is an account rich
in irony —

> Mother travelled first-class in the hold,
> her Risorgimento black and gold casket
> was like Napoleon's at the Invalides....
>
> While the passengers were tanning
> on the Mediterranean in deck-chairs
> our family cemetery in Dunbarton
> lay under the White Mountains
> in the sub-zero weather.

The endings of this and the second poem should give rise to considerable discussion. Here are the last four lines:

> In the grandiloquent lettering on Mother's coffin,
> *Lowell* had been misspelled *LOVEL*.
> The corpse
> was wrapped like *panetone* in Italian tinfoil.

Is Lowell simply callous, unfeeling, making cheap jibes? What do the two endings tell us of his relations with his parents?

One of the most remarkable things about this sequence is how vividly the poems build up the relationship between Robert and his parents. More accurately, we see both parents a bit indifferent to the child, and perhaps unaware of his feelings, while he is almost obsessed with them, particularly his father. As a portrait in verse 'Terminal Days at Beverley Farms' has few equals, and it repays close study, for which I can only give a few pointers here. 'A subject, a way of saying it, a coherence that is controlled' – 'structure ~~rises out of~~ follows matter and experience'. This poem provides a fine illustration of these observations of its author. It is shapely – look at the formal structure, with the 13-line 'portrait' first, then three roughly equal stanzas dealing with the place, the car and his father's 'work', leading to the dead-pan final four lines describing his death. The apparent casualness of the ending is deceptive: note how it is prepared for even in the opening stanza by the ominous sign of blood pressure 'a shade too ruddy', and by the third line of the second stanza reinforced by the sombre overtones of the images of the shotgun, and the sumac 'multiplying like cancer'. The first line of stanza three, a noncommittal statement of fact – 'Father had had two coronaries' – prepares us for the ending; we expect a third to be fatal. As we consider the structure and direction of the poem we are made sharply aware of the significance of 'Terminal' in the title. The actual physical frailty of his father gives a growing sense of pathos to his little self-deceptions, the trivial touches to which he attaches so much importance, like the 'indigo cummerbund', his evident pride in his 'vitally trim' figure, we pick up the irony of 'vitally' – and the treasured 'little black Chevie', with its oddly ostentatious absence of chrome. The quotations from his father's way of talking fill out the portrait with a vivid sense of actuality.

There is much more to this poem. In particular, I have not dwelt on Lowell's rhythmic control, nor his way of selecting detail – like the 'boulder' with which the poem opens. (Useful discussion can be stimulated by asking why he should start the poem in this way.) His imagery also repays close attention, particularly when one can study it together with the other poems, and with '91 Revere Street'.

STAGE 2   WRITING

One advantage of this model, if you have referred to the prose narrative, is that it encourages the pupils to start by writing their own bits of prose autobiography. Once they are focusing on their own experience in this way, it is possible to suggest picking out one facet for similar treatment to the shorter poems 'Father's Bedroom' or 'For Sale'. Geoffrey Summerfield's analysis of the latter is useful here. Possible comparable subjects might be: their room when they were much younger or living in another house; a treasured toy; a pet's illness; an accident in the home; quarrel or difference of opinion between parents; a parting (e.g. with a relative or close friend going overseas, or leaving a holiday house, caravan or campsite).

It would not be realistic to aim at the production of five poems by each class member. A more modest and achievable target might be a three-stage piece of writing, one of which could be in prose, one short poem just referred to and finally a longer pen-portrait on the lines of the first poem in the group. It is important that the subject of this should be very close to the writer – a parent or other close relative is the ideal. The close study of poem 2 should have given some positive advice for constructing this poem of their own, which should be seen as the most important part of the project.

STAGE 3   REVISION

It is helpful if pupils can work in pairs for this stage. As they have been encouraged throughout to stress the 'confessional' nature of the writing, it would be unfair to expect them all to share their work with the whole class; but most of them should be prepared to work closely with a friend in the class. Those who wanted could submit their final versions for inclusion in a class anthology for which it would be appropriate to borrow Lowell's title *Life Studies*.

This project takes some considerable time to work through fully, perhaps half a term. Obviously it is an on-going piece of English work, taking its place with other aspects of their English, like the study of a set text or oral work. Its purpose is to drive home the truism that the best poetry comes from within, or in Yeats's more portentous words:

> Whatever flames upon the night
> Man's own resinous heart has fed.

In Chapter 5 I emphasized the close connection between the reading and writing of poetry. 'Study of the poetry of others, whether our pupil's peers or established writers, constantly leads to or stems from their own writing' (p. 35). Many of the ideas for poetry work in other chapters bear this out; thus, my suggestions for thematic English work (Chapter 6) include several that lead children into writing poetry using the stimulus of the theme context as a starting point (e.g. Nos 2, 3, 7, 12, 14, 15). In the chapter dealing with the techniques of rhyme and metre (Chapter 7) there are further suggestions (pp. 80–82), including one that we shall take up again here, the *haiku* form (p. 82). And in the chapters on those central matters imagery and rhythm (Chapters 9 and 10) there are opportunities for putting into practice some of the theoretical points raised (see pp. 121, 129–35).

The present chapter has not therefore aimed at comprehensiveness but has concentrated on the central questions raised by any attempt to teach the writing of poetry in the classroom. We need to acknowledge that a classroom is usually far from being the ideal place for such an activity. Great things are being achieved by teachers and writers in contexts more naturally conducive of sustained poetic effort, like the Arvon Foundation centres. Some teachers have arranged weekend residential courses or day schools for their own senior pupils interested in developing poetic skills. The stimulus of being with a group of like-minded students, free of the pressures and distractions of school, can lead to remarkable results. The 'Writers in Schools' scheme sponsored by the Arts Council, and 'Poets in School' (The Poetry Society) (see Part Three) can often be used in conjunction with such projects. In the other direction, sponsorship enabling professional writers to become resident poets has sometimes made it possible for 'poetry workshops' of various kinds to be set up in schools, drawing interested pupils out of lessons to participate.

None of this exonerates the English teacher believing in the centrality of poetry from work on poetry writing as part of the normal curriculum.

12

POETRY IN A
MULTI-ETHNIC CONTEXT

This book is intended for use in all classrooms where the principal medium of teaching is English. Most of those would still have a majority of pupils who are white native-born English. Even where as many as one third of the pupils are first, second or third generation immigrants, it is possible to ignore or play down the new dimension this should bring to English teaching, and particularly to poetry lessons. However, the multi-ethnic classroom immediately confronts us with linguistic and sociological problems and tensions deriving from what has been well described, with reference to West Indians in Britain, as their 'permanent temporariness'. Because of the 'exposed' nature of the poetry teaching process as I have tried to expound it in this book, we cannot ignore these pressures. Indeed, with the kind of tactful guidance that an English teacher should be capable of giving they can become the dynamics of the pupils' own poetry as well as stimulating interest in the speaking, reading and discussion of poetry. Writing, speaking and reading poetry – particularly speaking for those with African roots – can also have the spin-off effect of encouraging children to take a more direct interest in their fellow pupils and thus help to break down barriers of hostility and incomprehension within the classroom. This short chapter can do no more than point to some of the new dimensions of the multi-ethnic context, and suggest one or two approaches I believe to be appropriate to it. There is now a growing awareness and understanding of the problems, and more school-books and material are becoming available. Part Three includes a section on these (pp.238–45).

I referred to the tensions of the multi-ethnic situation as linguistic and sociological. The two are of course interlinked, as the following quotation illustrates. It comes from a recent survey of 'Westindian-British poetry' in *Poetry Review* by the West Indian poet James Berry:

> Caribbean Creole uses an African response to language and changes standard English into simpler and speedier communication. It selects the words it wants from an English sentence and often alters them, or simply injects new rhythms and different nuances, changing their sounds, allowing the Westindian to communicate with emotional tones inherited from Africa and coloured by the Caribbean experience. Edward Kamau Brathwaite has pointed out that the refusal to use the English language as it stood was perhaps the most effective slave plantation rebellion of all. When political independence came to the Caribbean, many new art forms had to be found. Straight English and its forms could not and cannot express Caribbean people's experience accurately and satisfactorily. Establishment poetry of the past had dwelt on beauty of landscape, in self-consciously poeticising language, and had omitted numerous aspects of Caribbean life and experience. Many recent poets have made good this loss.

Earlier in the article Berry writes that

the poetry insists on getting attention. Unspoken behind it is an apprehension, a dread, that it may all fall on deaf ears. We see that an urgent intensity has inspired this poetry to date. It has a quality of directness. While it is not unnatural that writers who are close to oral traditions would reflect this in their writing, the poetry suggests an end of patience, with a fear of being misread, being wrongly interpreted, being misunderstood.

The same insecurity is diagnosed skilfully by the black London teacher Keith Ajegbo, who compiled the anthology *Black Lives, White Worlds*:

> When I started to teach black pupils, I found that though they might be confident with each other in relations with the white world, often of authority, they were defensive in the extreme. I also discovered that many of the pupils of a West Indian background had an image of Africa, as I had, conditioned by a popular white perception of it. They laughed at anything African as being primitive and savage and refused to recognise their link with Africa. It also seemed to me that many of them created, as I had done, a persona to cover up their fear of what their blackness really meant. It depended on creating an aggressive but cool style; a sophisticated veneer that made sure that people didn't connect them with their 'primitive' roots. It was this style that developed in the seventies into an anti-school, anti-authority stance. Black pupils fed on images of the dark continent, far behind in the race to civilisation and progress as defined through western eyes, were given little confidence in their ability to shine academically and they needed a defence against the possibility of failure at school.

Ajegbo also reminds native-born English teachers that unless they are aware of and sympathetic to such differences of perception they may unwittingly fall into xenophobic attitudes, particularly with blacks:

Black people were allowed certain qualities. The music teacher at school was very surprised that I, in particular, had no talent for singing. I remember also, at an early school sports day, that people were astonished that I didn't win the sports events. But while expecting those talents, they didn't expect me to be good at school. In the minds of many people I sensed that a black skin invited images of a primitive world that existed for the moment and for the pleasure and belonged continents away. This image, of course, was fuelled by nearly every schoolbook available in my school days that dealt with Africa. Mud huts, drums, nakedness, savagery were, I felt, images of Africa and of black people that existed just below the surface of many imaginations.

Native English teachers of multi-ethnic classes need to know themselves in this regard before they can bring to the poetry classroom the necessary openness of response. Two short studies from the Institute of Race Relations are invaluable preparatory reading for all such teachers: *Roots of Racism* and *Patterns of Racism*. These two short books have been described by two London teachers in these terms:

The two books should be essential reading for all teachers in all schools. The breadth of perspective has much to offer all those whose own education was Eurocentric and whose view of the world is founded in the generally held assumptions about Britain's imperial past. But the books are primarily for school (and other) students and there is no comparable material that we know of at present which handles these issues with such clarity while maintaining the necessary complexity. In our view, they will have immediate appeal to school students, probably over an unexpectedly wide age range (Hugh Betterton and Keith Kimberley, in 'Tackling Racism', *Teaching London Kids* (TLK) 19, London, 1983.)

It would not be appropriate to detail lesson suggestions for poetry teaching in the multi-ethnic classroom. There is no reason why the schemes described elsewhere in this book should not be adaptable for this purpose with suitable alternative texts where necessary; and to suggest that multi-ethnic classes need special (quasi remedial!) work schemes would be both presumptuous and counter-productive. Instead I want to put forward just two possible starting-points for poetry teaching.

Sharing experiences

The first is the sharing of backgrounds. Teachers accustomed to single nationality neighbourhood schools and classes, or the even more artificial selective teaching groups in grammar and public schools, can easily overlook the tremendous advantages of such homogeneity, in terms of what can be taken for granted. The effect of it on a newcomer from overseas can be distressing. Here is a 15-year-old Bengali girl describing her first days at an English secondary school:

> In the lunch time I never went out to the shops. I used to have school dinner so that I didn't have to go to the shops. Then I sat quietly looking out of the window. I used to watch other people playing outside and sometimes I used to read Bengali books. In the school there was a group of girls. They used to come near me and started asking me some questions. Sometimes I understood and sometimes I didn't understand what they were saying to me. I was really frightened of them. After one day I didn't want to go to school again. After four months I started to go to the Language Centre and I began to learn English more quickly. Now I don't feel lonely because I have lots of friends in the Language Centre. All my friends are foreigners. I think it is much easier to make friends with a foreigner because foreigners have similar problems. Some people feel lonely at school so they want some friends to talk

to. When you meet them you can make friends with each other, but you can't make an English friend like this because they have their friends already, they don't need any more. Also some people don't like to be friends with a foreigner. They hate foreigners. (Rukea Razzaque)

However, the booklet this comes from, published by the Lambeth Language Centre (1982), is an excellent – and quite unpretentious – example of how much racially mixed classes have to offer that single-nationality ones miss. The contributors come from Vietnam, India, Bangladesh, Turkey, Madeira and Chile. What a source of inspiration for a future citizen of the world! And what a range of opportunities for comparing experiences, environments, families, clothes, food, manners and behaviour. It only takes a little sympathetic probing to elicit details, family photos, samples of food and clothing and so on – all the stimuli one could desire for poetry writing of many kinds as detailed elsewhere in this book. Here are a few titles. Some might be used as focal points for wall displays, group projects, class or inter-class exhibitions or performances; others might act as 'starters' for individual writing or oral composing on tape, perhaps led into by means of preliminary class and/or group discussion:

Our big day
The feel of . . . (article of clothing)
'Lonesome traveller'
We all live here
Friend or foe (pet animals?)
Fancy dress
Treats to eat
Food for all
Colours – skin, clothes, food
Home
Hands across the sea
My black/white friend
The best smells

My street/your street
The sun shines all day long
Mixed marriage
Shopping for a family meal
Here and there
River/sea
Inside my skin

Choosing poems

The other point concerns the actual choice of poems for reading, performance or study in the multi-ethnic classroom. The principles for choosing suitable poetry remain the same as outlined in Chapter 5. However, there are two important new elements. The first is a practical one, and concerns the question of availability. In a recent article about the way girls are 'disadvantaged' in English studies, Margaret Sandra points out that any survey of school poetry anthologies reveals a pervasive male bias. In four popular school collections, she found nineteen women poets amongst a total of 250. The bias is even more noticeable when one looks for poetry by non-whites or other English-speaking races, and we can safely categorize the typical school anthology poet as white, male, middle class and Anglo-Saxon – not too promising a mix for presenting to West Indians, Bangladeshis or Turks, however tolerant they may be towards their new environment. There is now a new recognition amongst poetry publishers of the need to break down British insularity in the poetry world, and Commonwealth, African and (especially) Caribbean poetry, in forms of English that are sometimes startlingly far from 'received standard' (RSE) are becoming more accessible to the general reader. As usual, there is likely to be a time lag of several years before much of this finds its way into school anthologies, so teachers have to look out for themselves. I have given some details of sources in Part Three, (see pp.238–45), but would here like to refer particularly to the work of Joan Goody of the ILEA

Multi-ethnic English Centre and to three West Indian poets who have made significant contributions, James Berry, Linton Kwesi Johnson and Edward Kamau Brathwaite. An English poet who has done much to enhance children's awareness of the new sources is Michael Rosen, whose books and school television programmes are well known. Joan Goody collaborated with Lorna Cocking to produce her *Caribbean Anthology*, which remains the most thorough teaching collection available of English poetry from overseas. Pupils' copies (plain texts) are available in a pack, together with a Teachers' Book and taped reading of all the poems, mostly by their authors. This is particularly helpful for poems like John Agard's 'Woodpecker' or James Berry's 'Sunny Market Song', which depend for their main effect on the characteristic syncopated African rhythms. The biographical notes in the Teachers' Book on the twenty-five writers contributing to the Anthology, together with the booklists there, are a useful source of information on the most significant Caribbean English writers today.

James Berry has lived in England for more than thirty years but has done more than most writers to celebrate and bring to public consciousness his Jamaican home. His poetry is forceful, allusive, often angry, sometimes difficult:

> ... We say,
> in making disorder of a people
> a State makes other ordered areas
> In having harvests of happiness out of them
> the State empties a people of their happiness.

but much of it, like the delightful 'Seeing Granny' (included in the Appendix) is readily accessible to children.

It is Berry who pointed out in the article already referred to that 'with its ethnic form and style, the poetry of Linton Kwesi Johnson is having an infectious effect on pupils in schools. Other poets are emerging.' Johnson's poetry, like Brathwaite's, looks strange, even alien, on the page:

> noh baddah blame it pan di black working claas
> mistah racist
> blame it pan di rulin claas
> blame it pan you capitalis baas
> we pay di caas
> wi suffah di laas
> an wi naw goh figet New Cross
> nat a raas
> wi naw goh figet New Cross
>   (from 'Wat About Di Workin Claas')

but there is no doubt that it speaks with the authentic voice of black Jamaica in Britain. His performances and publications are reaching school children for whom more traditional poetry is a closed book. The same is true of the third West Indian voice I want to draw attention to, Edward Kamau Brathwaite, an older poet (now in his fifties) from Barbados. He is an academic, editor and performer of his own work as well as a writer with many books to his credit. Michael Rosen describes his poetry as 'the talking voice of Black British people, whose parents or grandparents came from the West Indies'. In Rosen's lively teaching anthology based on his Thames Television series *I See a Voice* he includes Brathwaite's 'Limbo' as a good example of the centrality of rhythm in much West Indian and African poetry, as well as its ability to alert us to new significances. 'A poem is a new way of looking at an idea. The rhythm of a poem can take us to the idea, can link one idea to the other' – in this case, the connection between limbo-dancing in the Caribbean and the slave trade, when many of the chained and shackled Africans in the slave ships survived only through limbo-dancing – their sole means of exercise.

I have concentrated on West Indian English poetry here because these are at present the most accessible texts for teachers, as well as some of the most eloquent expressions of the permanent temporariness that is familiar to so many of our fellow inhabitants of this small island. For poetry that will get across to other ethnic groups we often need to explore the collections of poetry in translation. The magazine *Modern Poetry in Translation* was founded in 1965, a result of what Ted Hughes called 'the unique tidal wave of poetry translation that swept through English in the sixties and early seventies'. After forty-four issues it has now become an annual volume of new poetry, published by Carcanet, full of interest and stimulus to English teachers. The poetry magazine *Agenda* has always taken a liberal and exploratory line towards poetry from overseas, though much of what appears there is at a level inaccessible to school pupils. Collections of oral poetry like Denys Thompson's *Distant Voices: Poetry of the pre literate* or the more recent *Penguin Book of Oral Poetry* (Ruth Finnegan) can also yield interesting material for school use, and not only in multi-ethnic classes. In the latter book it is salutary to encounter Somali poetry, for instance, which has so much more central a place in their culture than poetry – or for that matter any imaginative literature – has in ours. Ruth Finnegan reminds us:

> In Somali culture interest in poetry is universal and the recitation and discussion of poetry is part of everyday life. Poets sing far into the night around the camp fires in desert oases or gatherings under a shady tree, while in the town, people gather in tea shops for poetry and song. Among the Somali, poetry is seen as having many effective *uses* beyond just providing or commemorating private experiences. It is common for it to be used as a powerful weapon to win friends, revile enemies, praise traditional chiefs or modern political leaders, or broadcast public events.

Finally, there are the complete collections devoted to different countries, of which one of the most varied and lively I have come across recently is a collection of James Kirkup's translations, *Modern Japanese Poetry*.

13

CRITICAL
APPRECIATION

This book is concerned directly with the experience of poetry for children in the secondary age range – their encounters with poems, whether through performance, listening, reading or writing. In a sense all of these involve the developing of critical perceptions, a process William Carlos Williams recorded when he said of the first line of poetry he ever wrote (in his teens): 'The thrill. The discovery. At once, at the same instant, I said to myself, "ridiculous, the rain can't drive the clouds" so the critical thing was being born at the same time.' However, the more systematic critical appreciation of poetry really lies beyond the scope of this book as it is more appropriate to the study of literature in sixth forms and colleges, and many books are already available for teachers. I shall comment on some of these later in this chapter, but first I want to point out the route towards those more advanced studies and to suggest some preparatory classroom activities for fourth- and fifth-year pupils (14–16-year-olds). The lower limit of fourteen is a considered one. Some teachers have experimented – often quite successfully – with poetry criticism with second- and third-year classes (12–13-year-olds) but I believe such work is best done within the contexts and schemes of work already discussed in this book. The danger of attempting a kind of watered-down 'lit. crit.' with junior classes is that the teacher is almost forced to distance herself or himself from her or his pupils, and to teach from a position of superior insight or understanding of the poem (or poems) under scrutiny – a process that is counterproductive to the kind of poetry teaching/learning advocated here.

Asking questions: a group approach to criticism

The following scheme owes much to the pioneering work of a Bristol English teacher, Bernadette Fitzgerald, which she has described in a booklet *Approaches to Poetry* available from Avon County's Resources for Learning Development Unit, (RLDU, Bishop Road, Bishopstone, Bristol BS7 8LS). It developed from an attempt to solve two problems: (*a*) when teaching 'bright' (probably ability-streamed) middle school children (13- and 14-year-olds) how to get away from the traditional method of setting teacher's or textbook's questions on a poem being studied; and (*b*) how to break down the reluctance and sometimes hostility of less able fourth-year pupils towards poetry in any form.

GROUPS

Small group discussion within a normal classroom can be difficult to control, especially if the room is over-resonant. This last may seem a small point, but can have a marked effect on the success of group work. Carpets and curtains in an English classroom are worth striving for. It is best to work with groups of four to six pupils, i.e. a maximum of six groups in one class. (It is helpful in this scheme of work to have an even number of groups.) If the noise level is too high it is possible to organize the work so that only half the groups are engaged in discussion at any one time, the others doing individual work or reading.

METHOD

Stage 1   Pair the groups, so that from the outset of the work each group knows for whom it is preparing its questions. The idea is to get pupils to devise their own questions on a poem read and studied together, so that the questions they provide could lead other readers within their peer-group into a better appreciation of the poem.

Stage 2   The questions and poems are then exchanged, and the groups work through them *critically*, i.e. they discuss, while doing so, how well the questions set by the other group elucidate the poem and enhance their appreciation of it.

Stage 3   The pairs of groups come together and discuss the two poems together. It is useful at this stage to have the groups who are not involved as an audience. The teacher takes the role of a sort of 'informed umpire', mediating between the groups and adding any points he or she feels have been neglected in relation to the poems under study.

AIMS

a)   To provide an academic context for the close study of poetry that is adjusted to the age and the ability of the pupils;

b)   To provide a structured environment for group discussion;

c) To encourage the actual practice of finding language appropriate to poetry criticism.

NOTES

1   In choosing poems for this work, the teacher should keep in mind the possibility of finding points of comparison and contrast in the two poems set for each pair of groups. A list of suggested poems is given below but it may also be helpful to use some of the linked poems in the other piece of critical work suggested in this chapter (pp. 183–6).

2   While the set of questions arrived at in each group constitutes an 'end product' that pupils themselves can appreciate, 'the really educative element in such work is the experience of inter-active discussion not necessarily the end product which is produced' (B. Fitzgerald). A useful by-product for the teacher is that the range, quality and depth of the questions are a valuable indication of the degree of engagement and understanding the pupils have achieved.

3   It may be helpful to give the instructions Bernadette Fitzgerald gave to her class groups:

   i)   Read your poem silently once.

   ii)   Ask a member of your group to read your poem quietly out loud.

   iii) Re-read your poem silently.

   iv)   Discuss, within your group, the poem's sense, feelings (expressed and aroused), tone, intention, language, imagery, form, impact, etc.

   v)   Compose a set of questions whose answers would reveal how well another pupil had reflected on and understood the poem. (In doing this the members of the group had to agree: *a)* which aspects of the poem should be featured in the questions; *b)* the precise wording of the questions; *c)* the most logical sequence of questions.)

Follow up: the pupils were then asked to supply the answers which they would expect to see in response to their questions.

POEMS FOR STUDY

The following twenty poems from accessible anthologies in use in schools are suitable for this work:

The Rattle Bag, ed. Seamus Heaney and Ted Hughes
1 William Blake, 'London'
2 Elizabeth Bishop, 'The Fish' (also in *Voices 2*)
3 M. Holub, 'A History Lesson'
4 Thomas Hardy, 'The House of Hospitalities'
5 Sylvia Plath, 'Mushrooms' (also in *Poetry Workshop*)
6 Robert Graves, 'Legs'
7 Howard Nemerov, 'The Vacuum'

The New Dragon Book of Verse, ed. M. Harrison and C. Stuart-Clark
8 W. Wordsworth, 'Composed upon Westminster Bridge'
9 Charles Causley, 'Timothy Winters' (also in all other anthologies)
10 Philip Larkin, 'Mr Bleaney'
11 Dylan Thomas, 'Fern Hill'
12 Laurie Lee, 'Town Owl'
13 Ted Hughes, 'Wind'
14 Norman MacCaig, 'An Ordinary Day'

Poems 2, ed. M. Harrison and C. Stuart-Clark
15 Edwin Brock, 'Song of the Battery Hen'
16 Michael Rosen, 'Here is the News'

Poetry Workshop, ed. M. and P. Benton
17 Norman MacCaig, 'Moorings'
18 Seamus Heaney, 'The Early Purges'
19 Jeremy Hooker, 'Winter Moon'

Voices 2, ed. G. Summerfield
20 Robert Frost, 'Out, Out –'

As a transition between the scheme of work just outlined and the other one in this chapter it may be instructive to include an account of some group work on poetry carried out by Geoffrey Fenwick in Liverpool. This was an experimental project involving several secondary schools over two terms. 'Experimental' discussion groups, each of five third-year pupils of wide-ranging ability, were given fifteen poems for study and group discussion during the period of the experiment. In order to assess the effectiveness of this scheme 'control' groups of similar size and ability were asked to discuss the first and last poems, apart from which they studied poetry in a more conventional way in class. Discussions were taped. Fenwick writes:

> Invariably the commentaries of the final poem in a series revealed those of the experimental groups to be the more lengthy. So much for quantity. The old Yorkshire saying, 'tha's talkin' a lot but tha's sayin' nowt' serves as a reminder that in group discussion quality is also important. It was pleasing to note than on many occasions members of both experimental and control groups revealed considerable insight in their observations. There was much more consistency, though, within experimental groups. In their examination of words and phrases they showed persistence as they teased out sense and meaning. In the following extracts, Andrew Young's 'Hard Frost' was being examined:
>
> A What does stalicities mean?
> B They are like icicles. They hang from ceilings....
> C Stalicities! (*Laughter*) It's stalactites.
> D Yes, stalactites.
> E Stalactites aren't icicles.
> B What are they, then?
> E It's like water ... and over hundreds ... and thousands ... of years it's formed into rock.

C   Yes, it's not ice, it's limestone.
D   It can be icicles or limestone.
C   And stalactites are the ones coming down.
     (*Later, related phrases were being discussed*)
C   Well, what does that mean then?...
     'On the windows ferny ambush weaves'
A   D'you know ... like when....
B   He means Jack Frost's been at the windows again.
A   Yes, that's what it looks like....
C   I don't get that ... 'ferns on windows shoot their ghostly
     fronds' ... I don't even know what a frond is. What's a
     frond?
B   Neither do I.
D   It's a branch ... one part of it ... coming out.

Compare the extracts above with the following from a
control group. Less practised, its members by no means
lacked insight but they tended to lack persistence, often
moving from one problem to another before any solution
had been achieved.

A   The first line, 'frost called to water – Halt!' – that's
     stupid
B   Halt!
C   I don't understand this ... 'lurks under gluey glass'
D   'Moist snow with sparkling salt'
B   'The sun will strike him dead and strip his armour'
C   I don't get that.
A   'In the hard rutted lane'
D   'The sun will strike him dead and strip his armour'
     means like the sun melts the ice....
E   'And ferns on windows shoot their ghostly fronds' What
     does it mean?
B   Ghostly....
C   Ferns are plants.
D   It might be shadows of ferns.

E   What are fronds?
C   Don't know.... I'm your friendly frond (*giggles*).

Experimental groups were also more inclined to relate their own experiences to a poem. For example:

C   'At every footstep breaks a brittle pane' It reminds me, you know ... sort of this on this rocky thing ... it's all like witched, it's just like over it ... the ice is just over it. When you touch it, it just cracks up when you walk along.
A   D'you know ... once I went ice skating ... I went to the middle of the pond and I fell in.
D   When it says 'and windows ferny ambush weaves' well, it reminds me of when I was on holiday. When I woke up in the morning and looked in the window and it had sort of all like ... icicles on it ... like in a ... pattern.

They were also likely to make comments about the structure of the poem:

C   I mean like 'frost' and 'host'. What is that supposed to mean? Everything rhymes apart from 'frost and 'host'.
A   And there's another thing as well ... 'armour' and 'warmer'.
B   No, they sort of rhyme. It's not as bad as 'frost' and 'host'.

Generally, the experimental groups were more versatile, commenting upon the effects of words and phrases and the overall quality of poems. What was not in evidence at all was the ability to draw a number of diverse strands together into a coherent whole unless a poem was a straightforward narrative. None of the pupils concerned, however, was older than thirteen and this might well be a skill which they will develop later on.

Comparing poems

This is a well established classroom practice in the teaching of poetry and does not require detailed treatment here. It has the advantage of being adaptable to many different kinds of classroom practice. A school anthology that has helped to establish it amongst current English teaching techniques is Raymond Wilson's *Poems to Compare*, and I quote from his brief account of 'aims and method':

> Our understanding of poetry, like our understanding of everything else, grows with our ability to form comparisons. Even very intelligent pupils, when invited to comment on an isolated poem, often find it difficult to express more than their liking for or their dislike of it; but give them the same poem together with *another poem related in theme* and spontaneous discussion almost always follows.... Using this method, I have found that the first steps in practical criticism can be taken very much earlier than is usual in secondary schools. When we give a class, not isolated poems, but two or more poems that are so related that they invite the reader to make comparisons and establish contrasts, we are creating in little for the pupil the sort of background necessary to all literary evaluation. In considering one poem in relation to another, it usually happens that both poems are illuminated: each throws some light on the other and serves to place it in perspective.

Wilson includes 108 pairs or larger groups of poems in his anthology and his choices will not all meet with the same kind of approval, nor are they all by any means appropriate to fourth-year classes. Below I take just three of his pairings, together with one from a slighter collection compiled by an imitator (or perhaps 'emulator' is a better term), A. F. Bolt, *Double Take*, London, Harrap, 1976, and a fifth provided by me, and add some notes on how each pair might be used to develop powers of critical appreciation. It is particularly helpful to have individual or group copies of the poems under discussion, preferably on paper that can be written on. Page references are given for Raymond Wilson's book, but most of the poems are also readily available in other anthologies. I have included in the Appendix the full text of three which may be less familiar.

Let us start with a pair that includes the poem just discussed. I shall include rather fuller notes for this pair than for the others, to indicate how a teacher can help to 'open out' the pupils' apprehension of the poems under discussion. Similar methods can be applied to the other pairs.

First pair: Andrew Young, 'Hard Frost'
Charles Tomlinson, 'Winter-Piece'
(Wilson, pp. 98–9 and see Appendix)

a)   It is obviously helpful to reserve discussion of this pair until you have appropriate weather conditions. Before the poems are introduced, a short general class discussion will help. The poems are almost solely descriptive, so the discussion might be discreetly directed towards a comparing of what the pupils have seen, heard, felt. Both are country scenes but both include dwellings, so there will be points of contact with their own experience whether you are in town or country.

b)   The discussions transcribed above give some indication of where problems of comprehension might arise with Andrew Young's poem. Tomlinson's is in some ways more direct and sensuous ('grained', 'snap like gunshot', 'bladed', 'iron flanges', etc.), and his eye for exquisite detail, e.g. 'In a perfect web / blanched along each spoke / and circle of its woven wheel / the spider hangs, grasp unbroken / and death-masked in cold.' may appeal more strongly than Young's slightly more bookish images ('interns', 'ambush', 'strip his armour').

c)   It is helpful to draw pupils' attention to the contrast between the impersonality of Young's poem and the direct personal involvement that characterizes Tomlinson's – e.g. '*you* wake ... as *you* handle them' compared with Young's 'hard-rutted lane' (does this come over as strongly as 'ruts with iron flanges'? – a good point for discussion). For Young 'the fierce frost' is made into the protagonist, compared with 'you', 'the rooks' and 'the spider' in Tomlinson's poem – all actually living, and not requiring the device of pathetic fallacy.

d)   Work on this pair might conclude with a return to actual experience. It could even involve a walk round the school grounds, to test the validity of the poet's descriptive skill and find out whether the pupils' responses are more alert. If class interest has been sustained, the work could conclude with a written assignment – poem or prose – on a related theme, or could lead to further exploration of poetry books for analogous poems, e.g. Wordsworth's 'Skating' passage from *The Prelude*.

Second pair: William Shakespeare, 'Hal Muses before Agincourt'
(*King Henry V*, IV. i, 278–301)
William Shakespeare, 'Henry IV on his Sleeplessness'
(*King Henry IV Part II*, III. i, 4–31)
(Wilson, pp. 140–1)

a)   The choice of this pair for study need not depend on whether the plays are being read in school, though it would obviously help if pupils had seen either or both of them performed. It should only be necessary to sketch in a little of the context before studying them. In doing so, there is some point in stressing that the speeches are by father and son, each before an impending battle.

b)   Both passages are concerned with 'degree' or social levels and relationships. This provides a good point of comparison. Does rank involve responsibilities to the same extent today?

c) Study of these passages should include a consideration of the mode of language. What differences of tone, manner, etc. are demanded by dramatic poetry?

Third Pair: Edmund Blunden, 'The Pike'
Ted Hughes, 'Pike'
(Wilson, pp.174–5)

a)   The common subject-matter highlights differences of tone, language and attitude to subject, the study of which is very instructive.

b)   The way each poet uses his chosen mode of ordering the poem – rhyme for Blunden, four-line stanza for Hughes – can be studied.

c)   To what extent is the fish anthropomorphized in each poem?

d)   The relationship of humans to the fish in each poem needs attention.

e)   The two endings make an interesting contrast.

Fourth pair: Edwin Brock, 'Five Ways to Kill a Man'
John Betjeman, 'Inexpensive Progress'
(Bolt, pp. 2–3)

a)   The central point for study is *irony*. Each poet achieves it through adopting a mode of language at variance with the subject-matter.

b)   At first reading, both poems might be thought to lack feeling. What is the actual feeling, and how conveyed in each case?

c)   The endings both record disillusionment with our times. Are they justified? Which appeals more?

Fifth pair: Alistair Elliot, 'Touch of Death'

J. P. Ward, 'The M1 Dream'
(see Appendix)

a)   The common ground here is the personal nature of the two poems. Each records a single isolated experience, neither particularly significant until the poet endows it with significance. This can lead to consideration of the function of poetry.

b)   How important is our awareness of and sympathy with the speaker in each poem? How are these established and sustained?

c)   Develop the comparison implicit in the words 'cold, slack and ... dead?' / 'powerless' (Elliot) 'a mere word / we ignorantly drove / mindless' (Ward).

d)   Does the rhyme in one poem add anything?

The exercises and ideas set out above can provide practice in critical appreciation that points the way to more advanced study. Many books have been written to cater for the needs of senior students and their teachers, since the study of English literature developed into a major university course in the second quarter of this century. I have a particular stake in this, having collaborated in a re-write of one of the earliest of them, *Reading and Discrimination* by Denys Thompson and Stephen Tunnicliffe. This book for sixth-form study has been in print continuously for nearly half a century (from 1934 onwards), so can claim to depict fairly accurately what critical appreciation involves in many senior classes. However, during the thirty years or so since the 'New Criticism' began to influence university studies in the 1950s, there has been a proliferation of such books for school use, not always justifying their existence by offering any new approach or insights. Meanwhile, weaknesses and dangers in the subjectivity implied by the New Criticism have been identified, notably by George Watson (in *The Discipline of English*), who advocates a return to the confident objectivity of such early critics as Saintsbury, while recognizing the changed literary environment we inhabit.

Watson's approach is refreshing in its directness and pragmatism: 'How, then, should a critic look at language? The first essential is that he should indeed look at language in its instances, rather than at a theory of language. Theory is parasitic: if it does its work at all, it can only summarise what the individual instances tell.' It is a pity that Part II of his book, purporting to establish 'the tools of the trade' of a literary critic, is too sketchy to be of much help to English teachers, though there is valuable advice on using libraries and dictionaries, and other – rather piecemeal – useful hints, like ways of getting over 'writer's block'.

A more far-reaching critique of what she calls 'expressive-realist criticism' comes from Catherine Belsey, *Critical Practice:*

> Review pages and departments of literature come to function like consumers' associations whose main purpose is to write reports advising readers on the best (spiritual) buys, with additional details concerning, for instance, the distinctions between short-term topical worth and longer-term intellectual investment. Its value, usually seen as universal and eternal, inheres in the text itself and the reading process mysteriously transmits this essence to the reader. Criticism, presented as non-theoretical, neutral and objective, is seen as facilitating this transmission process, impartially advising and assisting the reader to derive the maximum benefit from the (freely-chosen) commodity.

Her strictures are borne out by such comments as these, from books aimed at sixth forms: 'We hope that our analyses of modern poems will persuade readers to look with pleasure *and profit* at the large number of good and sometimes great poems being written today' (C. B. Cox and A. E. Dyson, *Modern Poetry: Studies in Practical Criticism*, London, Edward

Arnold, 1963). 'Through Practical Criticism you can refine and deepen your appreciation of the poet's art ... the reader at best can have *a double bonus*: enjoyment of first reaction, and an awareness of how the artist gives the enjoyment' (Millar and Currie, *The Language of Poetry*). Belsey affirms that traditional Anglo-American critical practice has tended to 'smooth out' the diversities inherent in any literary text, by an over-emphasis on a single 'meaning' derived from the author: 'In thus smoothing out contradiction, closing the text, criticism becomes the accomplice of ideology.' A recent book setting out to provide an introduction to the close reading of prose and verse (T. Gibbons, *Literature and Awareness*, London, Edward Arnold, 1979) provides an apt example. Gibbons asks readers, with admirable objectivity, to consider every work of literature as 'simply a list of words, shorter or longer, in a certain order'. However, he is soon explaining that 'when we speak of "its" diction here, we really mean its author's ... his choice of words. ... The words which an author uses are clearly the means by which he communicates his meaning to the reader, and if we can make some general remarks about the kinds of word which he employs, then we have already begun to go some way towards recognising the particular aspects of reality which interest an author, and which he wishes to single out and comment upon to his reader.'

In contrast to this, Catherine Belsey's 'deconstructing' of a literary text aims to establish 'not the unity of the work, but the multiplicity and diversity of its possible meanings, its incompleteness, the omissions which it displays but cannot describe, and above all its contradictions'. This more open and exploratory approach to the study of literature seems to me a better model for English teachers, and a more productive way of leading their pupils into a true appreciation of the richness and variety of English poetry.

14

ASSESSING AND EXAMINING POETRY

Responsible English teaching constantly involves the teacher in some assessment of children's writing. Each teacher will develop (and if the work is taken seriously, systematize) his or her own methods; I shall refer later to one teacher's attempt with regard to poetry assessment. It is tempting to see the external examinations that conclude most pupils' secondary–school careers as continuing the same process, and no doubt some teachers, especially those involved in the examination system itself, really see GCE, CSE, 16+ and the rest in this light. A few years ago a chief examiner wrote in the Introduction to a course book he had devised: 'Any syllabus leading to an external examination in English literature will have as one of its main aims the intention of encouraging young people to respond with judgement and sensitivity, and in some depth, to prose and poetry of quality. This is a worthy aim and one with which this book is entirely in sympathy.' (David Clarke, *The Language of Literature*). He begins the next paragraph, 'it is sad to see how seldom this aim is fully achieved in the examination room'. We can begin to understand this teacher/

examiner's viewpoint when we find in one of his 'twenty test papers' on literature later in the book the following question set on a poem: 'The poem consists of five sentences. Summarise briefly each of these five sentences in order to bring out clearly the poem's meaning.' Such bland insensitivity – in this case to what constitutes poetic meaning – was what led Brian Jackson to say, as long ago as 1965, in *English versus Examinations*: 'Between English and the characteristic school examinations, there must be a tension. At every point, from primary school to university, examinations through their side-effects threaten the most precious and vulnerable parts of English teaching.' This is confirmed by a New Zealand educationist, Rachel McAlpine, who concludes a study of poetry teaching in New Zealand high schools with this remark:

> As it stands, the poetry question in the School Certificate Examination has little to do with what is specific to poetry (such as playful language, deliberate ambiguity and the provocation of a strong personal response). It offers little incentive to students or teachers to work enthusiastically at the topic during the year. Many fifth formers are so edgy about the coming examination that they question the 'use' of work which isn't obviously related to it. These factors must play their part in hostility to poetry in the fifth form. (*Song in the Satchel*)

This inescapable chasm between poetry in the classroom and as examination fodder is seen more clearly if one reads between the lines of examiners' comments, published annually after the mass reading of GCE and other scripts. Here are just three, chosen almost at random:

> Where poetry is seen not as a means of expression but merely as a statement then such statement as 'Bavarian Gentians' (by D. H. Lawrence) makes appears extremely thin. Hardly ever did comment go beyond this depressing process of reduction to prose paraphrase. ('O' level)

The poverty of candidates' comments on verbal effect and poetic technique is hardly improving. There is no merit in a display of technical terms unless the purpose of the technique can be demonstrated in context and related to meaning. Also mere displays of memory in the quotations of long sections of verse without comment earn no credit. (16+)

Nowhere was this absence of critical comment more apparent this year than in the response, or lack of it, to poetry.... Many candidates were only able to repeat the content of poems, often in a very superficial manner. Far too many candidates seem unpractised in looking at the way poetry particularly uses language in an emotive or heightened manner. ('O' level)

The clear implication behind these comments is that the candidates have been poorly taught. This is possible; if so, it justifies a book such as the present one. But I would also submit that the remarks provide convincing corroboration of Brian Jackson's view just quoted. For good measure here is a *cri de coeur* from an 'A'-level examiner that may raise a wry smile or two from English teachers to whom poetry really matters. It refers to candidates' response to a queston asking them which of two poems set for critical appreciation they prefer and why:

Most candidates gave the impression of having already said all they had to say, and of being taken aback by the invitation to express a personal opinion. They generally responded by way of the cautiously hedging statement that 'both poems are successful'.... Expressions of preference for poem X 'because it is easier to understand' were not welcomed with much enthusiasm when understanding had not been demonstrated earlier. It was not, of course, necessary to express a preference, and no one was penalised for not doing so. But where are all the independent-minded young people, intolerant of spoon-feeding and rote-learning, and bursting to enter into contention with received opinion, about whom we are always told? They don't seem to enter for this examination.

Perhaps they don't. And perhaps they are wise not to do so, if they wish to retain a love of poetry. The growing recognition of this stultifying effect of the traditional external English 'sit and deliver' type of examination, particularly on the more creative — or 'expressive/poetic' — modes of language, has led to an increasing reliance on course work within the examination system, involving teacher assessment on a continuous basis, with more or less elaborate schemes of 'moderation' to try to ensure comparability. One Board even has a system of moderating the moderators. (Those interested in the role of course work in the English examination system should read NATE Examination Booklet No. 3, *Course Work in English: Principles and Assessment*.)

The place of children's writing of and response to poetry within the established examination system, then, resolves itself into course work for the former and critical appreciation or 'practical criticism' questions for the latter. At CSE and 'O' level the latter often turns out to be little more than a comprehension exercise. This has the deleterious effect of leading examiners to seek poems for 'unseens' that are examinable (and unknown to the students) first, good poetry second. Appreciation questions deriving from set texts avoid this, and a recent example from London Region Examining Board's CSE English examination indicates a refreshingly open style of question, which might, however, make the task of standardized marking a difficult one. This is a question set in 1982 on R. S. Thomas's poem 'Iago Prytherch' — which was in the set anthology but was also printed in full above the question: 'Write as fully as you can on the content of this poem and the way it is written. You could consider the following ideas:

— how you are made to "see" Iago;
— what the author finds lacking in him;
— what the author admires in him;
— how the use of important words helps to express the ideas;

– what expressions there are that you find especially interesting.'

The chief danger of such a liberal approach is that by its wording '... as fully as you can on the content' it positively invites a prose paraphrase, which takes us straight back to the 'summarize the meaning' type of question; it would be relatively easy for the candidate to avoid the harder but far more worthwhile task of recording his or her *response* to the poem.

We are left with course work. The assembling of representative pieces of work for a course-work folder can involve teacher and pupil together in a process of assessment and validation that is very much closer to the approach to poetry in the classroom that I have been advocating in this book. The rest of this chapter is devoted to one teacher's attempt at establishing criteria for such assessment, and to a number of examples of actual children's work assessed. As Anthony Adams and John Pearce said in their excellent little handbook *Every English Teacher*: 'It is important for teachers to make explicit for themselves the linguistic as well as the literary attributes of pupils' writing which constitute the real criteria in their assessments.'

The novelist, poet and teacher C. J. Driver was bold enough in 1977 to commit himself to print – in the form of an article in *The Use of English* (28, 3 Summer 1977) – on the subject of 'marking poems'. I have, as shall be clear soon enough, strong reservations about his method; nevertheless, I must record here my thanks to him for tackling the subject at all, and thus clearing the ground for 'followers' like me. Driver suggests that most teachers assess children's poems according to 'at least three models'. By 'models' I think he means methods based on particular concepts of poetry-writing. His first two are, respectively, to assess work solely in relation to the writer's stage of development (A) and to assess it according to criteria derived from study of 'real' (i.e. professional) poetry (B). He dismisses both these as inappropriate and takes refuge in his third 'model'. This involves a set of eight 'values' by means of which he judges his pupils' poems and assesses them as good or bad. He lists them as follows (I give them *verbatim*, but without his incidental glosses and illustrations):

1   Verbal skills: has the writer found the exact, the precise word each time? Has he/she written economically, concisely? Has he/she syntactic power? Does he/she concentrate on nouns and active verbs, not on adjectives, participles and adverbs?
2   The particular, not the general.
3   Imagery: 'Imaginative' literature need not use images ... there are good completely imageless poems. But the imagery must, of course, be, when used, new.
4   Sensory perceptions: 'Above all I wish to make the reader "*see*"' and I add, 'hear, taste, smell, touch'.
5   Rhythm: which I mean in the sense of a wider category than metre, and use Hopkins's idea of 'sprung rhythm' – and the play of line-length against syntax (why is this poem divided in lines and stanzas?) as my initial values.
6   Humanity: is there room for other people, other lives, other voices? Room for laughter? For empathy, sympathy, antipathy? For uncomfortable feelings as well as nice ones?
7   Speech in their own voices: poems are a good way of getting pupils to start with 'expressive' writing – to be local and colloquial – and then to move into 'poetic' without losing the strength of the local and colloquial.
8   Honesty: in terms of their own perceptions as well as their voices, in terms of knowledge as well as sensation.

At first sight these seem to constitute a helpful yardstick against which to measure pupils' poems. When one considers them more closely, doubts arise. Are these, in fact, a third 'model' at all? How can, for instance, No. 7, and for that matter 6 and 8, be judged except through a knowledge of the writer's development (model A)? They all involve a consideration of the writer's sincerity. It is surely too much to expect conformity to any ideal standards of 'humanity' or 'honesty'. Nos. 2 and 4 seem to me to be two aspects of the same thing; for certain kinds of poems they might be useful criteria, but I suspect they could only be made meaningful by reference to poetry in general (model B), and Driver's references, in his description of the two points, to Pound, Conrad and Wallace Stevens suggest that he thinks so too. I have already devoted a chapter each to Nos. 3 and 5, evidence enough that both these features of poetry are too wide and complex to be itemized in such a way – although a teacher involved in assessing children's poetry obviously needs some understanding of them. Finally, to say that in judging children's writing one needs to consider 'verbal skills' is no more than a truism, if not a tautology. Writing involves words: good writing involves the skilful handling of words. To then limit one's idea of verbal skills as dogmatically as Driver does seems unnecessarily rigid. In effect, Driver has demonstrated well the problems one encounters when one tries to adopt any set scheme for assessing children's poetry writing. The good teacher is bound to place considerable stress on his knowledge of his pupils, and relate their work to their progress in general, and their grasp of language in particular (Driver's model A). It is not possible to demonstrate that here: Geoffrey Hawkes gives a good example of the kind of approach needed in commenting on an adolescent boy's attempt at a 'ballad' in a chapter of *English versus Examinations* (pp.105–6).

Instead of attempting to establish an abstract 'set of rules' for marking poems, I want to conclude this chapter and this section of the book by considering a few examples of children's writing. The comments that follow are intended as examples of the way a teacher can arrive at some idea of a student poem's merit or promise. They are *not* offered as examples of what the writers themselves should be told about their work. For this Rachel McAlpine (op. cit.) has some excellent advice:

We should absolutely refrain from any negative comments.

Praise can be a potent teaching tool. There is no call for insincerity or gushing. On the contrary, there is a danger of overkill and students detect phoniness right away. But every poem can be praised for some quality. In the classroom, I have seen a cynical, surly fifth former light up at the words, 'That's O.K. You said you couldn't do it, but that's O.K.' When students are writing in class, the best help the teacher can give is often to point out words or lines that seem to have energy in them. 'I like that line' is all that is needed. When it comes to comments on a finished poem, the teacher has an obligation to be specific in praise. The task is not just to make the student feel good but to draw attention to some matter of technique. . . . The student poet typically has a strong interest both in writing authentically and writing well. To hand the teacher a poem written for private reasons is a kind of publication. It transforms the poem from a private object to a vehicle of communication. It is important for teachers to make it possible for young people to take this step without fear.

Last Thoughts
My last ten minutes are given to you
In writing this will.
The last day of battle
And the French are ten thousand strong.
I have not long to live.
To my wife I give
All the flowers in a hundred acres
And my blessings go with all of them.
To our only son
I leave a choir of nightingales
Conducted at your command.
But to the enemy I am fighting
I leave the darkness of a hundred generations
And the Devil's curse.
Now I must leave for the pounding of hooves

Are drumming in my ears
And the roar of the cannon
And the shouts of the soldiers
Are ringing through my head.

(Ben Owen)

This is one of four examples Sandy Brownjohn gives of poems on death by her primary school pupils. She approaches the subject with her customary directness and honesty, explaining that because 'children are quite fascinated with the subject of death' they need to be offered opportunities to write about it. 'The idea of writing a last will and testament', she goes on, 'is an attempt to bring in an almost positive side to this subject, and to make the children think of the joys of life which they might wish to leave to someone.'

There are many positive features in the poem. The principal one is the way the writer has used the idea of the will as a *focus* for a dramatic picture of the battlefield – obviously the aspect which most interested him about the exercise. This is an object-lesson to teachers: the fact that individual pupils are likely to approach any subject in many different ways and with different emphases. It would be quite wrong to suggest to this boy that he hasn't really done what the teacher wanted (i.e. concentrate on what 'joys of life' he might leave and to whom). Any teacher of poetry has to learn to respond to the unexpected in his or her pupils' work. How has the immediacy of the scene been achieved? His main device is *contrast*. The oasis of 'my last ten minutes' is emphasized by contrast with 'the drumming in my ears' that terminates it, and the contrast is heightened by the 'flowers' and 'nightingales' bequeathed to his wife and son. The formal organization of the ideas is remarkably effective in supporting this, particularly the setting of 'a hundred acres' of flowers against 'the darkness of a hundred generations' – both bequests suggesting life going on, growth and continuity, and thus adding poignancy to 'I have not long to live'. The handling of rhythm is assured and varied; it is interesting to note how the

– perhaps chance – rhyme of live/give has been absorbed into the rhythmic structure, so that the new line after 'give' has a rhythmic unity that is appropriate as the first 'bequest'. If the writer wanted to re-work the poem it could be suggested to him that the two other bequests might be given a similar dramatic emphasis if they each had a line to themselves. In each case 'I leave' weakens the line's rhythm. The only other points one might discuss with the writer are:

a) The uneasy switch from second to third to first person ('given to *you*'/'to *my* wife'/'to *our* only son'/'at *your* command'). Does it serve any special purpose?
b) The rather flat tone of 'now I must leave', in which the shift from the previous meaning of 'leave' seems to be unnecessarily confusing;
c) The grammatical solecism of 'the pounding .../are drumming...'. (There is some advantage in keeping the plural to match 'are ringing' in the last line, but some re-wording of line 15 might be possible.)

> *The Dreams of a Stone*
> Here I stand in solitude,
> As oval as an egg,
> Waiting for my solid body to change,
> Every day a boring nothing.
>
> My shadow forms from nothing
> Till the long, black streak appears,
> Then dissolves again to nothing,
> Always nothing.
>
> The night shrouds in
> Till the moon and stars
> Give a boring change from nothing,
> A silvery change, though not what I want and need.
>
> But there is still hope.
> In a thousand, maybe a million years of nothing

It will happen,
I will change at last from a nothing life
To some part of something, great and glorious
Some part of a volcano.

Why a volcano, with its fiery funnel?
Why not a mountain
With its shadows cast by small
Insignificant flowers on the bleak graveyard sides?

It could be a mountain
So why do I want a volcano?
Is it because the hollow funnel
Is the front door to my home town?

Or is it because if I journey there,
Some day I will actually be larger,
Maybe a lot larger?
Perhaps I will even grow to a desolate mountain.
                    (Boy, aged 11, name unknown)

As a stimulus for this poem the boy was given a sea-rounded
pebble to hold. The device of getting children to write as if they
were the subject of the poem is a well tried one; here it has
worked remarkably well, in giving the boy's obviously lively
imagination plenty of scope. One of the most effective points is
the way the poem is constructed – two three-stanza sections,
with a longer transitional stanza marking the change of mood
from 'a nothing life' (a vivid and surprising phrase taking up
the key word of the first section and shifting the emphasis by, as
it were, demoting it to an epithet) to 'some part of something'.
The growth and 'dissolving' (good word) of the shadow is an
effective way of conveying the passage of time, and the
darkness of night is well drawn by the expression 'the night
shrouds in'. In the second half the writer's gift of 'seeing' his
subject is again evident in his comment on the 'shadows cast by
small/insignificant flowers'. Another indication of his lively

imagination comes with the volcano's 'hollow funnel' being 'the front door of my home town'.

As against this, there are quite serious weaknesses in this poem, which are themselves instructive. The tone is uncertain, indicated by lapses into prosaic language which weakens the rhythmic unity. The repetition of 'boring' is one example and 'silvery change' (with its distracting and obviously unintentional overtone of money – small change) is another, as is the rest of that line: 'want and need' is clumsy. The writer's use of repetition generally is uncertain – e.g. 'some part' stanza 4, 'is it because' stanzas 6 and 7; and his delight in the details of his poem beguiles him into overloading them, particularly with adjectives – '*small, insignificant* flowers', '*bleak* graveyard' '*hollow* funnel', '*desolate* mountain'. A poem like this, with marked strengths and weaknesses, can be a most useful teaching device.

The Wind
The wind blows across my garden
Taking with it leaves and flowers,
Birds are tossed and blown about.
Please stop blowing wind.

He's blowing little children over,
Blowing washing off the line,
He's whistling round the gable end
Please stop blowing wind.

He woke me up this morning
About six thirty a.m.
He blew my brother and I off to school
Please stop pushing wind.

He made my hands bitterly cold
He made my ears numb
He blew my hat off my head,
Please stop freezing wind.

He's cold and strong, he pushes things around
Sometimes he bends trees right over
Please go away wind.

(Girl, aged 11)

It is quite surprising to consider this poem after the two previous ones. Some readers may feel that it suggests inadequte teaching that a child of the same age as the writers of 'Last Thoughts' and 'Dreams of a Stone' should be capable of so much less in her response to so potentially dramatic and powerful a phenomenon as a gale-force wind. It is partly for this reason that I choose to include it, in spite of its cosiness. One way of encouraging children to be more adventurous in their writing is to see what happens when they restrict themselves to the most obvious and immediate ideas. What we are discussing so far is the *level* of the poetic response. While this affects the language and structure of the poem – it was partly a mismatch between the two that led to weaknesses in the previous one – we can still recognize in 'The Wind' a directness and accuracy in the actual language as far as it goes, and in the simple but effective verse-pattern. (These, in fact, are what made it so suitable for the lesson in Chapter 7.) The last line plea makes an effective refrain, tautening the structure and giving the poem as a whole a satisfying shapeliness – except for the final stanza which is not sufficiently innovative in ideas to justify breaking the pattern, even in pursuit of a way of rounding off the sequence. However, when one looks more closely, one is aware of a poverty of vocabulary that matches, and indeed is partly responsible for, the unadventurousness of the ideas. Does the repetition of 'blows', 'blown', 'blowing' 'blew' really serve any function? Are the other verbs – 'taking', 'whistling' (a little better), 'pushing', 'made', 'bends', 'go away' doing the work suggested by the theme of portraying a gale's power? The personification of 'wind' is probably the main culprit in reducing the scope of this poem. The image is of a bigger, more boisterous school-child, perhaps an older brother, as the third line from the end with its feeble 'things' makes clear. By domesticating the wind in this way the writer drains the theme of its true potential.

Many teachers will have been presented with 'poems' of this kind, though one hopes not after the first form in secondary school. It is sometimes helpful to keep a few in reserve until the children concerned are a little older, then either use them anonymously in the way I have indicated, with a different class, or privately with the pupil herself to illustrate what she has grown out of.

For the last two examples of pupils' poems we turn to more mature work – two outstanding poems by adolescents. I do not know whether either of these people has continued writing poetry, nor does it really concern us. What is indisputable is that within a normal educational environment it was possible for them to produce writing of originality and power. In itself this already provides a yardstick against which to measure other adolescent poetry. I shall show that by attempting to assess more accurately how, and to what extent, the poems succeed we can refine and deepen our powers of discrimination as teachers of poetry.

> *My Love*
> Now you have come I will introduce you.
> Here is my peace. See, I am content.
> Look how my still pool gleams in the sun
> And grey-green moss breathes the heavy scent
> Of damp earth. No. Say nothing, only feel.
> Do not jangle the sweetest peace
> With harsh words. See how my silver tree
> Lovingly shelters me from the breeze
> And kisses the hard grey lumps of rock
> Which sleep in the evening sun and so
> Humbly cluster together. My pool
> Is deep purple with bell-heather, low
> In the still water of solitude.

Be careful what you might say! Careful.
The smallest thoughtless word will wound me.
Do not say that my secret is dull,
It is alive, vibrant and thrilling.
Exposed, open, I am myself here.
I hope, Oh I hope you understand.
Vulnerable to your cruelty, I fear
You do not like it. Please do not crash
My world about me. I see my dreams
In the pool. I am in love with all this.
To understand is enough; but if it seems
Childish, useless, then it is no good.
I have no need of you then
I have no need of you.
                              (Karen Elizabeth Kirk, aged 16)

This poem demonstrates well how writing poetry can involve deeper layers of personality than any other school activity. Adolescent love is more intense, more tortured and often more incoherent than any other experience. Yet because of this any sincere attempt to articulate it in poetry is valuable. Here the writer has succeeded in expressing both the intensely personal, secret nature of her feelings and the realization that to follow her urge to share them she has to risk exposure and even destructive ridicule. It is interesting that although we are made very conscious of the writer's femininity, this is not an overtly sexual poem. The images do move towards sexuality – and I shall show that the uncertainty of tone in the second half is related to this – but the sharer/intruder addressed could be male or female.

The poem's strength derives mainly from two sources: its precise choice of vocabulary which is particularly evident in the descriptive details – 'grey-green moss breathes the heavy scent/ of damp earth' – and its firm structure, reinforced by the steady and entirely convincing (in conveying the actual tone of a speaking voice) 4-stress metre in a sensitively handled 'sprung' rhythm. The poem is set out almost as formally as a sonnet: the first part consists of thirteen lines ending with 'solitude', the second of twelve lines with a final 'couplet' or pair of lines summing up, in its plaintive repetition, the ambivalences of the whole poem, and making explicit the 'need' to share that is a mainspring of the theme. The opening address immediately sets up the relationship, creating a context as much from what is implied as from the words themselves: 'Now you have come' (i.e. 'after all this waiting' or 'at last!'). We are intrigued by 'I will introduce you' – to whom? or to what? The illusion of a particular moment is sustained by 'here', 'see', 'look', and of a response from the person addressed by 'No. Say nothing...', etc. The mood of stillness and peace is held throughout this section. My only reservation concerns the final line 'In the still waters of solitude' which seems weak. Perhaps the writer was beguiled by the lulling rhythm combined with the slightly biblical overtones of 'still water'. The line does not add anything to the image of the 'still pool' so brilliantly conveyed already.

The sense of completeness, as though even the companionship the poet seeks was unnecessary, has been conveyed by the image of the 'silver tree' which '*lovingly*' shelters her and '*kisses*' the hard rocks. But this last suggests an over-emphasis on submission – the rocks 'humbly cluster together' – which leads us into the more disturbed second half. Here the poet acknowledges how precarious this peace is. A single insensitive word might destroy it but ... perhaps to another it might seem merely 'dull'? It is here that I feel the writer loses control a little: 'alive, vibrant and thrilling' – this is surely over-written and the tone of 'I hope, Oh I hope', seems to falter. It might be argued that it is necessary here to disturb the smoothness of the poem, so as to bring out the threat of 'cruelty'. At any rate, the effect of the rather uneasily shifting tone in lines 17–21 is to diminish a little the intensity built up in the first part. 'I am in love with all this' sounds almost apologetic beside 'See, I am content' in line 2. I feel that some of this uncertainty derives from the writer's inability to handle poetically the strong, almost combative feelings aroused by the thought of having to remain 'vulnerable' to the intruder. 'Expose, open' is soon followed by 'cruelty', and the idea of the world *crashing* about her. The reality of the first section then becomes no more than 'dreams' (line 22). Obviously any conclusions about what the girl writing this poem wished to convey can only be speculation and if I were in a teaching relationship with her it would involve talking out precisely what she was aiming at, and whether there was any other way of achieving it. A powerful and largely successful poem like this demands to be assessed more stringently than one which attempts less. It is my experience that school writers of this calibre are particularly appreciative of having the highest standards applied to their work.

> *Flood Tide in My Affairs*
> Yes, this would be the time, I think, around
> The summer, when we played at the Town Hall:
> The 'Schools' Brass Band' we were, and duty-bound
> To play there now and then, for the Lord Mayor,
> Who always somehow mixed us up and all.
> Sometimes we'd 'played in Cheltenham' or 'in York',
> 'With great success'. And we'd all snigger, stare
> Then smile among ourselves, politely talk
> In serious tones of how we'd won
>
> This 'cup', that fictional 'gold medal', then
> We'd play, and show them all how bad we were.
> And at the end, he'd ask us back again,
> 'Sometime in June', an old-age pensioners' do,
> Reception, buffet, or some such affair
> We knew we'd hate: 'Our youth, I'm glad to say,
> Is not all bad', he'd say, 'I'm sure that you
> Have listened with enthralment to the Band
> Tonight' (like hell they had), 'we've heard them play
> Some really lovely pieces, and

It goes to show how great a deal of good
Is coming from the young of Liverpool.
We always hear today' (we knew this crud
Three times by heart) 'of all the bad, the harm
The young are said to do, at home, at school,
Within the community as a whole',
(It is a hole), 'but here' (out came the arm),
'Yes, *here* we see our young folk doing well'.
They'd all applaud; and, finding this too droll,
We'd smile and wish them all in hell.

They gave us something afterwards; that is,
The sandwiches left over, sausage rolls,
Vol-au-vents, lemonade without the fizz.
We talked together, laughing, about love,
I quoted 'Ask not for whom the bell tolls',
Then my bell tolled: 'She fancies you, you know'.
Joan meant Christine, and shouted it above
The noise. I went quite red. The moment passed,
A disappointment, since I loved her too.
The ebb-tide then. The die uncast.
                    (Michael V. T. Sharpe, aged 17)

It is good to be able to end this chapter with a poem in a
rather different *genre*, particularly as, like the one we have just
been looking at, it is both highly accomplished verse (by any
standards) and still unmistakably the voice of an adolescent.
The form is narrative, and the reader's interest is immediately
caught and held by the deceptively casual tone as much as by
the details of the story. In telling it the narrator adopts and
sustains a nicely satirical mode of story telling, colouring his
account in such a way as to establish firmly his identity as
'youth', one of an age group used but misunderstood by the
older generation represented by the speechifying Lord Mayor
and his audience of (presumably) respectable citizens. What is
particularly remarkable is that the writer has managed to do all
this within an elaborate verse-form, a 10-line stanza with an

extended kind of *terza rima* involving five rhymes and with the tenth line shortened to four iambic feet instead of five. Senior students with a gift for handling language – which always means also with a wider than usual experience of it, usually through reading – often like the challenge of an elaborate rhyme- or metrical-scheme, but it is rare that such a student can get beyond the 'fascination of what's difficult' so far as to subordinate the technique to its proper role as servant to a poetic purpose. This writer has succeeded almost entirely. The (rather self-mockingly portentous) title prepares us for the idea of a significant moment; 'Yes, this would be the time …' emphasizes it further; yet not until the fourth line of the last stanza does it come, almost casually, with the surprising word 'love'. After the consciously world-weary cynicism of the rest of the poem, we too feel embarrassed for the speaker as he 'went quite red' at the shouted revelation that his chosen girl 'fancied' him as well. As we complete our reading of the poem we realize that the clever, cynical comments on the band's public reception were not merely frivolous. The poem sets out to contrast what actually matters, what actually touches teenagers, with the way older people see them.

So far my assessment of this poem has concentrated on its very considerable achievements. However, I do not think that its author would claim that it succeeded completely, and within his ambitious scheme it is not surprising that there are some less successful moments. The most serious one, I think, is in the handling of the all-important conclusion. The reader is left puzzling and unsatisfied by the vagueness of the moment. Was Christine there? We are not told. What was the speaker's disappointment? At hearing that Christine 'fancied' him? If so, why, since, as he says, he 'loved her too' – apparently taking 'fancied' as synonymous with 'loved'. My guess – and the incomplete ending leaves it as nothing more – is that the speaker wishes to suggest that he might, in other surroundings, have been able to use the chance revelation to speak out to his girl about his feelings for her, but here was unable to do so. If this is the intended meaning, I think the reader needs more guidance towards it. My other reservation concerns the excessively negative responses to the Lord Mayor's speech. It is legitimate – and incidentally quite entertaining – to criticize what is seen as the Mayor's patronizing and hypocritical manner towards the youth band. But does this justify their lying about their successes (that fictional 'gold medal')? And do they really 'hate' appearing (stanza 2 line 6), or 'wish them *all* in hell' (stanza 3, line 10)? The lively social aftermath in the last stanza suggests otherwise. The apparent violence of the writer's animus against the official sponsorship of the band is disproportionate and reduces the effectiveness which it is the poem's main purpose to express.

I have tried to show by means of these five examples of students' work, how assessment and validation can be used positively in the teaching of poetry. I hope it has become clear that, while rejecting, as I said earlier, the idea of applying an 'abstract set of rules' when assessing children's poems, I do in fact have a fairly systematic method for arriving at my conclusions.

a) First approach. The first couple of reads-through are really 'for pleasure'. I try to let the poem say what it has to say in its own way and adjust my expectations accordingly. In the context of normal English teaching this process is bound to be influenced a good deal by one's knowledge of the writer as it would be in reading, say, a personal letter. The fact that you know the writer becomes a positive help in deciding, for instance, at what level the letter is pitched – is it serious or flippant, considered or hasty, reflective or purely utilitarian?

b) First response. Once the poem has 'settled down' in one's consciousness one can set about articulating – putting into words as clearly and simply as possible – what it has achieved within the limits it has set itself. This will involve assessing how well the writer has used his or her chosen technique: the verse-form, rhyme, repetition, imagery, etc. whether they are used consciously or instinctively. (Often you can surprise a pupil: 'I didn't know I was using assonance/rhythm etc.' is a response familiar to teachers.) The aim is to accentuate the positive, to show the writer first, then other readers, the successes of the poem, taken on its own terms.

c) *Second response.* At this point, when the poem has become really familiar, one can bring in comparative standards, weighing the poem against that of other writing in a similar *genre*. The *aim* is important here: it is not to denigrate or diminish the writer's achievement in any way, but to show him or her how, *within the terms of the poem itself*, more might have been achieved. Two points need to be kept in mind: *i*) in a normal teaching context one's knowledge of the writer can be a valuable aid. How much criticism can he or she take? Has she or he the verbal experience to appreciate this point about monotony? Have they the staying power to tackle a rewrite or the potential to make it more successful than the previous attempt? *ii*) Is the poem worth treating in this way? This is not as harsh as it may sound. In my experience a pupil is the first to acknowledge that he or she did not put enough effort into a piece to warrant too detailed an analysis of it.

d) *Next step.* This may be a re-write or a new attempt at a similar idea. It may involve following up reading references – poems, stories, even reference works (e.g. on ballads, or sonnets, or narrative poems, etc.). Or it may be more productive to leave the work altogether and move on to something new.

References

For fuller lists see Part Three.

INDIVIDUAL POETRY COLLECTIONS

ABSE, Dannie *Collected Poems 1948–1976* (London, Hutchinson, 1977)

BIDGOOD, Ruth *Not Without Homage* (Swansea, Christopher Davies, 1976)

BROWNJOHN, Alan *A Night in the Gazebo* (London, Secker & Warburg, 1980)

CAUSLEY, Charles *Collected Poems 1951–1975* (London, Macmillan, 1975)

COOK, Stanley *Word Houses: Poems for Juniors* (Huddersfield, The Polytechnic Department of English, 1979)

DALE, Peter *One Another* (London, Agenda Editions, 1978)

DUNN, Douglas *Terry Street* (London, Faber & Faber, 1969)

HILL, Geoffrey *Mercian Hymns* (London, Deutsch, 1971)
   Tenebrae (London, Deutsch, 1978)

HOBAN, Russell *The Pedalling Man* (London, World's Work, 1969)

HUGHES, Ted *Moonbells and Other Poems* (London, Chatto & Windus, 1978)
   Moortown (London, Faber & Faber, 1979)
   Remains of Elmet (London, Faber & Faber, 1979)

JENNINGS, Elizabeth *Growing Points* (Cheadle, Carcanet, 1975)

LOWELL, Robert *Life Studies* (London, Faber & Faber, 1959)

MORGAN, Edwin *From Glasgow to Saturn* (Cheadle, Carcanet, 1973)
   The New Divan (Manchester, Carcanet, 1979)

MURPHY, Richard *High Island* (London, Faber & Faber, 1974)

ORMOND, John *Definition of a Waterfall* (London, Oxford University Press, 1973)

THOMAS, R. S. *Laboratories of the Spirit* (London, Macmillan, 1975)

The Way of It (Sunderland, Ceolfrith Press, 1977)

ANTHOLOGIES (see also pages 225–7)

CAUSLEY, Charles (ed.) *The Puffin Book of Magic Verse* (Harmondsworth, Penguin, 1974)

FIACC, Padraic (ed.) *The Wearing of the Black* (Belfast, Blackstaff Press, 1974)

KIRKUP, James (transl.) and DAVIS, A. R. (ed.) *Modern Japanese Poetry* (Milton Keynes, Open Univerity Press, 1979)

LOWBURY, E. (ed.) *Night Ride and Sunrise* (Aberystwyth, Celtion Publishing Co., 1978)

ROSEN, Michael (ed.) *I See a Voice* (London, Hutchinson, 1982).

STEINER, George (ed.) *Penguin Book of Modern Verse Translation* (Harmondsworth, Penguin, 1966)

SUMMERFIELD, Geoffrey (ed.) *Worlds: Seven Modern Poets* (Harmondsworth, Penguin, 1974)

OTHER BOOKS

ADAMS, A. and PEARCE, J. *Every English Teacher* (London, Oxford University Press, 1974)

ALLEN, David *English Teaching Since 1965* (London, Heinemann Educational, 1980)

BELSEY, Catherine *Critical Practice* (London, Methuen, 1980)

COX, C. B. and DYSON, A. E. *Modern Poetry: Studies in Practical Criticism* (London, Edward Arnold, 1963)

JACKSON, Brian *English versus Examinations* (London, Chatto & Windus, 1965)

SUMMERFIELD, Geoffrey *Topics in English* (London, Batsford, 1965)

SUMMERFIELD, G. and TUNNICLIFFE, S. (eds.) *English in Practice: Secondary English Departments at Work* (Cambridge, Cambridge UniversityPress, 1971)

THOMPSON, D. and TUNNICLIFFE, S. *Reading and Discrimination* (new edn) (London, Chatto & Windus 1979)

PART THREE
SOURCES AND RESOURCES

SECTION I:
FROM THE CLASSROOM

Teachers' ideas

As a secondary school English teacher with twenty-five years of continuous teaching behind him (unmitigated by such interludes as in-service courses, schoolteacher fellowships, spells in higher education or even hospital) I hope I may claim that the perspective of this book is that of a practising classroom teacher for whom poetry matters.

In addition to my own experience, Part Two draws on the practice of other poetry teachers and teacher/poets. The list that follows indicates the main sources:

i)   General (*passim*) – the work of Sandy Brownjohn, as incorporated in her two books (see p.232)

ii)   Chapter 6 – this chapter is based on the work of many teachers, including the team of six who prepared the *Cambridge Resources for English Teaching*, Malcolm and Jenny Lewis, Lindsay Harford, Frances Glendenning, Michael Routh and myself (see p.235 for full references).

iii)   Chapter 8 – the work of the folk-singer and scholar Roy Palmer informs this chapter. He was for many years headmaster of a multi-ethnic comprehensive school in Birmingham. For his books, see p.238.

iv)   Chapter 11 – includes the teaching work of Barrie Wade (on *haiku*), Neil Powell (on poetic form), David Young (on the use of direct stimuli for poetry writing) and Peter Abbs (on revising poems). An Advisory English Teacher in Essex, Bill Deller, has also done useful work on teaching *poetic forms*, believing as he does that 'concentration on form can release [children] to write what they feel'. He has prepared a useful short paper, 'Forms of poetry' (available from County Language and Teaching Centre, Sawyers Hall Lane, Brentwood, Essex).

v)   Chapter 12 – the black teacher Keith Ajegbo makes a valuable contribution to this chapter. Another useful source of ideas is an article by the poet Jon Silkin, written some years ago, and printed in the *Times Educational Supplement* for 14 July 1978 under the title 'Vital Verses'. Under Silkin's guidance his pupils compiled *The Aylestone Anthology* (originally supplied direct from the school, Aylestone School, Aylestone Avenue, London, NW6). The school had at that time a 70 per cent immigrant population.

vi)   Chapter 13 – incorporates the work of a Bristol teacher, Bernadette Fitzgerald (see p.175), and Geoffrey Fenwick from Manchester.

vii)   Additional points from teachers (in letters to the author):

a)   comment on a school anthology: 'I was surprised to find that the selection for this book must have been made before 1965: I think this is quite unsatisfactory for reader and poet.' (Pauline Spence, Ruislip).

b)   A Lancashire teacher, A. E. Gilmore, has done interesting work with the lyrics of pop songs. Those used in class include many from the Beatles, Led

Zeppelin ('Stairway to Heaven'), Supertramp ('The Logical Song'), Pink Floyd ('The Wall'), and The Police ('Spirits in the Material World'). (A. E. Gilmore, 34 Mickering Lane, Aughton, Ormskirk, Lancs.)

c) David Hughes, (a teacher at St Peter's School, York, YO3 6LY), writes interestingly and at length on poems he has found teachable. He has made a point of involving local poets in his work. His letter concludes: 'All this makes me realise how I mostly just use what comes to hand. It comes down to a question of what I *do* with the material rather than what the material is. The effect I aim for is to make poetry seem something that one reaches for without premeditation; and although that obviously means I try to stay familiar with quite a lot of poetry, it also means I prepare apparently little in the short term.'

d) A teacher in Sevenoaks, Audrey Third (Walthamstow Hall, Sevenoaks, Kent, TN13 3DJ), sent me a useful list of poems she has used successfully, from which I take the following:

1st and 2nd year pupils: Border Ballads, 'Alison Gross', 'Sir Patrick Spens' – approached after a good reading aloud – through the making of 'comic-strip' pictures individually – followed by selected pictures on OHP transparencies and the making of a sound track with the poem and appropriate sound effects to accompany the pictures. 'Sent as a Present from Annam', trans. Arthur Waley (in *Iron, Honey, Gold* Book I, ed. D. Holbrook, Cambridge University Press) – used as a pattern for short poems about their own treasured possessions.

4th year: 'The Almond Tree', Jon Stallworthy – always very well received by 14–15-year-old girls. Evokes discussion of subject-matter and imagery at quite a profound level.

School poetry stocks

The following lists have been compiled from the results of a questionnaire sent to all secondary schools belonging to the Schools Poetry Association (see Section III for details of SPA). Those returned reflect fairly faithfully both the range of secondary schools in Britain (though with a higher proportion from England) and the wide variations in school poetry stocks, except that the sample included a rather higher than average proportion of independent, single-sex schools (some 25 per cent of the total).

A typical secondary school is a mixed comprehensive school with between 600 and 1,000 pupils of all abilities – including those sometimes classified as ESN or 'remedial' – aged between 11 and 18. However, there are also significant and perhaps growing numbers of 11–16 and 13 or 14–18 comprehensives of a similar size. Sixth-form and 'tertiary' colleges fall outside the age range with which this book is chiefly concerned.

School poetry stocks vary greatly, and tend to reflect more the enthusiasm (or lack of it) of particular heads of English than the availability of funds. I know from my own bitter experience that many heads of English use their funds (*a*) to stock up with examination texts, (*b*) to buy class sets of past examination papers (source of many a soul-destroying fourth- and fifth-form English 'lesson'), (*c*) to fill in gaps in class sets of so-called 'course books', (*d*) to buy 'readers'. Only after all these have laid their voracious claims does he or she look round for such 'luxuries' as poetry. I hope that any English teacher reading this book will subject the values leading to such use of available resources to close critical re-appraisal.

We must assume that members of SPA are all alerted to the value of poetry in secondary English; so I hope we can safely conclude that the school in the lead as regards poetry stocks, with some forty different anthologies, represents the best we are likely to find, whereas the school recording the poorest poetry stock is probably far from being the most deprived, poetically speaking. Since the latter listed only three anthologies in stock, one being Palgrave's *Golden Treasury* and the other two certainly having been in circulation when I started teaching in 1952, that is not a particularly encouraging prospect. If they do nothing else these findings should alert readers to the need for a more enlightened and disciplined approach to the stocking of the English department with sufficient quantities of appropriate poetry.

It is almost impossible to devise a fool-proof classification for school poetry anthologies. One cannot nowadays even usefully separate poetry from prose; many good English collections contain both, perhaps with a common theme or some other unifying idea. I have grouped the books loosely under five headings, followed by a short list of 'favourites'. It will be evident that even so general a grouping is flawed; I shall mention just one point. The first 'general' list (A) undoubtedly includes collections that are principally or exclusively of twentieth-century writing, and could therefore as suitably be included in list B. It was felt worth while nevertheless to list separately those collections which included a reference to recent or contemporary origin in their titles, as this implies a more deliberate emphasis on modernity for its own sake or for a consciously educational purpose.

A GENERAL COLLECTIONS (* indicates series)

As Large As Alone	Copeman, C. and Gibson, J.	(London, Macmillan, 1969)
Billy The Kid	Baldwin, M.	(London, Hutchinson, 1963)
A Choice of Poets	Hewett, R. P.	(London, Harrap, 1968)
*Conflict**	Hacker, G. (Bks I & II) Robinson, R. and Learmouth, J. (Bk III)	(London, Nelson, 1976)

*Discovering Poetry**	Marland, M.	(London, Longman, 1970)
Dragonsteeth	Williams, E.	(London, Edward Arnold, 1972)
*Enjoying Poetry**	Parker, E. W.	(London, Longman, 1953)
Every Man Will Shout	Mansfield, R. and Armstrong, I.	(London, O.U.P., 1964)
*Happenings**	Wollman, M. and Grugeon, D.	(London, Harrap, 1964/1972)
Here, Now and Beyond	Martin, N.	(Oxford, O.U.P., 1972)
Here Today	Hughes, Ted (intro.)	(London, Hutchinson, 1963)
I See a Voice	Rosen, M.	(London, Hutchinson, 1982)
*Impact**	Poole, R. H. and Shepherd, P. J.	(London, Heinemann, 1967)
*Iron, Honey, Gold**	Holdbrook, D.	(Cambridge, C.U.P., 1965)
*Junior Voices**	Summerfield, G.	(Harmondsworth, Penguin, 1970)
Looking Glass	Williams, E.	(London, Edward Arnold, 1973)
Many People, Many Voices	Hidden, N. and Hollins, A.	(London, Hutchinson, 1978)
The New Dragon Book of Verse	Harrison, M. and Stuart-Clark, C.	(Oxford, O.U.P, 1977)
*Pegasus**	Simpson, A. A.	(London, Bell, n.d.)
Poems 1 and 2	Harrison M. and Stuart-Clark, C.	(Oxford, O.U.P., 1979)
Poems of Spirit and Action	Smyth, W. M., 2nd edn.	(London, Edward Arnold, 1971)
Poetry Workshop	Benton, M. and P.	(London, Hodder & Stoughton, 1975)
The Poet's Tongue	Auden, W. H. and Garrett, J.	(London, Bell, 1945)
The Poet's Way	Parker, E. W.	(London, Longman, 1953)

Poets' World	Reeves, J.	(London, Heinemann, 1972)
Reach Out*	Blackburn, T. and Cunningham, W. T.	(London, Nelson, 1968–9)
The Road Ahead	Parker, E. W.	(London, Longman, 1953)
Rhyme and Reason	O'Malley, R. and Thompson, D.	(London, Hart-Davis, 1974)
The Rhyming River	Reeves, J.	(London, Heinemann, 1959)
Say It Aloud	Hidden, N.	(London, Hutchinson, 1972)
The Sheldon Book of Verse	Smith, P. G. and Wilkins, J. F.	(Oxford, O.U.P., 1959)
A Sudden Line	Mansfield, R. and Armstrong, I.	(Oxford, O.U.P., 1976)
Tapestry	Williams, E.	(London, Edward Arnold, 1974)
Telescope	Williams, E.	(London, Edward Arnold, 1974)
Thoughtshapes	Maybury, B.	(Oxford, O.U.P., 1972)
Touchstones (1–5)*	Benton, M. and P.	(London, Hodder & Stoughton, 1969–72)
Tunes on a Tin Whistle	Crang, A.	(Oxford, Pergamon, 1967)
Viewpoint	Skelton, R.	(London, Hutchinson, 1962)
Voices (Books 1–3)*	Summerfield, G.	(Harmondsworth, Penguin, 1968)
Watchwords (1–3)*	Benton, M. and P.	(London, Hodder & Stoughton, 1979–82)
The Winchester Book of Verse	Lee, H. D. P.	(London, Harrap, 1959)
Wordscapes	Maybury, B.	(Oxford, O.U.P., 1971)

Words In Your Ear	Deadman, R.	(London, Evans, 1973)
You Tell Me	McGough, R. and Rosen, M.	(Harmondsworth, Penguin, 1979)

B   NEW AND RECENT POETRY

The Albemarle Book of Modern Verse	Finn, F. E. S.	(London, John Murray, 1962)
Contemporary British and North American Verse	Booth, M.	(Oxford, O.U.P., 1981)
A Junior Book of Modern Verse	Wollman, M. and Hurst, D. M.	(London, Harrap, 1961)
*Modern Poets 1–4**	Hunter, J.	(London, Faber & Faber, 1968)
The New Poetry	Alvarez, A.	(Harmondsworth, Penguin, 1962)
Nine Modern Poets	Black, E. L.	(London, Macmillan, 1966)
Poetry 1900–1980	Macbeth, G.	(London, Longman, 1982)
Poetry of the Nineteen-Thirties	Rodway, A. E.	(London, Longman, 1967)
Poets of Our Time	Finn, F. E. S.	(London, John Murray, 1976)
Ten Twentieth-Century Poets	Wollman, M.	(London, Harrap, 1975)
Voices of Today	Finn, F. E. S.	(London, John Murray, 1980)
Worlds: Seven Modern Poets	Summerfield, G.	(Harmondsworth, Penguin, 1974)

C   SPECIFIC GENRES: COLLECTIONS

Ballads Old and New	Atkins, S. H.	(London, Hulton, 1968)
A Book of Ballads	Bird, Alan	(London, Longman, 1967)

Famous Poems	Bebbington, W. G.	(Huddersfield Schofield & Sims, 1962)
A Golden Treasury of Longer Poems	Rhys, E.	(London, Dent, 1954)
English and Scottish Ballads	Graves, R.	(London, Heinemann, 1957)
The Narrative Art in Verse	Clay, N. L.	(London, John Murray, 1941)
The Poet's Tale	Evans, A. A.	(London, U.L.P., 1957)
Stories in Modern Verse	Wollman, M.	(London, Harrap, 1976)
The Windmill Book of Ballads	Serraillier, I.	(London, Heinemann, 1962)

D   THEMATIC COLLECTIONS

Conflict and Compassion	Skull, J.	(London, Hutchinson, 1969)
Extra-ordinary	Glendenning, F.	(Cambridge, C.U.P., 1979)
Friends and Enemies	Harford, L.	(Cambridge, C.U.P., 1977)
Men Who March Away	Parsons, I. M.	(London, Chatto & Windus, 1978)
Poets of the First World War	Stallworthy, J.	(London, O.U.P., 1974)
The Puffin Book of Magic Verse	Causley, C.	(Harmondsworth, Penguin, 1974)
The Puffin Book of Salt-Sea Verse	Causley, C.	(Harmondsworth, Penguin, 1978)
Seven Themes in Modern Poetry	Wollman, M.	(London, Harrap, 1968)
Stone, Wood, Metal, Plastic	Tunnicliffe, S.	(Cambridge, C.U.P., 1975)
*Themes**	Jones, R.	(London, Heinemann, 1969)

E   SINGLE-AUTHOR COLLECTIONS

(As there are many different books and editions of some authors it is impossible to give a fully detailed list. The authors listed are those most commonly included in school poetry stocks.)

Most frequent:

T. S. Eliot	Gerard Manley	D. H. Lawrence
Robert Frost	Hopkins	Mersey Poets (especially
Thomas Hardy	Ted Hughes	McGough)
Seamus Heaney	John Keats	Wilfred Owen
	Philip Larkin	Michael Rosen

Less frequent:

W. H. Auden	Douglas Dunn	Sylvia Plath
Hilaire Belloc	Thom Gunn	Stephen Spender
William Blake	Rudyard Kipling	Dylan Thomas
Charles Causley	Laurie Lee	Edward Thomas
S. T. Coleridge	Robert Lowell	Alfred, Lord
Walter de la Mare	Spike Milligan	Tennyson
John Donne		W. B. Yeats

POPULARITY

Of the books listed above (A to E), the following appear most frequently in school stocks. Sometimes this is due to their status as 'set' texts for GCE or CSE (indicated thus ˢ). Those listed first are the most popular.

i) *Choice of Poets* (Hewett)

   Dragonsteeth (Williams)
   ˢ *Here Today* (Hughes)
ii) ˢ *Every Man Will Shout* (Mansfield)
   I See a Voice (Rosen)
   ˢ *Ten Twentieth-Century Poets* (Wollman)
iii) *As Large As Alone* (Copeman)

   ˢ*Rhyme and Reason* (O'Malley)
   Touchstones (Benton)
   ˢ*Voices* (Summerfield)
   Thoughtshapes (Maybury)

   Watchwords (Benton)
   Wordscapes (Maybury)
   Worlds (Summerfield)
   Poems 1 and 2 (Harrison/ Stuart-Clark

Happenings (Wollman)

Here Now and Beyond (Martin)

Junior Voices (Summerfield)

New Dragon Book of Verse (Harrison/ Stuart-Clark)

The New Poetry (Alvarez)

Nine Modern Poets (Black)

Pegasus (Simpson)

Poetry Workshop (Benton)

Poet's World (Reeves)

Seven Themes in Modern Poetry (Wollman)

Tapestry (Williams)

Telescope (Williams)

Viewpoint (Skelton)

Windmill Book of Ballads (Serraillier)

EDITORS

A high proportion of the poetry at present available in schools is due to the editorial work of eight people (one of them supplemented by a ninth). These are:

Michael and Peter Benton
F. E. S. Finn
R. P. Hewett
E. W. Parker (supplemented by Michael Marland)

Geoffrey Summerfield
Eric Williams
Maurice Wollman

Some useful anthologies

(For additional collections suitable in multi-ethnic classes see below, (p.237))

1 *The Children's Book of Comic Verse* Logue, C. (London, Batsford, 1979) (paperback edition, Pan Paperbacks)

2 *Double Take: Book of Verse Comparison* Bolt, A. F. (London, Harrap, 1976)
This, and the rather larger collection by Raymond Wilson

(below, no. 11), make use of the well-tried technique of comparing poems with similar themes. This book is suitable for 4th and 5th year pupils.

3　*Hard Lines: New Poetry and Prose* Dubes, F. (London, Faber & Faber, 1983)
The casual and 'laid back' format and style make this a useful collection for senior — perhaps reluctant — classes.

4　*I Like This Poem* Webb, K. (Harmondsworth, Penguin, 1979)
All the poems have been chosen by children as their favourites. Suitable for 1st and 2nd year classes.

5　*The London Book of English Verse* Read, H. and Dobree, B. (London, Eyre Methuen, 1977)
Although rather old-fashioned, having been first published in 1949, this, in its paperback version, is quite a bargain, including in its nearly 900 pages a very wide range of poetry. A resource 'quarry' rather than a class anthology.

6　*Let The Poet Choose* Gibson, J. (London, Harrap, 1973)
Forty-four poets were asked to choose their own favourites from their work and add a personal comment. This makes it an interesting teaching aid. As with too many anthologies, there is a strong male bias — only five of the poets are women.

7　*Modern Poetry in Translation: 1983* Weissbort, D. (Manchester, Carcanet, 1983)
This is the first of an intended annual series, replacing the magazine of the same name. It includes a selection of prose poems and folk poetry, and interesting observations by translators.

8　*The New Dragon Book of Verse* Harrison, M. and Stuart-Clark, C. (Oxford, O.U.P., 1977)
One of the best of recent general school anthologies, and particularly good value in its paperback form. It is arranged thematically (8 themes), but — infuriatingly —

lacks any contents page at the beginning, so the plan is easily overlooked.

9 *The Penguin Book of Oral Poetry* Finnegan, R. (Harmondsworth, Penguin, 1982)
A wide-ranging collection of poems 'from thirteen cultures', with much interesting editorial material. It relates to Chapter 8 in Part Two.

10 *The Penguin Book of Women Poets* Cosman, C. and Weaver, K. (Harmondsworth, Penguin, 1979)
An article in the ILEA magazine *Teaching London Kids* (TLK) drew attention to the heavy male bias of most school anthologies, e.g. *Here Today* – 1 female, 43 male poets; *Every Man [sic] Will Shout* – 16 female, 78 male; *The Rattle Bag* (see no. 12 below) – 10 female, 127 male. This anthology and no. 13 may help to redress the balance, but teachers also need to read and cull from the poetry magazines, which are more conscious of the outstanding work of women poets today.

11 *Poems to Compare* Wilson, R. (London, Macmillan, 1966)
See no. 2 (above).

12 *The Rattle Bag* Heaney, S. and Hughes, T. (London, Faber & Faber, 1982)
An enormous assorted 'bag' of poetry of all ages for young people. It is arranged alphabetically by title, leading to unexpected and often provocative juxtapositions.

13 *Scars Upon My Heart: Women's Poetry of the First World War* Reilly, C. (London, Virago, 1981)
See no. 10.

14 *Young Writers (24th Year [1982])* (London, Heinemann, 1983)
Most teachers will have collections of children's poetry ready to hand. The television education programmes have generated much poetry through competitions, and there are many others. The collection above comes from the longest established national children's poetry competition.

SECTION II:
PUBLISHED SOURCES
AND RESOURCES

Poets on poetry – a select list

AUDEN, W. H. *The Dyer's Hand and Other Essays* (London, Faber & Faber, 1963)
Forewords and Afterwords (London, Faber & Faber, 1973)
Certain World: Commonplace Book (London, Faber & Faber, 1982)

Cookson, W. (ed.) *Agenda 10/4 and 11/1* (double no.), and *Agenda 11/2–3* (double no.) (London, Agenda (5 Cranbourne Court, Albert Bridge Road, SW11 4PE) 1973)

Special issues on rhythm, the second being an American supplement. They include replies by many poets to a searching questionnaire on rhythm. Those who replied included W. H. Auden, Basil Bunting, Donald Davie, Thom Gunn, Adrian Henri, Robert Lowell, George Oppen, Kathleen Raine and Charles Tomlinson. This is an essential source-book for those interested in modern poetry, and has special reference to Chapter 9.

DAVIE, DONALD *Articulate Energy* (London, Routledge & Kegan Paul, 1955)

Thomas Hardy and British Poetry (London, Routledge & Kegan Paul, 1973)

ELIOT, T. S. *Selected Essays* (London, Faber & Faber, 1932)

Poetry and Drama (London, Faber & Faber, 1951)

Selected Prose (Harmondsworth, Penguin, 1953)

On Poetry and Poets (London, Faber & Faber, 1969)

Haffenden, J. (ed.) *Viewpoints: Poets in Conversation With John Haffenden* (London, Faber & Faber, 1981)

HUGHES, TED *Poetry in the Making* (London, Faber & Faber, 1967)

This book arose out of a series of broadcasts in the BBC 'Listening and Writing' series. It is useful for thematic poetry work and is illuminating about Hughes's own poetry.

JARRELL, RANDALL *Kipling, Auden & Co: Essays and Reviews 1935–64* (Manchester, Carcanet, 1981)

The fourth and final book of criticism by this fine poet and critic.

JONES, DAVID *Epoch and Artist* (London, Faber & Faber, 1969)

Letters to Vernon Watkins, ed. Ruth Pryor (Cardiff, University of Wales Press, 1976)

The Dying Gaul and Other Writings (London, Faber & Faber, 1978)

I include these prose writings of this major twentieth century poet both for their intrinsic merit and to draw attention to the persistent neglect David Jones still suffers under.

LEWIS, C. DAY *The Poetic Image* (London, Jonathan Cape, 1947)

The Poet's Way of Knowledge (Cambridge, Cambridge University Press, 1957)

Lewis, Jenny (ed.) *Poetry in the Making: Catalogue of an Exhibition of Poetry Manuscripts in the British Museum* (London, Turret Books, 1967)

A useful little book, containing facsimiles of working drafts by Ted Hughes, Sir John Betjeman, W. H. Auden, Dylan Thomas, Philip Larkin and others.

PAULIN, TOM *Thomas Hardy: the Poetry of Perception* (London, Macmillan, 1975)

ROSEN, MICHAEL *I See a Voice* (London, Thames Television/ Hutchinson, 1982)

Although really an anthology, this book includes valuable notes and comments, some of which are expanded in the Thames handbook to the series 'The English Programme' (1982 and 1983 editions).

SKELTON, ROBIN *The Poet's Calling* (London, Heinemann, 1975)

Poetic Truth (London, Heinemann, 1978)

Summerfield, G. (ed.) *Worlds: Seven Modern Poets* (Harmondsworth, Penguin, 1974)

The seven poets represented here – Charles Causley, Thom Gunn, Seamus Heaney, Ted Hughes, Norman MacCaig, Adrian Mitchell and Edwin Morgan – contribute their own autobiographical comments.

THOMAS, DYLAN *Letter to Vernon Watkins* (London, Dent and Faber & Faber, 1957)

THOMAS, R. S. *Selected Prose* (ed. Sandra Anstey) (Bridgend, Poetry Wales Press, 1983)

TOMLINSON, CHARLES *Poetry and Metamorphosis* (Cambridge, Cambridge University Press, 1983)

Some Americans: a Personal Record (Berkeley, University of California Press, 1981)

WILLIAMS, WILLIAM CARLOS *I Wanted to Write a Poem* (London, Jonathan Cape, 1967)

A list of Williams's published poetry at the time (1958), with accompanying comments by the poet, throwing light both on his work and on the activity of writing poetry.

Teachers and critics of poetry

Arnstein, F. J. *Children Write Poetry* (London, Constable, 1967)

   This is a British edition of *Poetry and the Child*, published in USA in 1951; consequently parts seem a little dated. It is nevertheless a useful source of ideas, expounding the theory behind the teaching of poetry, with chapter-headings like 'Why poetry?', 'We like to write', etc.

Badham-Thornhill, D. *Three Poets: Two Children* (Gloucester, Thornhill Press, n.d.)

   An interesting idea that evidently went on the rocks before completion; the author had projected three such volumes, but only this one survives – and the book is not easy to find, alas! In it a girl of 11 and a boy of 14 interview three established poets (Leonard Clark, Dannie Abse, Vernon Scannell) about their work and methods.

Belsey, C. *Critical Practice* (London, Methuen, 1980)

   A close and valuable study of literary criticism with radical implications for much current English teaching practice. It relates to Chapter 13.

Bentham, N. *et al. Language Matters* (No. 382 'Poetry' 24pp.) (London, Centre for Language in Primary Education, 1982)

   A number of a periodical specially devoted to the teaching of poetry in primary schools. Much in it also applies to junior secondary classes. It includes a selection of children's poems.

Boyle, Bill *What's In a Poem?, 1 and 2* (London, Collins, 1983)

   In 1981 the author's school was awarded the Observer Young Poets Award. These books show how it came about.

Brownjohn, S. *Does It Have to Rhyme?* (London, Hodder & Stoughton, 1980)

Brownjohn, S. *What Rhymes With 'Secret'?* (London, Hodder & Stoughton, 1982)

   In his foreword to the second of these books by an inspired teacher of poetry Ted Hughes pinpoints the value of her work: 'She succeeds not just with the odd pupil ... but with a big proportion of her class.' As this book has made clear, I warmly endorse Hughes's view that 'Whatever is going on here, it is certainly worth very close examination by all English teachers.'

Burgess, C. *et al. Understanding Children Writing* (Harmonds-worth, Penguin, 1973)

Druce, R. *The Eye of Innocence: Children and Their Poetry* (2nd edn) (London, University of London Press, 1970)
In spite of its dated and rather embarrassing title this book has some useful advice for poetry teachers, as well as examples of children's work drafts.

Fitzgerald, B. *Approaches to Poetry: Group Question-Setting* (Bristol, Avon Resources for Learning Development Unit, 1982)
A record of an interesting project in do-it-yourself criticism in the classroom, by the teacher who initiated it.

Harding, D. W. *Words Into Rhythm: English Speech Rhythm in Verse and Prose* (Cambridge, Cambridge University Press, 1976)
The most thorough study of rhythm in English language available, by a former *Scrutiny* critic who was also a professor of psychology. It relates closely to Chapter 9.

Jackson, B. *English versus Examinations* (London, Chatto & Windus, 1965)

Koch, K. *Wishes, Lies and Dreams* (New York, Random House, 1971)

Koch, K. *Rose, Where Did You Get That Red?* (New York, Vintage Books, 1974)
Books by an American teacher with the same commitment to poetry as Sandy Brownjohn (above), and a similarly eclectic approach to his pupils. These are essential reading for serious teachers of poetry in school.

Langdon, M. *Let the Children Write* (London, Longman, 1961)
This little book, sub-titled 'An explanation of intensive writing', created quite a stir when it first came out. It reads

rather oddly today – especially beside Sandy Brownjohn's books, which reflect our less rigid classroom environments nowadays – but still has something to offer.

McAlpine, R. *Song in the Satchel: Poetry in the High School* (Wellington, New Zealand Council for Educational Research, 1980)

An unpretentious account of her work in New Zealand secondary schools by a poet and teacher.

Thompson, D. and Tunnicliffe, S. *Reading and Discrimination (new edition)* (London, Chatto & Windus, 1979)

Although this is written chiefly for use in post-O Level and CSE classes, it includes useful ideas, both theoretical and practical, adaptable to 14- and 15-year-old students.

Turner, K. *Possible Worlds: a discussion of Blake with thirteen-year-olds* (Warwick, Warwick University Press, 1979)

Finally, the termly magazine *The Use of English* Scottish Academic Press (33 Montgomery Street, Edinburgh EH7 5JX) frequently has articles relating to the teaching of poetry. No. 30/1 (Autumn 1978) was wholly devoted to poetry.

Themes (see chapter 6)

Since teachers and educationalists have come to recognize the advantages of thematically planned English work many textbooks and anthologies have followed suit. One of the most carefully planned series is the *Cambridge Resources for English Teaching*, compiled between 1974 and 1979 by six English teachers under my general editorship. We originally envisaged a series of six 'theme kits', three for junior secondary classes or middle schools and three for older children. Owing to the recession and a change of policy by the publisher only three were published. For each topic there is a theme book (an anthology of verse and prose), sets of colour-slides, work cards and duplicator masters and a pre-recorded cassette, together with a 'teacher's pack' containing the teachers' handbook and copies of two 'key texts' – popular children's novels related to the theme. Each element can be purchased and used separately, but careful cross-referencing makes it possible to use them together to approach the theme in many different ways, reinforcing the learning process visually, through talk and listening, drama, reading and writing. Throughout we placed considerable emphasis on poetry, as is clear from Chapter 6.

For convenience only the theme books of the CRET series are included below. The list covers only books wholly planned thematically and not included elsewhere in Part Three. Books are listed alphabetically by author/editor except where no single person can be named.

Adams, A. *The Sea* (Anchor Books) (Edinburgh, W & R. Chambers, 1976)

Adams, A., Leach, R., Palmer, R. *Feasts and Seasons* (4 vols.: *Spring, Summer, Autumn, Winter*) (Glasgow, Blackie, 1978)

Connexions: a series of topic books (Harmondsworth, Penguin, 1970) e.g. Allsop, K. *Fit to Live in? The future of Britain's countryside*

Glendenning, F. *Extra-ordinary* (Cambridge Resources for English Teaching) (Cambridge, Cambridge University Press, 1979)

Harford, L. *Friends and Enemies* (Cambridge Resources for English Teaching) (Cambridge, Cambridge University Press, 1977)

Heath, R. B. *Theme and Variations* (London, Longman, 1965)

Horner, S. *Plans: English Teachers at Work* (York, Longman/ Schools Council) (Longman Resources Unit, 33–5 Tanner Row, York YO1 1JP)

This is not an anthology, but includes two valuable 'case studies' of teachers using thematic material with fourth-year classes.

Jones, Rhodri *Themes* (series of thematic anthologies) (London, Heinemann, 1969)

Preludes (four thematic anthologies for junior classes) (London, Heinemann, 1971)

Parker, T. H. and Teskey, F. J. *Themes to Explore* (Glasgow, Blackie, 1970)

A series of twelve theme collections, with such titles as 'Animals in captivity', 'Inland waters', 'This human frame' etc.

Skull, J. *Themes: A Series of Poetry Anthologies* (London, Heinemann, 1970)

Stokes, C. G. *Poetry Themes* (London, Collins, 1973)

Themes ('Rebels', 'Aggression', 'Roman Britain') (London, Routledge & Kegan Paul, 1969–72)

Tunnicliffe, S. *Stone, Wood, Metal, Plastic* (Cambridge Resources for English Teaching) (Cambridge, Cambridge University Press, 1975)

Wollman, M. & Grugeon, D. *Seven Themes* (London, Harrap, 1968)

Recorded and oral material

Most living poets of established reputation have been recorded reading their own work – an indispensable tool, even when the voice itself is monotonous or unpractised, for serious study of particular poets. Much poetry of the past is also available, usually read by professionals. The *Gramophone* catalogues give full lists of current discs and cassettes. *Argo* have been the pioneers for spoken poetry on disc; in cassettes, *Caedmon Cassettes* offer the widest range. The Poetry Society Bookshop (see Section III below) supply lists of titles in stock, under separate headings for 'UK and Irish', 'American and Canadian' and 'Dylan Thomas'. Faber publish cassettes of some of the poets whose work they publish, e.g. Ted Hughes, Seamus Heaney, Tom Paulin. It is worth investigating also the collections of dialect poems now available, of which an outstanding example is:

Northumbrian Voice: Poetry in the Dialect, by Fred Reed, (White Meadow Records, Mount Hooley, Whittingham, Alnwick, Northumberland NE66 4RN).
Recordings relevant to multi-ethnic classes are included below (see p.243).

The poet Alan Brownjohn has compiled a useful and interesting book of oral poetry: *First I Say This*, Brownjohn, A. ed. (London, Hutchinson, 1969)
See also: *Say It Aloud*, Hidden, N. and Hollins, A. (London, Hutchinson, 1972)

FOLK AND TRADITIONAL

The widest range of material at present available, including Scottish and Irish, is produced by the indefatigable Topic Records Ltd (50 Stroud Green Road, London N4 3EF, phone 01–263 6403), who can supply full lists on request; more traditional Irish folk music is recorded by *Shanachie Records*, which are distributed by Topic. The following is a small selection of records I have found useful:

Bob Roberts, *Songs from the Sailing Barges* (see pp.98–101) Topic 12TS361.

Johnny Doughty, *Round Rye Bay for More* (full text provided – nb. 'Wreck of the Northfleet'), Topic 12TS324.

George Spicer, *Blackberry Fold* (esp. 'The Folkestone Murder'), Topic 12T 235.

Phoebe Smith, *Once I had a True Love* (esp. 'The Wexport Girl'), Topic 12T 193.

The Ling Family, *Singing Traditions of a Suffolk Family*, Topic 12TS292.

Walter Pardon, *A Proper Sort* (full text provided – nb. 'Van Diemen's Land'), Leader LED2063

ROY PALMER

Roy Palmer is a folk-singer and social historian of great distinction. He was also until recently head of a large

Birmingham comprehensive school, so has first-hand know-ledge of the impact folk-songs and ballads can have in a school setting. Only two (marked *) of his eleven collections of songs and ballads currently available have accompanying discs, but all of them include the melody lines of the tunes, two with guitar chords (marked †). Together they make an unrivalled collection of lively, accessible and unconventional teaching material:

Everyman's Book of British Ballads (London, Dent, 1980)

Everyman's Book of English Country Songs (London, Dent, 1979)

Love is Pleasing (Cambridge, Cambridge University Press, 1974)

The Painful Plough (record now OP) (Cambridge, Cambridge University Press, 1972)

Poverty Knocks (Cambridge, Cambridge University Press, 1974)

The Rambling Soldier (record Fellside FE 017) (Harmonds-worth, Penguin, 1977)†*

Rigs of the Fair (Cambridge, Cambridge University Press, 1976)

Room for Company (separate edns. melody and piano) (Cambridge, Cambridge University Press, 1971)

Strike the Bell (Cambridge, Cambridge University Press, 1978)

A Touch on the Times: Songs of Social Change 1770 to 1914 (Harmondsworth, Penguin, 1974)†

The Valiant Sailor (record Topic 12TS232) (Cambridge, Cambridge University Press, 1973)*

For the multi-ethnic classroom

ANTHOLOGIES

African Poetry for Schools (Books 1 & 2) Machin, N. (Harlow, Longman, 1978)

An Anthology of Swahili Poetry Jahadhmy, A. A. (London, Heinemann (African Writers series no. 192), 1975)

An Anthology of West African Verse Bassir, O. (Ibadan (Nigeria), Ibadan University Press, 1957)

Attachments to the Sun Blackburn, D. *et al.* (London, Edward Arnold, 1978)

Bite In (3 vols) Gray, C. (London, Nelson, 1977)
This is a three-year secondary course for Caribbean students.

Bluefoot Traveller (new edn) Berry, J. (London, Harrap, 1981)
A new edition of this well-known collection of West Indian poets in Britain.

Breaklight Salkey, A. (London, Hamish Hamilton, 1971)
One of the most comprehensive collections of Caribbean poetry.

Caribbean Anthology Cocking, L. and Goody, J. (London, ILEA (Learning Materials Service), 1982)
An attractive school anthology produced in three forms: teacher's edition, with editorial material; pupil's edition (text only); cassette – the poems mostly spoken by the poets themselves. ILEA schools get one-third discount.

Caribbean Voices (Books 1 & 2) Figueroa, J. (London, Evans, 1966)

Commonwealth Poems of Today Sergeant, H. (London, John Murray, 1967)

Distant Voices: poetry of the pre-literate Thompson, D. (London, Heinemann, 1978)

Heritage: a Caribbean anthology Jones, Esmor (London, Cassell, 1981)

Jamaica Woman Mordecai, P. and Morris, M. (London, Heinemann, 1982)
Unusual in being the only recent anthology of poems written only by women. Fifteen Jamaican women poets are represented.

Mango Spice: 44 Caribbean Songs Conolly, Y. *et al.* (London, A. & C. Black, 1981)

This collection is for singing, and is suitable for children from 4 to 14. A separate tape is available, and the book includes a score.

Many People, Many Voices Hidden, N. and Hollins, A. (London, Hutchinson, 1978)

More suitable for senior classes. The range is world-wide from English-speaking countries. Arranged thematically.

Merely a Matter of Colour: Ugandan Asian anthology Markham, E. A. and Kingston, A. (Edgware, 'Q' Books, 1973)

The Minority Experience Marland, M. and Ray, S. (London, Longman, 1978)

An anthology of prose, verse, TV documentary and photographs.

Modern Indian Poetry Nandy, P. (London, Heinemann, 1974)

Mother Goose Comes to Cable Street Stones, R. and Mann, A. (Harmondsworth, Penguin, 1980)

Although, as its name suggests, a collection of nursery rhymes, this book can be useful in secondary classes because of its multi-cultural and skilful illustrations.

Oral Poetry from Africa Mapanje, J. and White, L. (Harlow, Longman, 1983)

Poems from East Africa Cook, D. and Rubadiri, D. (London, Heinemann, 1971)

Poetry from Africa Sergeant, H. (Oxford, Pergamon, 1968)

Poets to the People (new edn) Feinberg, B. (London, Heinemann, 1980)

An anthology of the best-known black South African poets.

Seven South African Poets Pieterse, C. (London, Heinemann, (African Writers series no. 64), 1971)

The poets represented are: Dollar Brand, Dennis Brutus, Choonara, C.J. Driver, Timothy Holmes, Keorapetse Kgoositsile and Arthur Nortje.

The Second Tongue Thumboo, E. (Singapore, Heinemann Educational (Asia) Ltd, 1976)

This is sub-titled 'an anthology of poetry from Malaysia and Singapore'. It is an attractively produced paperback, edited without fuss by one of the thirty-eight poets represented. It is available in UK.

A Selection of African Poetry Senanu, K. E. and Vincent, T. (Harlow, Longman, 1976)
  A teaching anthology, with quite full notes, commentary and questions on most of the poems.

Shaking the Pumpkin: Traditional Poetry of the Indian North Americas Rothenberg, J. (ed.) (New York, Doubleday, 1972)

Sunflower of Hope: Poems from the Mozambican Revolution Searle, C. (London, Allison & Busby, 1982)

Talk of the Tamarinds Forde, A. N. (London, Edward Arnold, 1971)

The World in a Classroom Searle, C. (London, Writers and Readers Publishing Cooperative, 1977)
  An anthology of prose and poetry by a London teacher.

You Better Believe It Breman, P. (Harmondsworth, Penguin, 1973)
  A collection of black verse in English from Africa, the West Indies and the United States of America.

Children's collections

Talking Blues (London, Centreprise, 1976)
Hey, Mr Butterfly Aston, A. (ed.) (London, ILEA, 1978)
Note: The poet Michael Rosen's anthologies (see p.231) reveal a sympathetic awareness of the multi-cultural London classroom.

INDIVIDUAL POETS

Agard, John *I Din Do Nuttin and Other Poems* (London, Bodley Head, 1983)

Angira, Jared *Silent Voices* (London, Heinemann (African Writers series no. 111), 1971)

Brown, Wayne *On the Coast* (Trinidadian) (London, Deutsch, 1972)

Chakravarti, Prithvindra *Chharaa* (Baroko, Papua Pocket
Poets (Vol. 27) [1975])

Cheyney-Coker, Syl *Concerto for an Exile* (London, Heinemann (African Writers series no. 126), 1973)

de Veaux, Alexis *Don't Explain: a song of Billie Holiday* (New
York, Harper & Row, 1980)
A long story-poem for children giving the life-story of Billie
Holiday. It draws upon the African tradition of praise, and
swings in the black music tradition, telling of the white
exploitation of black artists.

Huntley, Accabre *At School Today* (London, Bogle l'Ouverture, 1975)

Huntley, Accabre *Easter Monday Blues* (London, Bogle
l'Ouverture, 1983)
Two collections by a talented school-child.

Johnson, Linton Kwesi *Dread Beat and Blood* (London, Bogle
l'Ouverture 1975)

Johnson, Linton Kwesi *Inglan is a Bitch* (London, Race Today
Publications, 1980)

Mtshali, Mbuyiseni Oswald *Sounds of a Cowhide Drum*
(Johannesburg, A. D. Donker, 1982)

Nandy, Pritish *Riding the Midnight River* (New Delhi, Arnold
Heinemann, 1975)

Okigbo, Christopher *Labyrinths, with Path of Thunder* (London, Heinemann (African Writers series no. 62), 1971)

Parthasarathy, R. *Rough Passage* (Delhi, Oxford University
Press, 1977)

Scott, Dennis *Dreadwalk: Poems 1970–1978* (London, New
Beacon Books, 1982)

Senghor, Leopold Sedar *Prose and Poetry* (ed. and tr. J. Reed
and C. Wake) (London, Heinemann (African Writers
series no. 180), 1976)

Shange, Ntozake *Nappy Edges* (New York, St Martin's Press,
1972)

Soyinka, Wole *A Shuttle in the Crypt* (London, Eyre Methuen,
1972)

Thomas, Joyce Carol *Black Child* (New York, Zamani
   Productions, 1981)

ORAL MATERIALS

(see also ANTHOLOGIES, collections by Cocking and Goody,
Mapanje and White, Thompson, Conolly)
An Evening of International Poetry (cassette) (London, Bogle
   l'Ouverture, 1983)
   Artists include James Berry, Edward Kamau Brathwaite,
   Linton Kwesi Johnson, E. A. Markham.

MAGAZINES

Dragon's Teeth (three issues per year) 240 Lancaster Road,
   London W11.
The English Magazine (three issues per year) The English
   Centre, Sutherland Street, London SW1.
Inter-Racial Books for Children Bulletin (eight per year) CIBC,
   1841 Broadway, New York, NY 10023.
   Vol.13.8(1982) is an index to vols. 7–13 (1977–82)
Multicultural Teaching (three issues per year) 30 Wenger
   Crescent, Trentham, Stoke-on-Trent ST4 8LE.
Multiracial Education Jo Rex, 745a Finchley Road, London
   NW11.
TLK (Teaching London Kids) (twice yearly) 40 Hamilton
   Road, London SW19.
   Some poetry magazines (see p.245) have good coverage of
   poetry from other cultures, e.g. *Poetry Review* vol.73.2
   (June 1983) includes a long essay on West Indian poetry by
   James Berry and a wide selection of poems; *Ambit 91* (1982)
   was a Caribbean special issue.

REFERENCE

ILEA *Multi-Ethnic Education Review* (annual) is published by the ILEA Multi-Ethnic Inspectorate, County Hall, London SE1.

Edwards, V. *Language Variation in the Multicultural Classroom* (Reading, University of Reading, 1982)

Klein, Gillian *Resources for Multi-Cultural Education: An Introduction* (York, Longman/Schools Council, 1982)

Studdert, J. & Wiles, S. *Children's Writing in a Multicultural Classroom* (London, ILEA Centre for Urban Educational Studies, 1983)

BOOKLISTS

Books in a Multi-Cultural Society: an annotated bibliography of fiction, autobiography and poetry for schools by W. Whitehead. (Sheffield, Sheffield City Polytechnic Language Development Centre, 1982)

Indian Literature in English: a checklist compiled by R. J. Warwick. (London, Commonwealth Institute, 1979)

Multi-Racial Books for the Classroom (3rd edn) compiled by J. Elkin. (London, The Library Association, 1980)

Penguin Multi-Ethnic Booklist compiled by R. Stones. (Harmondsworth, Penguin, 1982; new edn forthcoming, 1985)

We All Live Here: a multicultural booklist for young children selected by Anne Kesterton. (London, The National Book League, 45 East Hill, London SW18 2QZ, 1983)

A Wider Heritage: a selection of books for children and young people in multi-cultural Britain compiled by R. Ballin, J. Bleach and J. Levine. (London, The National Book League (address above), 1980)

Note: The following also produce special lists: Oxford University Press, Heinemann, Soma Books (38 Kennington Lane, London SE11).

SOURCES

The Arts Council Poetry Library, 105 Piccadilly, London W1.
The Centre for Education in a Multi-Ethnic Society, Robert
Montefiore School, Underwood Road, London E1 5AD.
This Centre has a useful library, carries a good range of
magazines, and is the base for the Schools Council 'Mother
Tongue Project 1981–4'.
The Commonwealth Institute Library Resource Centre, Kens-
ington High Street, London W8.

Poetry magazines

'While the major publishers are cautiously weighing up the
present the poetry magazines are already mapping out the
future.' With this brave sentence S. T. Gardiner concluded his
comments on poetry magazines in the 1978 (and, alas!, the
final) *Poet's Yearbook*. When that remarkable publication
went to press in 1977 there were some 174 poetry magazines in
existence. No one has had the dedication – or perhaps even the
knowledge – to count them accurately since then, but the
number is almost certainly smaller now. Nevertheless, their
function continues to be at the frontiers of poetry. Earlier Mr
Gardiner wrote that poetry magazines – defined as those
'which regularly devote at least one half of their total space to
poetry and poetry matters' – together accounted for 'almost
half the contemporary poetry sold in the UK'. These facts point
clearly to the need for any English teacher who is serious about
poetry to make it his or her business to see *regularly* as many
poetry magazines as possible, either by subscribing to them (or
at the very least arranging for the school to do so), or by getting
access to a library which stocks them, if necessary insisting that
they are stocked. Even local librarians are prepared to take out
a subscription if you can convince them there is a potential
readership. It is then up to you to find the readers amongst your
colleagues or pupils.

A particular advantage of regular reading of poetry magazines is that most carry substantial and serious reviews of new
poetry, often by poets, rather than the standard two short
columns covering (or skating over) ten or so books which is all
that most newspapers and weeklies are prepared to counte-
nance. Moreover, whereas the latter tend to stick to the
products of 'respectable' publishers, the poetry magazines
include coverage of the now very significant output from the
increasing number of small private presses.

Where then to start? The national Poetry Society and your
Regional Arts Association (see Section III p. 256) are the first
places to contact. (The central body, The Arts Council of Great
Britain, funds a few well established journals like *Agenda* and
PN Review.) Most Regional Arts Associations either publish
themselves or substantially assist a regionally 'weighted'
magazine of some kind, e.g.

Poetry South-East (South East Arts Association)
Poetry Durham (North East Arts Association, with Durham
   University)
Poetry Wales (Welsh Arts Council)
Chapman (Scottish Arts Council)
Honest Ulsterman (Northern Ireland Arts Council)

The Poetry Society publishes, under guest editorship, its own
substantial quarterly *Poetry Review* (free to members), which
remains, in spite of a certain air of respectability and some blind
spots, about the most wide-ranging poetry magazine in Britain.

It would be fruitless to attempt any complete list of other
extant magazines. Many are short-lived; others may die or be
born at short notice. Few extend their circulation beyond
hundreds, though their influence may be out of all proportion
to their apparent numerical insignificance. It is worth saying
here that a magazine's demise is no safe indication of failure;
indeed, it may mean precisely the opposite, as two outstanding
examples in recent years show – Harry Chambers's innovative
and lively *Phoenix* and Norman Hidden's unassuming but

adventurous *New Poetry* (originally *Workshop New Poetry*). The latter, whose final number appeared in the winter of 1980/81 after thirteen years, was a particularly severe loss to teachers as it actively promoted poetry in schools. Needless to say, both these dedicated editors are still closely involved in promoting new poetry.

The following classification is offered as the roughest of guides to what is currently available. The magazines listed are examples only.

A   LITERARY OR ACADEMIC

Agenda, ed. William Cookson, 5 Cranbourne Court, Albert Bridge Road, London SW11 4PE.

Anglo-Welsh Review, ed. Gillian Clarke, 1 Cyncoed Avenue, Cardiff.

Aquarius, ed. Eddie Linden, 116 Sutherland Avenue, London W9.

Argo, ed. (UK) Hilary Davies, Old Fire Station, 40 George St., Oxford OX1 2AQ.

Babel, English and German, ed. K. A. Perryman, Gartenstr. 29, D-8913 Schöndorf-am-Ammersee, Federal Republic of Germany.

PN Review, formerly *Poetry Nation*, ed. Michael Schmidt, 208–212 Corn Exchange Buildings, Manchester M4 3BQ.

The Present Tense, ed. Michael Abbott, 115 Princess Victoria Street, Clifton, Bristol BS8 4DD.

B   GENERAL

Chapman, ed. Joy M. Hendry, 3 Duddington Park, Edinburgh EH15 1JN.

The Honest Ulsterman, ed. Frank Ormsby, 70 Eglantine Ave., Belfast BT9 6DY.

London Magazine, ed. Alan Ross, 30 Thurloe Place, London SW7.

Other Poetry, ed. Anne Stevenson *et al.*, 2 Stoneygate Ave, Leicester LE2 3HE.

Outposts Poetry Quarterly, ed. Howard Sergeant, 72 Burwood Road, Walton-on-Thames, Surrey KT12 4AL.

Poetry Durham, Dept. of English, University of Durham, Elvet Riverside, Durham DH1 3JT.

Poetry Matters, ed. Harry Chambers, Treovis Farm Cottage, Upton Cross, Liskeard, Cornwall PL14 5BQ.

Poetry South-East, ed. Anthony Thwaite, 9–10 Crescent Road, Tunbridge Wells, Kent.

Poetry Wales, ed. Cary Archard, 56 Parceau Avenue, Bridgend, Mid-Glam.

Stand, ed. Jon Silkin and Lorna Tracey, 19 Haldane Terrace, Newcastle-upon-Tyne NE2 3AN.

Thames Poetry, ed. A. A. Cleary, 160 High Road, Wealdstone, Harrow, Middlesex HA3 7AX.

C   SPECIALIST AND EXPERIMENTAL

Akros, ed. Duncan Glen, 25 Johns Road, Radcliffe-on-Trent, Nottingham NG12 2GW.

Ambit, ed. Martin Bax, *et al.*, 17 Priory Gardens, London N6 9QY.

Bananas, ed. Emma Tennant, 2 Blenheim Crescent, London W11.

Iron, ed. Peter Mortimer, 5 Marden Terrace, Cullercoats, N. Shields, Tyne and Wear NE30 4PD.

New Departures, annual, ed. Michael Horovitz, Piedmont, Bisley, nr Stroud, Gloucestershire GL6 7BU.

Voices, Federation of Worker Writers, 61 Bloom St., Manchester M1 3LY.

Writing Women, no ed., 19 Osborne Road, Newcastle-upon-Tyne NE2 2AH.

There are also literally dozens of cheaply produced periodicals, sometimes no more than a few duplicated sheets or photocopied pages, with names like *Dowry, Graffiti, Litmus, Ore, Poetic Licence, Sea-Legs, Spectrum* and *Tops*. It does not do to dismiss these, which are often the seed-bed of genuine new talent. Finally come the more local products, often resulting from regularly meeting local poetry groups or workshops.

The Arts Council Poetry Library (see Section III, p. 253) carries a good selection of poetry magazines and welcomes browsers. It can supply lists and other information. For general advice on submitting poetry for publication see the annual *Writer's and Artist's Yearbook* (A. & C. Black).

Publishers

(As full addresses are easily obtainable – e.g. in *Whitaker's Almanack* or *The Writer's and Artist's Yearbook* – names only are given here.)

A MAJOR PUBLISHERS

The lion's share of poetry publishing in this country other than in magazines is taken by five publishers, the first four being major firms with general lists, the fifth a specialist poetry publisher: Chatto & Windus, Faber & Faber, Oxford University Press, Secker & Warburg, Carcanet Press.

A second group of the major firms regularly publish new poetry, though not to the same extent: Jonathan Cape, J. & M. Dent, André Deutsch, Dobson Books, Gollancz, Heinemann Educational, Hutchinson, Penguin Books, Routledge & Kegan Paul.

A few other major publishers produce a book of new poetry in their lists now and then: W. H. Allen, Allen & Unwin, Calder, Calder & Boyars, Eyre Methuen, Hamish Hamilton, Hart-Davis, Macmillan, John Murray.

B   LITTLE PRESSES AND MAGAZINE EDITIONS

The poetry produced by these is often more noteworthy and exciting, because it is less tied to established reputations. Thus, for instance, Alan Tarling of Poet and Printer (30 Grimsdyke Road, Hatch End, Middx HA5 4PW) comments:

> The policy of this particular press has always been to produce inexpensive pamphleteered collections partly as a taster for the poetry reader and partly as a testing-ground for the poet.... Its output is necessarily small (usually 500 copies or less) and it is doubtful that such presses could ever be a financial success, most of them cultivating, editing, printing and selling their output as a one-man venture.

Many of the 'little presses' belong to the Association of Little Presses (272 Randolph Avenue, London W5). The 'magazine editions' are offshoots from current or defunct poetry magazines. It would be impractical to try to list all such organizations; the following are the most productive:

Little Presses

Anvil Press	Poet and Printer
Bloodaxe Books	Priapus Press
Ceolfrith Press	Sceptre Press
Enitharmon Press	Sycamore Press
Hippopotamus Press	Trigram Press
Hub Publications	Writers & Readers Publ. Coop.

Poetry Magazine editions

Agenda Editions	London Magazine Editions
Akros Publications	Outposts Publications
Harry Chambers/	Poetry Wales Press
Peterloo Poets	Workshop Press

C PARTICULAR NATIONALITIES

A significant group of smaller publishers cater for particular nationalities or races, of which the following are productive examples:

Wales – Christopher Davies, Gwasg Gomer
Black writers – Bogle l'Ouverture
Ireland – Blackstaff Press
Scotland – M. Macdonald Publishers

(D) REFERENCE

Two easily accessible works of reference between them list a high proportion of the entire *corpus* of new poetry published in English since the First World War. They are:

British Poetry Since 1970 (National Book League, 1977)
Arts Council Poetry Library Catalogue (revised edn 1981, distrib. Carcanet Press)

Copyright

The Publishers Association has supplied a summary of the current legal position relating to photocopying in poster form to all schools. This is derived from a pamphlet, *Photocopying and the Law*, published in 1970 by the British Copyright Council (29 Berners Street, London W1). As the rigidity of the existing law leads to widespread infringements in schools negotiations are in progress for a 'blanket' licensing scheme for educational authorities, libraries, etc. This is supported by the Authors Lending and Copyright Society (ALCS) and the Society of Authors who are currently (1984) engaged in talks about it with the Publishers Association.

Footnote on poetry publishing

One distinguished poetry publisher, Menard Press, has within the last three years found it necessary to change its policy. I cannot do better than quote from its *Cambridge Poetry Festival Keepsake*:

> Until recently Menard was a poetry press – for poetry was and is vital to this publisher. But poetry pre-supposes future, pre-supposes continuity: there must be a world for poetry to be vital in, and that world is held in trust by each generation for its children. Menard is now concerned exclusively with its nuclear series, a concern it takes to be normal in the face of the terminal crisis the earth is fated to experience unless we halt the nuclear arms race. 'The time has come' – in the words of Octavio Paz – 'to build an ethics and a politics on the poetics of the now.' Menard believes that the fundamental divide is not between 'unilateralists' and 'multilateralists' but between 'disarmers' and 're-armers', and calls upon serious people to re-examine their positions in the light of this adjusted conceptual framework. Then, together on reclaimed common ground, they must find the resources to change their lives in order to prevent the final violence that will destroy our children and our world.

SECTION III:
PUBLIC BODIES,
COMPETITIONS,
POETRY COURSES

The Arts Council of Great Britain

The Literature Panel has to decide on the allocation of substantial public funds (e.g. £875,000 in 1983–4) and to administer various projects associated with the promotion of literature. It consists of writers, publishers and regional representatives, under a salaried Literature Director. It can provide bursaries for practising poets, grants to enable translations into English of poetry from other languages, and help to publishers, magazines and book distributors.

One particular activity of direct value to English teachers is the Arts Council Poetry Library housed at 105 Piccadilly, London W1V OAU, containing an unrivalled collection of twentieth-century poetry in English. Membership is free, and there is a mailing scheme for members outside London. Closely associated with the Library is the Poetry Book Society, whose Assistant Secretary is Jonathan Barker, the Poetry Librarian. He has provided the following notes:

One simple way of building a school library of contemporary poetry

As anyone involved with contemporary poetry knows, the future readers and writers of poetry come from young people whose imaginations at some time have been captured and educated by the poetry already available in books. There is no great difficulty in purchasing cheap paperback selections of the work of our own poets of the past. We all know, or think we know who is essential reading from Chaucer to, say, A. E. Housman. But once it dawns upon us that poetry is a living thing being produced by countless contemporary poets we come across a sudden network of problems. Who is the best? Which books of theirs are essential reading? Where can copies of their most recent books be found? How much will they cost? Who can offer advice on all this?

It was questions like these which led to the founding of the Poetry Book Society in 1953, in order to promote 'knowledge, appreciation and enjoyment of the published works of contemporary poets.'

T. S. Eliot, a founder member, spoke on ways in which the Society could help schools at a press conference in 1956. He said:

> If every secondary school in the country joined the Poetry Book Society and had a shelf in its library exhibiting the books of new poetry, and just left them there for the boys and girls in the upper forms to discover for themselves and find out what they liked, we would be doing a very great service, because it is in the years between 14 and 18 if ever that people become readers of poetry and lovers of poetry, and also amongst those readers will be the poets of that generation.

This is precisely the service we have offered to schools ever since, although from the small number of school libraries which have bothered to enrol one could be forgiven for thinking that English teachers chose to disagree. The embarrassing truth is that far and away the majority of our members are private individuals, many living away from large bookshops, who are individually concerned enough with contemporary poetry to pay for a subscription each year.

In 1974 Philip Larkin, then a member of the Board of Management and now (1983) its Chairman, wrote a letter aimed specifically at teachers and school librarians encouraging them to subscribe, in which he said:

> As a librarian I know that coverage of new poetry can present a problem. It is easy to buy the later volumes of established writers, but this doesn't allay the suspicion that one ought also to be investing in books by younger or less known writers who may themselves be established in ten or fifteen years' time, when these early works will be collectors' pieces. Unfortunately, library funds are short, and young poets are extremely productive. How is one to know what to buy?
>
> If you have answered this question to your own satisfaction, read no further. If not, then consider whether it would not at least be a start to receive the Poetry Book Society's modestly priced quarterly Choices, and to have its Recommendations as a guide for further purchases.

Following this persuasive plea individual memberships continued to come in but school membership still stuck at its surprisingly low level. Two of our most distinguished poets had spoken up for the Society and the teachers they tried to address had not heard.

The time has surely come for a change of heart. Membership is a practical way of helping the dissemination of contemporary poetry. It is also a simple and effetive way of building up a representative library collection of the best contemporary poetry. The Society provides its members with four books of new poetry a year, chosen by selectors who are practising poets or critics, and supplied at a substantial discount. The selectors also recommend books of special merit. The Choices come with a quarterly Bulletin which includes contributions from the authors about their work and themselves.

Membership also brings a special 64-page supplementary anthology in December of previously unpublished poetry, edited by one of the selectors.

The closing words of T. S. Eliot's 1956 press conference can hardly be ignored by teachers of English, who are directly responsible for the taste of future generations of poetry readers:

> I have always held firmly that a nation which ceases to produce poetry will in the long run cease to be able to enjoy and even understand the great poetry of its own past.

(Enquiries to the Assistant Secretary, Poetry Book Society – address above.)

Scottish and Welsh Arts Council; Regional Arts Associations

Much of the government's support for literature has now been decentralized. Your local library can supply the address of your own area's Arts Council or Association; it is worth contacting the Literature Officer to ask for details of their activities and support for poetry. One that is particularly relevant to English teachers is the *Writers in Schools* scheme, which subsidizes visits to schools by creative writers, including poets.

The Poetry Society

This Society has now been in existence for over eighty years. It receives about one third of its income from the Arts Council, and raises the remainder through its various activities. The staff member (out of a complement of ten) with special responsibility for schools is the Education Officer, who should be contacted by all teachers interested in making use of the organization. Activities of particular relevance to poetry in schools are:

i) A children's poetry competition (now sponsored annually by Puffin Books);

ii) Poetry workshop sessions for teachers and pupils;

iii) 'Poets in Schools', a scheme sponsored by W. H. Smith;

iv) The National Poetry Secretariat, which administers a special fund for poetry *readings*;

v) Examinations in spoken poetry and prose. These have been organized by the Society for more than 75 years on a nation-wide basis;

vi) A critical service for poets, run by Norman Hidden (formerly editor of the poetry magazine *Workshop New Poetry*).

The Poetry Society's Bookshop, at the same address, 21 Earls Court Square, London SW5 9DG, is the best stocked poetry bookshop in the country. It issues free stock lists under various headings, and runs a mail-order service.

The National Book League

This organization, now, alas! housed in a rather inaccessible part of South London (Book House, 45 East Hill, London SW18 2QZ) instead of its former appropriate and dignified premises in Albemarle Street, issues book lists and other publications of interest to teachers, and runs travelling exhibitions from time to time. Of particular relevance to poetry teaching are two lists:

Guide to Literary Prizes (1979)

British Poetry Since 1970, sel. M. Mackenzie (1977)

A new list of '200 best poets writing in English' is in preparation, in collaboration with the Poetry Society.

Schools Poetry Association

This lively organization was formed a few years ago (at Twyford School, Winchester, Hants, SO21 1NW), largely through the enthusiasm and dedication of its founder and present secretary, the poet and teacher David Orme. The most recent membership figure I have (November 1983) is 'over 350'; there is no doubt that it is providing a new stimulus to poetry in schools. The Association publishes a magazine, *Schools Poetry Review*, a series of A3 size poem posters called 'Broadsheet Poets', and now a series (free to members) of 'Poemcards'. One particular merit of the organization is its practice of allowing members to photocopy any of the Association's publications for use in school. It also encourages and is prepared to support the formation of local groups of members.

The Arvon Poetry Foundation

This charitable Foundation owns two large country houses (Lumb Bank, Hebden Bridge, W. Yorks and Totleigh Barton, Sheepwash, Reaworthy, Devon, EX21 5NS) where it arranges residential writing courses for adults and young people over 16. Grants towards the cost of the courses are available from Regional Arts Associations. These courses, held in intimate and comfortable surroundings set in beautiful countryside, provide unique opportunities for keen young writers and their teachers to meet established poets on equal terms in a 'workshop' context.

Poetry competitions

Details of most national competitions are available from the Poetry Society and the Arts Councils and Associations, and from the Society of Authors (84 Drayton Gardens, London SW10 9SD). Individual magazines, journals and newspapers also run their own competitions from time to time. See also the NBL *Guide* referred to above (p.257).

My own feelings about the value of such contests in relation to the pursuit of poetry are ambivalent; 'competition' often has commercial overtones and implications that are antipathetic to poetry. Some comments the poet Adrian Mitchell once made on advertising have some relevance:

> You get a kind of anti-poetry in advertisements. I would call it anti-poetry because, although it uses the same skill as poetry, and some poets work in advertising, I think that's a Judas job for a poet. I think poetry's a search for the naked truth and that's serious. Advertising is a search for money, and money is the opposite of truth, as far as poetry goes. Money is one of the enemies of poetry.

With this *caveat* in mind, it may still be helpful in particular instances to encourage individual students to try their luck in a competition. The following are characteristic examples of what is currently available at a national level:

The Eric Gregory Trust Fund Award (eight awards annually worth £10,000) for writers under 30 (administered by the Society of Authors).

The Dylan Thomas Award (annually, £1,000) poet or short-story writer (administered by the Poetry Society).

Redcliffe National Poetry Competition (£200, and 3 at £50) run in association with the poetry magazine *The Present Tense* (see p.247 above).

APPENDIX:
SOME POEMS

The main purpose of this little collection is to provide easy access to poems used in Part Two of the book. Some of them will be unfamiliar and for that reason, I hope, welcome as new classroom material. Cross-references are given where necessary.

The last poem is added as a *bonne-bouche*. Desmond Heath is a little-known but talented poet who is also a fine musician. The exact delicacy of his poetry may owe something to his experience as a baroque violinist. I am grateful to him for allowing me to end my book so appropriately.

The poems

Swallows

Steps on the creaking stairs
set panicking a nestful
of young swallows in an empty room,
their little bodies hurtling
through dead air to dirty window-panes.

'This shall be a quiet room', said the man
to his gipsy delicate girl, who gently
gathered swallows in her thin hands.
'We'll walk barefoot, keep silence here', he planned.
'Look!' she said, rapt, holding out to him
a tiny brittle swallow in each hand.

But it was only the future
that he could see and while he paced
its hopeful rooms, she opened the window
and set the moment free to go
on soft wings into summer and the past.

(Ruth Bidgood)

The Rule

I was ten when
the joiner came to measure
for the coal-bunker – ten

years squandering treasure,
fumbling innocent dust
into shapes – the fibrous pressure

of my fingers taught to mistrust
naive random responses,
to bridle aggressive thrust,

curb impulsive advances
in guiding the tempered edge
of chisel and plane – senses

subdued to the tools' judgement. How I despised the unlovely
products: the splintered bodge

of an egg-rack, rendered behovely
only by Mother's grace
in accepting the spirit of it, gravely

loading it with eggs, her face
tranquil, so filled with pleasure
I almost believed it. Chase

that memory away and treasure
instead the moment when
the joiner brought out his measure ...

A folded boxwood rule, brass tips and hinges
smoothed from his denim's friction
shining dully
every joint true and neat, the right angles
snugly righting themselves
to true the edge
as he clicked open the sections of warm wood.

Gnarled fingers, bent arms at first belied
the rule's exactitude
its notched inches,
but held in his square fist to parcel the bunker's space –
joints crooked and straight –
the two were knit
and an airy structure shaped itself to their laws.

The boxwood rule my cynosure
I watched the bunker – utile, prosaic – take shape
    Joints jostled together
    dovetails driven dead true down
    measurements marked immutable
    rigidly ruled
    perspectives of planks
    smoothed surfaces.

– for the joiner loved his wood,
stroked a true-grained piece with his old fingers
while I
round-eyed, oblivious,
longed again for the magic-working power-conferring
wand of wood and brass to make all right.
Idolatrous,
wayward eyes jerked parallel along
ruled lines – railed lanes
diminishing to adulthood.

(Stephen Tunnicliffe)

The Pebble

    Not a smooth, cold, sleek grey,
    Superior pebble,
    Nor a hot, rich, golden,
    Exotic pebble.
    But a humble, lumpy, bumpy,
    Rigid lined,
    Curved, streaked, spotted,
        dotted,
    Stone.

A homely, kindly, bumbly
Sort of a pebble,
Like an old, gnarled, oak tree
In a forest.
Or a comfortable, mellow, wall,
Carefully built,
Lovingly formed, by an old old
Craftsman.

(Francis Le Fevre, aged 12)

Ode

There was a time when meadow, grove, and stream,
The earth, and every common sight,
    To me did seem
    Apparell'd in celestial light,
The glory and the freshness of a dream.
It is not now as it hath been of yore; –
    Turn whereso'er I may,
    By night or day,
The things which I have seen I now can see no more.

II

    The Rainbow comes and goes,
    And lovely is the Rose,
    The Moon doth with delight
Look round her when the heavens are bare,
    Waters on a starry night
    Are beautiful and fair;
The sunshine is a glorious birth;
But yet I know, where'er I go,
That there hath pass'd away a glory from the earth.

III

Now, while the Birds thus sing a joyous song,
   And while the young Lambs bound
     As to the tabor's sound
To me alone there came a thought of grief:
A timely utterance gave that thought relief,
     And I again am strong:
The Cataracts blow their trumpets from the steep;
No more shall grief of mine the season wrong;
I hear the Echoes through the mountains throng,
The Winds come to me from the fields of sleep,
     And all the earth is gay;
      Land and sea
    Give themselves up to jollity,
      And with the heart of May
    Doth every Beast keep holiday; –
      Thou Child of Joy,
Shout round me, let me hear thy shouts, thou happy
      Shepherd Boy!
     . . . .
     Not for these I raise
    The song of thanks and praise;
     . . . .
    But for those first affections,
    Those shadowy recollections ,
   Which, be they what they may,
Are yet the fountain light of all our day,
Are yet a master light of all our seeing,
   Uphold us, cherish us, and make
Our noisy years seem moments in the being
Of the eternal Silence: truths that wake,
     To perish never;

Which neither listlessness, nor mad endeavour,
> Nor Man nor Boy,
Nor all that is at enmity with joy,
Can utterly abolish or destroy!
> Hence, in a season of calm weather,
> Though inland far we be,
Our souls have sight of that immortal sea
> Which brought us hither,
> Can in a moment travel thither,
And see the Children sport upon the shore,
And hear the mighty waters rolling evermore.

(William Wordsworth *Poems*, 1807)

NOTES ON THIS SELECTION

I am aware that purists and Wordsworth enthusiasts may object to my presenting these fragments from a famous poem for school study. My prime excuse is a practical one. I am advocating learning by heart in Chapter 8, and it would be pointless even to suggest that more than the fifty or so lines here could be committed to memory in a normal school context. Any pupil who voluntarily undertakes to learn this passage will certainly want to read the whole poem.

It is worth remembering that more than two years passed between the completion of the first part (lines 1–57) of the Ode and the writing of the remainder, so there is a respectable precedent for setting parts from each section, with an indicated break. In my second part the items referred to by 'these' in the first line – i.e. 'Delight and liberty, the simple creed/Of Childhood...', etc. – are in effect referring back to the opening lines, so I am not doing violence to Wordsworth's meaning. Similarly, in omitting the short section between '... praise;' and 'But for those ...' I am merely cutting out a second 'but' clause, and the general sense is retained.

Teachers may like to be reminded of some of the poet's own comments on this poem, as recorded by Isabella Fenwick in 1840, i.e. thirty-eight years after writing the first part:

> It was not so much from the source of animal vivacity that my difficulty came as from a sense of the indomitableness of the spirit within me. I used to brood over the stories of Enoch and Elijah, and almost to persuade myself that, whatever might become of others, I should be translated in something of the same way to heaven. With a feeling congenial to this, I was often unable to think of external things as having external existence, and I communed with all that I saw as something not apart from, but inherent in, my own immaterial nature. Many times while going to school have I grasped at a wall or tree to recall myself from this abyss of idealism to the reality.... To that dreamlike vividness and splendour which invest objects of sight in childhood, everyone, I believe, if he would look back, could bear testimony.

In Memoriam

Time doesn't heal the heartache
Or stop the silent tears
Or take away the memories
Of parents we loved so dear.

*   *   *

A life so faithful, true and kind
A beautiful memory left behind.

*   *   *

May the wind of love blow gently
On a quiet and peaceful spot
Where the one we loved lies sleeping
But never will be forgot.

*   *   *

His life was full of kindly deeds,
A helping hand to all in need,
A pleasant smile, a heart of gold,
No finer son and brother this world could hold.

*   *   *

Beautiful memories, silently kept
Of one I loved and will never forget.

(Anonymous – various sources)

Representational

His mother's wrinkled gloves have been warm enough
For the glass of the table where they lie to steam a bit:
These three are sat on gold-painted cane armchairs
In the middle of a spa, the man quite readily benign,
And smiling at the seven-year-old boy, though he hasn't
Much to say, and he sucks a thin cigar.

A lady
In a purple topcoat leaves the counter and brings,
On a green tray, coffees and orangeade, she glides
Into their circle deftly with a quiet, adaptable
Smiling. This December is cold, but the sweet
Orangeade shrills heavenly up the waxy straw, a cool
Perfect runnel over his tongue, it's 1974.

His mother
Is flushed and laughing with the man, there they are
In the great wall-mirror on the far side of the room,
Laughing and flushed the two of them, the freer selves
They could always be if this were only art
– Oh, if this were only art, or even fiction! But still,
Small rewards and mercies hold good . . .

                                                  And the little boy
Now draining the last sacramental droplets from the glass
Quite likes the man, and the sun is coming out.
The lady with her emptied tray makes an adult smile
For the adults, and a children's smile for the child;
Her petition forms on the counter, to which she returns,
Are nearly filled, so the Ring Road is nearly prevented.

                                                  The man
Will have paid off the Datsun in just another five months'
      time.

                                        (Alan Brownjohn, 1980)

What is Our Life?

What is our life? A play of passion,
Our mirth the music of division.
Our mothers' wombs the tiring houses be
Where we are dressed for this short comedy.
Heaven the judicious sharp spectator is
That sits and marks still who doth act amiss.
Our graves that hide us from the searching sun
Are like drawn curtains when the day is done.
Thus march we, playing, to our latest rest,
Only we die in earnest, that's no jest.

(Sir Walter Raleigh – set to music by Orlando Gibbons)

Gibbons matches the mood of this rather melancholy 'conceit'
with music that is predominantly slow-moving, but illuminates

the poem line by line in simple yet musically subtle ways. First the rhetorical question 'What is our life?' is stated firmly, with a lift on the word 'life' to add emphasis, and to lead into the expected reply. As it comes, the word 'passion' – sung in three syllables – derives poignancy and intensity through the discord that accompanies it. Now we start to move step by step through the development of the life/play metaphor. Our mirth, or laughter, becomes 'the music of division', that is, fast-moving note passages, and the music livens up, especially on the 'division' (four syllables) so as to illustrate the idea. As we trace life from 'our mothers' wombs' the harmony becomes less harsh in keeping with the intimacy of the image. However, plays have sharp, critical spectators, and for this play of life 'heaven' fulfils this role. Notice how Gibbons gives the word a high note, befitting its altitude. As Morley (another composer of the time) says, 'you must have a care that when your matter signifieth ascending, high heaven and suchlike, you make your music ascend.' The 'sharpness' of this critic's judgment finds its match in the increasing stringency of the harmony as the word 'spectator' is repeated. This gives way to the short, mocking notes of 'that sits and marks' – one syllable to a note – for all the world like a wagging admonitory finger. After this levity, however, comes a more solemn note. At the end of the play, curtains to draw across the scene; at the end of life, 'our graves'. Notice the solemn effect of the long notes here after the mocking crotchets that we have just heard. The harmonies give almost the effect of organ chords, with a poignant discord between soprano and tenor on the word 'searching' – 'the searching sun'. The music moves in a stately fashion, like the slow drawing of curtains it is illustrating, emphasized by the tranquil major key. Once again the mood changes for 'Thus march we', becoming strongly accented, a marching rhythm which leads us in almost spritely fashion – 'playing' still – to our 'latest (i.e. final, last) rest'. But the last mood is a bitter one – 'we die in earnest' – there is no jesting or play-acting about that event in our life. For this moment Gibbons has saved his most telling effect, the slow notes in the bass, mounting step by heavy step, almost like a man climbing the scaffold to the block. The finality here dramatically clinches poem and music.

(Quoted from *Discovering Shakespeare*, by Stephen Tunnicliffe, Studytapes Ltd.)

Reading Lesson

Fourteen years old, learning the alphabet,
He finds letters harder to catch than hares,
Without a greyhound. Can't I give him a dog
To track them down, or put them in a cage?
He's caught in a trap, until I let him go,
Pinioned by 'don't you want to learn to read?'
'I'll be the same man whatever I do.'

He looks at a page, as a mule baulks at a gap
From which a goat may hobble out and bleat.
His eyes jink from a sentence like flushed snipe
Escaping shot. A sharp word, and he'll mooch
Back to his piebald mare and bantam cock.
Our purpose is as tricky to retrieve
As mercury from a smashed thermometer.

'I'll not read any more.' Should I give up?
His hands, long-fingered as a Celtic scribe's,
Will grow callous, gathering sticks or scrap;
Exploring pockets of the horny drunk.
Loiterers at the fairs, giving them lice.
A neighbour chuckles. 'You can never tame
The wild-duck: when his wings grow he'll fly off.'

If books resembled roads, he'd quickly read;
But they're small farms to him, fenced by the pages,
Ploughed into lines, with letters drilled like oats:
A field of tasks he'll always be outside.
If words were bank-notes, he would filch a wad;
If they were pheasants they'd be in his pot
For breakfast, or if wrens he'd make them king.

(Richard Murphy
from *High Island*, Faber & Faber, 1974)

Terminal Days at Beverley Farms

At Beverley Farms, a portly, uncomfortable boulder
bulked in the garden's centre –
an irregular Japanese touch.
After his Bourbon 'old fashioned,' Father,
bronzed, breezy, a shade too ruddy,
swayed as if on deck-duty
under his six pointed star-lantern –
last July's birthday present.
He smiled his oval Lowell smile,
he wore his cream gabardine dinner-jacket,
and indigo cummerbund.
His head was efficient and hairless,
his newly dieted figure was vitally trim.

Father and Mother moved to Beverley Farms
to be a two minute walk from the station,
half an hour by train from the Boston doctors.
They had no sea-view,
but sky-blue tracks of the commuters' railroad shone
like a double-barrelled shotgun
through the scarlet late August sumac,
multiplying like cancer
at their garden's border.

Father had had two coronaries.
He still treasured underhand economies,
but his best friend was his little black Chevie,
garaged like a sacrificial steer
with gilded hooves
yet sensationally sober,
and with less side than an old dancing pump.
The local dealer, a 'buccaneer',
had been bribed a 'king's ransom'
to quickly deliver a car without chrome.

Each morning at eight-thirty,
inattentive and beaming,
loaded with his 'calc' and 'trig' books,
his clipper ship statistics,
and his ivory slide-rule,
Father stole off with the Chevie
to loaf in the Maritime Museum at Salem.
He called the curator
'the commander of the Swiss Navy'.

Father's death was abrupt and unprotesting.
His vision was still twenty-twenty.
After a morning of anxious, repetitive smiling,
his last words to Mother were:
'I feel awful.'

(Robert Lowell
from *Life Studies*, Faber & Faber, 1959)

Seeing Granny

Toothless, she kisses
with fleshly lips
rounded, like mouth
of a bottle, all wet.

She bruises your face
almost, with two
loving tree-root hands.

She makes you sit, fixed.
She then stuffs you
with boiled pudding and lemonade.

She watches you feed
on her food. She milks
you dry of answers
about the goat she gave you.

(James Berry)

Winter-Piece

You wake, all windows blind – embattled sprays
grained on the medieval glass.
Gates snap like gunshot
as you handle them. Five-barred fragility
sets flying fifteen rooks who go together
silently ravenous above this winter-piece
that will not feed them. They alight
beyond, scavenging, missing everything
but the bladed atmosphere, the white resistance.

Ruts with iron flanges track
through a hard decay
where you discern once more
oak-leaf by hawthorn, for the frost
rewhets their edges. In a perfect web
blanched along each spoke
and circle of its woven wheel,
the spider hangs, grasp unbroken
and death-masked in cold. Returning
you see the house glint-out behind
its holed and ragged glaze,
frost-fronds all streaming.

(Charles Tomlinson
from *A Peopled Landscape*,
Oxford University Press, 1963)

The M1 Dream

I entered in August at Daventry and felt immediately
Myself a mere word in a long, composite message down
Co-axial cable or three wires to important
London. It was hot; I, protected, who wear
Wool on the skin in summer this day had shirt
Alone, unbuttoned, both windows down, yet felt air
Like warm water still. Our tin column made South;
At 3 p.m. it darkened, sidelights came on and
Main beams. The rain fell like grapes on the windscreen.
Thunder clocked, I saw nearly nothing, nor dared dash
Out a lane; in my puny rain-jewelled mirror cars' and
Trucks' lanterns shimmered wetly and I could not place
    them.

Our three lines were submarine, great motorized fish
Coming by me. Yet on the surface the sky's black gods
Roared at us; lightning splintered the dislodged air.
A Porsche sluicing past close a parabola of water blinded
My side-window just as I wound the glass up. An empty
Lorry bumped by like a badly-dressed fat man; chains
Dangling, boards flapping, spraying the rain's saliva
Mannerlessly on us others there. In the Toddington
Service station I sat awed, the road under the bridge
Hissed and slammed with strewn vehicles, and I re-merged
With a nether tunnel of moving lights approaching the
      ownerless.
We ignorantly drove; our inevitable course, the sacred
Ecstasy in it history itself, London our moment, our
      revolution.
Our intellects, swaying, passed and being passed,
The dark mindless, the blue signs pleading. A transporter
Threatened to tip its load, someone mad as the day's
Weather sawed his eighty through the hacking rain as we
Pushed on, alone in risk, yet with splats and blobs of
Friendship as a face at a near-side window smiled.
Faded Jesus walked such water serenely; we drive on it,
Terrified gripping the wheel; yet a long way off a radio
Mast suddenly appeared, a piece of silk sky
Beyond it; and what I had most feared became a benevolent
Catastrophe merely, of recognition, a sun-shafted sky
And houses; and it was just an August after all.

                                              (J. P. Ward)

Touch of Death

Strange fingers woke me, fumbling at my brow.
My rooms were near a roof. I thought: Somehow
Someone's got in. The cold hand hit my nose.
Naked between the freezing sheets, I froze.
Then ... nothing happened. I became aware
Horribly slowly no one else was there:
Quite dark, but you could sense across the floor
The usual wooden quadrupeds, no more.
Was it a corpse's hand, put in my bed
By my best friend, who's studying the dead?
Surely he'd not do that ... The arm felt grey,
Somehow, and yielding, in a foul soft way.
It didn't smell, though. Feeling worse, and colder,
I ran my left-hand up it to the shoulder,
Expecting torn-out strings, a bulb of bone,
And wetness. Worst of all, it was my own –
I'd two right arms: one, warm beneath my head
And pillow, there; and this, cold, slack and ... dead?
I tried to touch the real one where I knew
It must be, but my fingers went straight through.
All the sensations of my arm lay there
In order, like a well-lit thoroughfare,
But not the arm. My soul is breaking free,
I thought: I'll lose the arm. I might lose me!
I grabbed the dead thing. It was powerless.
I rubbed the muscles, stroked and tried to press
The blood along, like air in a balloon.
But nothing made it feel. It would die soon,
If it weren't dead already. Then I thought
If I could swing it round, it might get caught

As it goes through its image. Can you fit
Your arm back in the space that matches it?
The elbows fused together as they met,
The wrists and knuckles too – a perfect set.
And even when I moved them on, they stayed
United as they'd been since they were made.
I felt the rushing happiness of a boy
Who's found the key he needs to wind his toy.
I slept then, I suppose. I don't recall.

You'll keep this quiet, won't you? After all,
Who'd ever shake this hand – with which I write –
Knowing it died and met its ghost one night?

(Alistair Elliot)

Flame

Windprint.

God if you like,
flowering blue on the cooker,
burning everything but himself.

Flame that can bear it,
dead centre of truth.

Moth-ash.

He was right
for a second absolutely right,
knew more of flame than flame,
brought it to life by dying,
entered his invisibility,

became a was-moth,
remembered pattern of himself
hurting what —

me at the centre of me,
able to bear myself,
or me oblique
seeing flame and wing
unthinkably touch?

Smooth as time it pours
light liquid
unimaginably soft,
deadliness miscast,
villainy in a fine tongue —

something is wrong —
flame does not hurt,
God is not like that,
singing insects into himself —
can't stand insects —
is an insect,

is in two minds
about eating candles anyway
the wind will tread him out.

That's nice — here he is in a match,
transmogrified, arcane as a seed.
I will turn this one that has not burned
into an ending.

(Desmond Heath
from *Rise Down Water)*

NAME INDEX

OF POETS